WE SHALL PERSIST

WOMEN'S SUFFRAGE AND THE STRUGGLE FOR DEMOCRACY
SERIES EDITOR: VERONICA STRONG-BOAG

The story of women's struggles and victories in the pursuit of political equality is not just a matter of the past: it has the value of informing current debate about the health of democracy in our country.

This series of short, insightful books presents a history of the vote, with vivid accounts of famous and unsung suffragists and overdue explanations of why some women were banned from the ballot box until the 1940s and 1960s. More than a celebration of women's achievements in the political realm, this series provides deeper understanding of Canadian society and politics, serving as a well-timed reminder never to take political rights for granted.

Books in the series:

One Hundred Years of Struggle: The History of Women and the Vote in Canada, by Joan Sangster

Our Voices Must Be Heard: Women and the Vote in Ontario, by Tarah Brookfield

To Be Equals in Our Own Country: Women and the Vote in Quebec, by Denyse Baillargeon

A Great Revolutionary Wave: Women and the Vote in British Columbia, by Lara Campbell

Ours by Every Law of Right and Justice: Women and the Vote in the Prairie Provinces, by Sarah Carter

We Shall Persist: Women and the Vote in the Atlantic Provinces, by Heidi E. MacDonald

HEIDI E. MacDONALD

WE SHALL PERSIST

Women and the Vote
in the Atlantic Provinces

UBCPress

VANCOUVER & TORONTO

32 31 30 29 28 27 26 25 24 23   5 4 3 2 1

Printed in Canada on FSC-certified ancient-forest-free paper
(100% post-consumer recycled) that is processed chlorine- and acid-free.

Library and Archives Canada Cataloguing in Publication

Title: We shall persist : women and the vote in the Atlantic Provinces /
Heidi MacDonald.

Names: MacDonald, Heidi, 1968- author.

Series: Women's suffrage and the struggle for democracy; v. 6.

Description: Series statement: Women's suffrage and the struggle
for democracy; v. 6 | Includes bibliographical references and index.

Identifiers: Canadiana (print) 20230158927 | Canadiana (ebook) 20230158951 |
ISBN 9780774863179 (hardcover) | ISBN 9780774863193 (PDF) |
ISBN 9780774863209 (EPUB)

Subjects: LCSH: Women—Suffrage—Atlantic Provinces—History. |
LCSH: Suffrage—Atlantic Provinces—History. | LCSH: Women—Legal status, laws,
etc.—Atlantic Provinces—History. | LCSH: Women—Atlantic Provinces—Social
conditions. | LCSH: Suffragists—Atlantic Provinces—History. | LCSH: Voting—
Atlantic Provinces—History. | LCSH: Women—Suffrage—Canada—History.

Classification: LCC JL192 .M33 2023 | DDC 324.6/2309715—dc23

Canadä

UBC Press gratefully acknowledges the financial support for our publishing
program of the Government of Canada, the Canada Council for the Arts,
and the British Columbia Arts Council.

Printed and bound in Canada by Friesens
Set in Humanist and Tundra by Artegraphica Design Co. Ltd.
Copy editor: Deborah Kerr
Indexer: Rachel Robinson
Cover and series design: Jessica Sullivan

UBC Press
The University of British Columbia
2029 West Mall
Vancouver, BC V6T 1Z2
www.ubcpress.ca

CONTENTS

THE CAMPAIGN FOR WOMEN'S suffrage in the Maritimes and Newfoundland was long, contentious, and rife with personal insults. Politicians in Atlantic Canada (composed of three provinces and the Crown colony of Newfoundland, later a dominion) defeated more than two dozen suffrage bills over three decades. Finally, in 1918, most Nova Scotia women gained the vote provincially and federally. Similar legislation followed in New Brunswick, Prince Edward Island, and Newfoundland (but not Labrador) in 1919, 1922, and 1925, respectively. Privilege and racism, however, remained well entrenched – perhaps most starkly for Indigenous women who were disenfranchised from band council elections due to their sex until 1951, barring them from voting on community issues that profoundly affected their lives. In other elections, they were disenfranchised based on their race. Nova Scotia and Newfoundland allowed them to vote when other women did, in 1918 and 1925, respectively. However, systemic racism was a strong deterrent, as were Nova Scotia's disqualifications for receiving government relief or not owning property between 1918 and 1920. In Labrador, where many residents were Innu, no one voted until the Confederation referendum in 1949, when the government finally provided the necessary infrastructure: ballot boxes. Federally, reserve-based Indigenous men and women gained the franchise only in 1960. New Brunswick and Prince Edward Island continued to exclude them from voting provincially until 1963. By then, Atlantic Canadian women had been toiling in the suffrage trenches for more than a century.

Female enfranchisement, as well as the long fight for it, was key to making Atlantic Canada what it is today. It legitimized the expansion of women's influence beyond the family into the public sphere. Although sexism thrived in many forms, suffrage curbed the most blatant political misogyny and prepared the way for more citizens' rights, including women's election to public office, minimum wage legislation, improved social assistance, and access to birth control. *Not* getting the vote, or getting it later, would have been a disaster for democracy and community well-being. And yet the slow appearance of women – especially racialized women – as political candidates and victors demonstrated the persistence of the fierce opposition mounted by anti-suffragists.

The declaration "We Shall Persist" captures both the long suffrage campaign and the subsequent years of disillusionment. The fact that suffrage failed to achieve equality for women has been underscored by the regional Me Too Movement's exposure of horrendous examples of inequality and by broader recognition that cis-gendered women (those whose gender identity corresponds with their birth sex) are far from the only historical (or contemporary) victims of sexual inequality. Suffrage victories in Atlantic Canada are no more than steps in a still unfinished and contentious process toward gender, race, and class equality.

A conservative stereotype has often substituted for research when non–Atlantic Canadian historians write about the area. As a result, traditionalism haunts its economic, religious, political, and gender history. Although Atlantic Canadians see themselves as outward looking, particularly due to their kinship with and commercial links to New England and Great Britain, history of global shipping and shipbuilding, and ethnic ties to other places, a persistent characterization of isolation, traditionalism, and marginalization developed. Atlantic Canada has often been dismissed as less engaged in suffrage than elsewhere, particularly the West. Its enfranchisement campaign has also been portrayed as less interesting.

Catherine Cleverdon, the author of the first and, until recently, the only national history of suffrage, *The Woman Suffrage Movement in Canada* (1950), highlighted Atlantic Canadian conservatism: "Nowhere has the traditional conservatism of the Maritime

Provinces been more apparent than in the securing of political rights for women … It was *natural* that these provinces should exhibit varying shades of apathy." She dismissed each Maritime province and Newfoundland in turn, while praising the progressivism of the Prairie provinces. Numerous scholars repeated her claims over the next seven decades, exaggerating what was in fact a relatively short delay in enfranchisement: Manitoba, Saskatchewan, and Alberta women in 1916; British Columbia and Ontario in 1917; Nova Scotia in 1918; New Brunswick in 1919; Prince Edward Island in 1922; Newfoundland in 1925; and Quebec in 1940. In *Liberation Deferred? The Ideas of the English-Canadian Suffragists, 1877–1918* (1989), Carol Lee Bacchi similarly gave Atlantic Canada short shrift, as did Sylvia Bashevkin, who lumped its suffragism with that of Quebec, referring to both as "slow to develop" in *Toeing the Lines: Women and Party Politics in English Canada* (1993). Unfortunately, only in 2018 did the *Canadian Encyclopedia* revise its claim that Maritimers lacked an interest in suffrage. As late as 2020, the *Famous 5 Centre of Canadian Women,* a display at Calgary's Heritage Park, dismissed Atlantic Canada. And so, erroneous claims persist in the face of inadequate research into suffrage in Atlantic Canada.

Writing history is inherently political. Even professional historians incorporate the biases of their society, era, training, and personal perspective, as they choose topics, gather evidence, and offer interpretation. Finishing up this book in 2021, during the Black Lives Matter movement and the discovery of the remains of 215 Tk'emlúps te Secwépemc children on the former Kamloops Indian Residential School property, I am reminded viscerally of how the legacies of slavery and colonialism shaped Atlantic Canada's citizenship rights and the suffrage movement's lack of inclusiveness. As a settler feminist historian, I assert the worthiness of examining suffrage as a step toward women's equality – a yet unfinished project – but I do not put suffragists or any other historical figures on pedestals. As a historian of Atlantic Canada, a region long stereotyped by historians as conservative and less relevant to Canada than Ontario, I am frustrated by the lack of attention its suffragists have received. Suffragists such as Julia Salter Earle and Jessie Ohman of Newfoundland; Mary Chesley and Eliza Ritchie of Nova Scotia; Ella Hatheway and Emma Fiske of New Brunswick; and Catherine Anderson and Elsie Inman of Prince Edward Island are as much a part of the story as their better-known sisters. They are not lesser because they are unknown. In the same vein, the exclusion of racialized and poor women is sadly consistent across the country.

We Shall Persist is the region's first book-length study of the Great Cause. In contrast to Cleverdon and those who echoed her findings, it traces a longer, more contentious campaign. In my search for a fairer portrait, I benefitted significantly from suffrage studies by Margot Duley and Elspeth Tulloch for Newfoundland and New Brunswick, respectively, as well as numerous smaller local studies and suffragist biographies. I have also researched primary (original) documents at thirteen provincial, municipal, university, and national archives.

The chapters that follow are organized by province because female enfranchisement provincially and in the Dominion of Newfoundland required amendments to mid-nineteenth-century voting legislation. Amendments could be made only by majority approval on three occasions in each respective House of Assembly: first, a bill had to be introduced and further consideration requested; next, it had to be approved at a second reading, usually preceded by a fulsome debate; and, finally, there was the third reading, usually at a committee level outside of the regular legislative sitting. Because provincial enfranchisement rules were also used federally until 1920, suffrage campaigns targeted provincial legislation change that would extend to the federal level. Distinct campaigns emerged in each of the Maritime provinces and Newfoundland against a backdrop of a broad interrogation of power and privilege, both inside and outside the four Houses of Assembly.

Each jurisdiction receives attention in the chronological order that it achieved the vote: Nova Scotia in 1918, New Brunswick in 1919, Prince Edward Island in 1922, and Newfoundland in 1925. Chapters demonstrate how suffrage campaigns unfolded within local political contexts; their connections to other human rights and social reform campaigns; the range of the suffrage groups; the significance of property; ethnic, age, and other voting qualifications; the effect of school board and municipal elections on suffrage campaigns at higher levels; and the impact of the First World War. Advocates everywhere trudged with determination and courage along similar but nevertheless distinctive pathways.

The Maritime provinces and Newfoundland had long, vigorous, strategic, and hard-won suffrage battles. Stubborn advocates fought fierce opponents thousands of times in hundreds of skirmishes in the press, the legislature, universities, churches, clubs, societies, and theatres – but also in living rooms, kitchens, and job sites. Dogged resolve won the day. Although during its long campaign, Newfoundland was a separate Crown colony of Great Britain rather than a province of Canada, its distinctive trajectory is part of the Atlantic Canadian story.

With due gratitude to [Attorney General of Nova
Scotia] Mr. Longley for his chivalrous desire to
save us from self-destruction, we will take the
risk of the strain upon our delicate "moral fibre"
of depositing a ballot once in four years ...

– M.R. CHESLEY, LETTER TO THE EDITOR,
HALIFAX HERALD, 23 MARCH 1895

ONE

SUFFRAGE CONTEXTS AND CHALLENGES IN THE MARITIMES AND NEWFOUNDLAND

Petition from residents of Lunenburg County
in favour of female suffrage, 1917.
Note that Mary Russell Chesley is the first signatory.

THE FIGHT FOR WOMEN'S suffrage was a series of provincial movements rather than a national one because it occurred before standard federal franchise requirements were set. Until the passage of the Dominion Elections Act in 1920, federal elections used the voting requirements of the provinces. Advocates for suffrage therefore focused on provincial voting legislation, all of which excluded women. The same pattern occurred in Newfoundland, whose suffrage campaign and legislation were separate from Britain's.

Although there were four distinct campaigns in Atlantic Canada, they shared legal, religious, economic, demographic, and cultural contexts. These included significant connections to organized religion, class and ethnic hierarchies, and challenges that caught the attention of politicians, given suffrage's chronological overlap with numerous political and economic crises. These shared contexts affected the ways in which suffrage emerged.

Female enfranchisement numbered among the key North American and European human rights reforms that also included married women's property and custody rights. The Maritime provinces and Newfoundland were among the many jurisdictions that renegotiated British common law in the mid- to late nineteenth century. Prior to the reforms, wives were represented by their husbands in all legal matters. In effect, they experienced a legal death upon marriage. They could not own or sell property, sue or be sued, control their wages, or initiate divorce. The same principle extended to the vote: husbands spoke for their wives at the polls. The common law enshrined their physical, financial, and emotional vulnerability. Its precepts energized wealthy families who feared that feckless husbands could potentially fritter away the fortunes of heiresses. These concerns, plus increasing recognition of the predicament of the growing mass of working women who were married to dissolute providers, incited some of the earliest reforms in Atlantic Canada, as elsewhere. Deserted wives' acts implemented between 1843 and 1860 denied claims on wives' wages or property to husbands who had abandoned their families. Over more than a century, amended laws allowed married women to control property with the same rights as men. That demand for equal marital rights fostered demands for suffrage.

In *One Hundred Years of Struggle,* the first volume in this series, historian Joan Sangster rightly characterizes the Canadian suffrage movement as a "circle of ideas and people that sits within two other social movement circles." In the inner sanctum, a select group of women (and men) championed the vote as the key recognition of full citizenship that would introduce a better world. Beyond them, a larger social reform circle distributed its energy across diverse causes, from public health and child welfare to criminal justice and religious equality, as well as politics. Farther beyond was a broad women's movement constituency encompassing a plethora of suffrage, reform, and religious groups, with causes ranging from the conservative to the truly radical.

RELIGION

Organized religion was vital to the suffrage movement in Atlantic Canada and the broader social reform movement. It motivated women, justified their new public roles, and provided organizational and leadership experience from which to draw. The vast majority of late-nineteenth-century Maritimers and Newfoundlanders identified as Christian, with Catholic, Presbyterian, Anglican, Methodist, and Baptist the main denominations. All shared assumptions about the distinctive roles of the sexes, particularly women's maternalism. Many, in what has been termed the "Protestant Social Gospel" and "Social Catholicism," were also committed to improving the world. Though atheists and agnostics were instrumental in the suffrage movement, many suffragists were driven by religious faith, a justification that made their views generally more palatable. Church allegiances affirmed them, not as threats to social relations, but as advocates of essential religious principles. Respectable groups such as the Anglican Church Women, Catholic Women's League, Baptist Women's Missionary Society, and the African United Baptist Association took up issues, such as temperance and child welfare, that set women on the path to a larger role in public life.

Not all challenges to the status quo were obvious. Catholic women found leadership and fulfillment in nearby or faraway religious orders, with hundreds of Maritime and Newfoundland women choosing vows of poverty, chastity, and obedience over families. Convents were rarely self-determining, but nuns elected their own leaders and had considerable economic independence. Such options may have reduced Catholic women's enthusiasm for secular reforms, including suffrage, which was condemned by the pope. In some Protestant evangelical churches, such as the Methodist and Baptist Churches, women gained opportunities to preach, despite Saint Paul's admonition that they remain silent in church. Maritime and Newfoundland women of faith such as May Coy (1771–1859), Mary MacKinnon Fletcher (1773–?), Mary Narraway Bond (1779–1854), Anna Towle (1796–1876), Susannah Lynds McCurdy (1776–1862), and Martha Jago (1807–75) expanded opportunities for their sex by speaking in churches, gospel tents, community halls, taverns, and other public spaces. Like nuns in large orders, Protestant overseas missionary societies, in sites as far afield as India and China, disproved myths of female weakness and passivity. Indeed, some women in missionary support groups were directly linked to the suffrage cause. Many members also worked on temperance campaigns and mustered for the Woman's Christian Temperance Union, which endorsed suffrage nationally in 1888.

POLITICAL AND ECONOMIC VULNERABILITY

The suffrage movement in Atlantic Canada was further affected by economic and political vulnerability. In the 1880s, the critical decade that laid the foundation of the movement, the futures of Nova Scotia, New Brunswick, and Prince Edward Island remained uncertain after their recent confederation with Canada. Newfoundland, which had rejected Confederation, remained a British dominion until 1949. With a combined population of just over 1 million, the four jurisdictions suffered an extended worldwide recession, which was compounded in the Maritimes by Ottawa's preoccupation with settling the Prairies and strengthening manufacturing industries in the central provinces to the detriment of those in the east. People and investments jumped ship from Atlantic Canada at unprecedented rates during the late nineteenth century. Although per capita income in the more prosperous jurisdictions of Nova Scotia and New Brunswick initially clung to the national average, it soon faltered.

By the end of the nineteenth century, the Atlantic region was caricatured as out-of-date, nearly moribund. Calls by Maritime business leaders and politicians for improving their integration into Confederation were ignored by Ottawa. At the same time, Newfoundland's relationship with Britain soured when London failed to deal with the controversial arrangement on the French Shore that gave France fishing rights to the western perimeter of the colony. Nostalgia festered for past glory days, with vibrant shipping and shipbuilding industries that had linked dozens of rural communities and urban manufacturing centres with global ambitions until the 1880s.

As primary industries employed most wage earners in the late nineteenth century, the economic downturn negatively affected per capita incomes. Agriculture was less lucrative than in other regions, timber sales fell sharply, and the fishery swung between feast and famine. In Saint John, Marysville, Halifax, Sydney, and Truro, factories of various sizes continued to refine sugar and to produce cotton, leather, and rope, but profits had dropped by the late nineteenth century. Coal mining surged in Cape Breton and western Nova Scotia, but gains were undercut by dangerous working conditions, diminishing wages, and labour unrest. Between 1871 and 1901, the lack of satisfactory local employment pushed nearly a quarter of a million Maritimers, especially women, youth, and anglophones, to factory and domestic work in the Boston States, which had the domino effect of further weakening the economy and the potential of a Maritime metropolis. All of these economic concerns distracted local governments from new causes, including women's rights and suffrage.

CLASS AND ETHNIC HIERARCHIES

Most suffrage leaders in Atlantic Canada were drawn from the dominant class and ethnicity, and were largely indifferent to the rights of those outside their circle. The area was well established by the late nineteenth century, with 80 percent of its approximately 1-million-strong population native-born and most arable land settled. This long history of predominantly European settlement contrasted with that of the vast area west of Ontario, where only 100,000 Euro-Canadian settlers and 60,000 Indigenous people lived at the time of Confederation in 1867. Between 1881 and 1911, however, some 1.5 million immigrants settled in the West, increasing the Euro-Canadian Prairie population from 3.2 to 22.2 percent of the national population and decreasing that of the Maritimes from 18.2 to 11.4 percent. Whereas western immigration peaked in the early 1910s, it occurred in the Maritimes during the 1830s and 1840s, when skilled and unskilled immigrants, mostly from the British Isles, had been attracted to the traditional resource industries as well as the shipbuilding and shipping industries of the Maritimes. In Newfoundland, the Irish and English arrived to engage in the cod – and to a lesser degree, seal and whale – fishery, 85 percent of them living in outport communities in the late nineteenth century.

The older settler society of the Maritimes may have encouraged religious, ethnic, and class fissures. British residents outnumbered the two main ethnic minority populations, the Acadians and Indigenous peoples, by almost nine to one. Smaller minority groups of Jewish, African, German, Lebanese, and Chinese descent residing in scattered enclaves faced overt discrimination, with higher rates of poverty and illiteracy, restricted social mobility, and exclusion from the governing and business elite. As in Europe and elsewhere in Canada, disputes between Catholics and Protestants could result in violence. These rifts made inclusivity in the suffrage movement improbable. Furthermore, the region lacked any boost of recent immigration from countries that supported enfranchisement, such as Iceland, whose female migrants to the Prairies in the 1870s and 1880s encouraged its suffrage movement.

Anti-French, anti-Catholic discrimination against the Acadians, the largest minority, led them to establish their own francophone newspapers, universities, and inter-provincial conventions during the late nineteenth century. These accomplishments, along with a high birth rate, made them a force to be reckoned with, including in provincial elections. This sometimes worked against the suffrage movement. When Catholic laymen (including not only the majority of Acadians but also large numbers of Irish and Scottish men) were elected to government, they upheld their church's official stance against enfranchisement until well into the 1910s. Catholic women rarely participated in mainstream social reform movements, including the campaign for the vote. Catholic charitable and social improvement efforts, such as the League of the Cross, a temperance group, were tied to the church.

Whereas Acadian women were rarely invited into the mainstream movement, Indigenous women were even more invisible to most suffrage advocates. In the mid-nineteenth century, Indigenous people made up approximately 2 to 3 percent of Atlantic

Canada's population. They included the Mi'kmaq and Wolastoqiyik in the Maritimes and the Mi'kmaq and Innu in Newfoundland. Greater prejudice, including exclusion from the franchise, meant that they did not possess the cultural traction of the Acadians. Not yet united with Canada, Newfoundland did not adhere to the Indian Act of 1876 or have any land treaties. Newfoundland Mi'kmaq tended to live on the western shores of the island, and the Innu populated Labrador. Although the region's only residential school, Shubenacadie (near Truro, Nova Scotia), was not established until 1929, several day schools opened 140 years earlier as part of church-based assimilation projects. Unlike in Australia and New Zealand, there is no evidence that late-nineteenth- or early-twentieth-century Atlantic Canadian suffragists had any interest in winning the franchise for Indigenous women. Furthermore, many Indigenous women were ambivalent about the provincial vote, the main focus of the suffrage movement, because of their stronger ties to the federal government and the Queen through treaties and the federally controlled Indian Act.

Descendants of African Canadians have resided in the Maritimes as long as Europeans, including enslaved Black people who toiled in the French fortress of Louisbourg during the early eighteenth century and more than three thousand free and enslaved Blacks who were part of Planter and Loyalist migrations of the late eighteenth century. Repeatedly, Maritime governments broke promises of providing arable land, education, and infrastructure to force free Black citizens into cheap labour. In the face of such overt, sanctioned racism, many moved on. The population grew back slowly, recovering to three thousand in the late nineteenth century, the largest concentration in Nova Scotia where it composed nearly 4 percent of the population. With the British Empire outlawing slavery only in 1833, elite Maritimers in the early colonial period kept enslaved people as domestic servants and labourers, courts upheld slavery, and the law supported returning escaped slaves to their American owners.

When slavery ended, racism and segregation continued. Despite early successful alliances from the 1830s to the 1850s, including with the Conservative Party in Nova Scotia and Liberal reformer Joseph Howe, African Maritimers and Newfoundlanders were again forced to find support outside the mainstream, primarily in Baptist churches. The African United Baptist Association, created in 1854, linked more than forty Black communities, provided needed leadership, and sought out practical ways around anti-Black strictures. In the 1890s, its conventions began to include female delegates, such as regular participant Louisa Ann Johnson (?–1911), a Halifax shopkeeper who was also a keen temperance advocate. As with Acadians, Black Atlantic Canadians saw the power of their own press. The *Atlantic Advocate,* a monthly journal "devoted to the interests of coloured people in the Dominion," began publication in 1915. Among its founding editors was Miriam A. DeCosta, a feminist forerunner to another Nova Scotia Black woman journalist, Carrie Best (1903–2001), who founded the *Clarion* in 1946. Although prohibited from training either as teachers or nurses, some Black women taught in local schools through special permission licences. A handful also ran small businesses in the late nineteenth century, including Halifax grocer and artist Edith Macdonald-Brown (1880–1956). As one historian summarized, from the end of slavery until the 1960s, "Black women in North America, and more specifically in Nova Scotia, suffered the overt effects of individual, institutional and cultural racism. The results were widespread illiteracy, underemployment, unemployment, economic deprivation, political powerlessness, social rejection, spiritual exclusion and other negative elements imposed on the Black community by white Nova Scotian society." Although a few Black women beat remarkable odds to achieve formal education, none are known to have participated in the suffrage movement.

DEFINING THE WORTHINESS OF VOTERS
In the nineteenth century, participation in elections was treated

as a privilege that was properly extended only to those who were seen as having a stake in society, most often landowning male taxpayers, rather than to everyone based on innate humanity or dignity. This long-standing ideology was most famously articulated by seventeenth-century political economist John Locke (1632–1704), who claimed that male landowners were instinctively committed to responsible government and could be trusted to vote in the best interests of the community. Governments rarely saw Acadian, Indigenous, Black, or poor Maritimers as deserving of the privilege. However, when it came to the franchise, ethnic and racial minority men had priority over all women because they were potential heads of households, breadwinners, and soldiers. Except for Indigenous men, they were included in late-nineteenth-century demands for universal male suffrage, which dropped property owning as a requirement. In contrast, women, like children, were identified as meaningfully represented by male family members. That their interests might differ from those of male kin was ignored. Indeed, suffrage was all the more feared because it might sharpen family disagreements, in effect exposing a reality of conflicting interests.

The tie between property and the franchise remained in place for women long after it faded for men. Before reforms in married women's property laws in the nineteenth century, only single women (never married or widowed) could hold property. As taxpayers without a male representative, they were seen to merit the vote more than married women (who were "represented" by their husbands) or unpropertied single women (who did not pay taxes). At the same time, single female adults were suspect for insufficiently investing in the patriarchal domestic order; their right to vote was based solely on the principle of no taxation without representation. A particularly strong commitment to a property franchise often allowed Atlantic Canadian municipalities, like those elsewhere in Canada, to become the first level of government to enfranchise qualified women. It also meant that municipal franchises were among the last to be fully democratized, since female and male tenants who could not afford the poll tax – a fee charged to non-property-holders for the privilege to vote – were not eligible to participate in some municipal elections. Halifax, for example, abolished its poll tax requirement only in 1949 and did not give married women the full municipal franchise until 1963.

Distinctive houses of assembly and political environments required Atlantic Canadian suffrage advocates to employ a number of strategies tailored to convince those who held power in each particular jurisdiction. At the same time, local orientation was offset by important transnational influences fostered in activist networks ranging into the United States and Britain, and to a lesser degree, the rest of Canada. Some links were created by immigrants as they shared correspondence, read newspapers, and joined national and international church, temperance, professional, and suffrage organizations. When suffragists in Saint John applauded the visiting American suffragist Julia Ward Howe in 1896, and the British suffragette Sylvia Pankhurst in 1912, they joined a global sisterhood. During extended family stays in Halifax in the late nineteenth century, Anna Leonowens, the Anglo-Indian author of *The English Governess at the Siamese Court* (1870), challenged provincial activists to join an international crusade.

OPPOSITION

The virulent opposition to votes for women provoked a long and exhausting struggle. Anti-suffragists – both male and female – commonly employed four arguments: women were already represented and protected by men; they lacked sufficient intellect; they would be drawn away from their primary domestic duties; and only a small, unrepresentative group wanted the vote. None were unique to the region, but local partisans made them personal, and therefore local. Opposition was never tied to evidence, making it all the harder to fight. For example, even when governments received suffrage petitions with thousands of women's signatures, the old argument that women had not demonstrated interest was inevitably trotted out by sanctimonious opponents. Atlantic Canada's suffragists never accepted the calumnies that were directed at them. As they insisted, women had aptitudes (such as for protecting children) that justified their involvement in issues that men knew less well; their successes in universities and the professions proved their intellectual capacity; the brief time needed to cast a ballot would not threaten domestic duties; and enough women wanted the vote to warrant it, whereas the disinterested would not be forced to vote. More broadly, suffragists fought deep-rooted assumptions about gender roles, particularly the stereotypes of the stalwart male breadwinner and the passive female homemaker. In fact, most households depended upon female labour, indoor and outdoor, stretching around the clock and involving significant mental and physical demands. Nor could many men guarantee the kind of secure incomes that would support the romantic visions of conservatives. Most Atlantic Canadian families, as elsewhere, were working or lower middle class. Entire households toiled to survive. From a twenty-first-century perspective, the assumption that only men were deserving citizens seems ludicrous.

Atlantic Canada's suffrage movement varied in membership, fields of action, choice of strategies, and opponents. No single suffragist embodies its rich history. Although the leadership tended to be female, white, urban, middle class, Protestant, English speaking, and educated, the tens of thousands of supporters, including those who signed petitions from the 1890s through the 1920s, represented a wider range of Maritimers and Newfoundlanders. Personal or observed experiences of social injustice, or a core faith in common humanity, could be a powerful motivation. Activist engagement in particular causes, such as Julia Salter Earle's fury at the appalling factory conditions in Newfoundland, or Edith Archibald's loyalty to British imperialism in Nova Scotia, often generated distinctive interests in the vote. Whatever their differences, suffrage champions met a common hostility. Women were routinely discouraged from entering public debates, and their capacity for rational discourse was ridiculed. Not surprisingly, their strategies commonly began with efforts to demonstrate their merits and contributions to a host of "good" causes, from child protection to public health.

Despite some early advances in higher education and the law, as well as the enfranchisement of certain propertied and often single women in some municipalities during the 1880s, Canadian women could not vote federally until the 1917 Wartime Elections Act. Even then, it was limited to military nurses or those who had close male relatives serving overseas in the armed forces. In 1918, federal enfranchisement was extended to all qualified women at twenty-one years of age. Newfoundland women waited until 1925 to vote for members of their House of Assembly. Exclusions remained significant: Newfoundland residents had to be twenty-five; property requirements persisted for decades; and Asian and First Nations women lacked the federal franchise until 1949 and 1960, respectively. Provincially, most women gained the franchise in Nova Scotia in 1918, New Brunswick in 1919, and Prince Edward Island in 1922.

All women are not heroines, neither are all men heroes, but the ordinary woman is not so stupid as some men would affect to believe.

– MARY FLETCHER,
NOVA SCOTIA STENOGRAPHER AND ACTIVIST, 1917

TWO

NOVA SCOTIA:
STEADY, DETERMINED, AND
STRATEGIC AGITATION

Edith Jessie Archibald was a founding
member of the Halifax branch of the Local Council of Women.
There she represented the Woman's Christian Temperance Union
and later served as branch president from 1896 to 1905.

MARY RUSSELL CHESLEY (1847–1923) demonstrated the fervour of Nova Scotia's suffrage movement by publishing a "scathing attack" on anti-suffragist attorney general J.W. Longley in the *Halifax Herald* in 1895. She shredded his justification that he was protecting women by not granting them the vote: "With due gratitude to Mr. Longley for his chivalrous desire to save us from self-destruction, we will take the risk of the strain upon our delicate 'moral fiber' of depositing a ballot once in four years ... Mr. Longley's high-flown rhetoric to the contrary, it is ballots not 'personal charms' that count with politicians." She pointed to jurisdictions that already benefitted from the vote and to the many failures of male legislators to defend women, including allowing fathers to determine the guardianship of offspring without reference to wives and mothers. Unfortunately, Chesley's compelling arguments did nothing to change Longley's opinion.

Although the Mi'kmaq called Nova Scotia home for at least five thousand years before European settlers arrived in the seventeenth century, little has been written about Mi'kmaw women's participation in their government before the twentieth century. The same is true for their association, if any, with the early voting of settler women or the emergence of mainstream demands for the franchise. Existing evidence leaves such questions as yet unanswerable, forcing a focus on the newcomers. Nova Scotia's settler campaign for suffrage built upon a long history of female leadership in religious and social reform societies and was propelled by advances in women's access to higher education and the property rights of wives. The province was noteworthy for some politicians' relatively early endorsement of the Great Cause, the near success of female franchise legislation in 1893, and the impact of the 1917 Halifax Explosion.

Between 1758 (the first colonial election) and 1851, property-owning Nova Scotian women were occasionally reported as voting, a right that was sometimes contested. Records are incomplete, but in 1793, at least six women, probably recently arrived Loyalists, cast their ballots in Windsor. Confirming that they met property, age, and other qualifications, the county sheriff observed that their eligibility was "good if women have a right to vote," but uncertainty remained. In an 1806 Amherst Township by-election, the unsuccessful candidate, Thomas Law Dixon, complained that "several women and persons having no legal qualification" had voted against him, but the legislature allowed their votes to stand. In 1851, Nova Scotia specifically excluded all women. Even so, the matter never entirely disappeared. In 1834, famed Nova Scotia politician and newspaper publisher Joseph Howe (1804–73) argued in a tongue-in-cheek editorial that the province should experiment with having women involved in politics. He reasoned that women were unlikely to do worse than men and that due to their physical inferiority, control would be easy to regain. Though his endorsement was semi-comic and its reception unknown, its appearance in the popular press suggests interest several decades before a mainstream movement emerged in the late nineteenth century.

The suffrage campaign erupted in two phases: 1885 to 1897 and 1904 to 1918. In both stages, white settler women ignored the enfranchisement of Indigenous women (and men) and discouraged the participation of Acadian and African Nova Scotian women. Prior to the campaign, Nova Scotia improved protection for deserted wives and married women's rights to property. These gains, in tandem with female involvement in the surging agitation for social reform, fostered a synergy that fed the drive for the vote and made the last decade of the nineteenth century especially memorable. Key activists materialized, among them the three Ritchie sisters: Ella (1844–1928), Mary (1850–1917), and Eliza (1856–1933); Edith Archibald (1854–1936); and Anna Leonowens (1831–1915), all members of the Halifax branch of the Local Council of Women (LCW); as well as Lunenburg resident and international peace activist Mary Russell Chesley. Aside from journalist Ella Murray (1874–1949), the Nova Scotia campaign did not produce a second generation of leaders: the pioneers persisted for almost four decades. Most had lived in either Britain or the United States, maintaining less contact with the rest of Canada, so they focused on the province rather than the region or the

Sisters Eliza, Mary, and Ella Ritchie were suffrage advocates and members of the Halifax LCW. At their parents' death in 1890, the three spinsters inherited enough to live together in Halifax, employ several live-in domestics, and pursue suffrage and other reform work.

Eliza, the youngest, was probably the first Canadian woman to earn a doctorate. She spent more than a decade in the United States, where she studied for her PhD in German philosophy at Cornell and taught at Vassar and then Wellesley. After returning to Halifax in 1899, she established a Dalhousie alumni association that, unlike the original, included women, and spearheaded the first women's residence on the Dalhousie campus in 1912, acting as an unpaid warden in the first year. Though a committed suffragist, Eliza was a pessimist who emphasized gradual steps. In the early twentieth century, she sat on the executive of the Halifax branch of the Victorian Order of Nurses and then headed the National Council of Women's country. Their strategies developed with an eye across the Atlantic and the international border. The first phase of the suffrage movement culminated in the early 1890s, when MLA Albert Hemeon (1873–1949) introduced four suffrage bills. These bills met increasingly spiteful opposition that was anchored by the powerful J.W. Longley (1849–1922), long-time attorney general.

DEMOGRAPHIC, ECONOMIC, AND POLITICAL CONTEXTS OF SUFFRAGE

Suffrage debates played out within Nova Scotia's dominant class, which had been formed over a long period. The location of Nova

committee on public health. Unlike the rest of her family, who maintained strong connections to St. Paul's Anglican Church, she identified as an agnostic Anglican.

Mary, considered the most religious of the sisters, was active in the Girls' Friendly Society of St. Paul's Anglican Church, which supported teenagers from downtown working-class neighbourhoods. It evolved into broader child welfare initiatives, including campaigns for supervised playgrounds, tree planting, and pasteurized milk. Her determination to obtain a female playground commissioner reflected her strategy of putting women into influential municipal positions at a time when they were barred from sitting on school boards and voting provincially.

The eldest, Ella, focused on the Victoria College of Art, serving on its board for four decades. Art was commonly seen as an appropriate hobby for women, so her interest could suggest relative conservatism. Though she was often described as charming and traditional, Ella too was a committed suffragist.

Scotia (or Acadie as the French called it) made it attractive, first to the Mi'kmaq and then to both French and British colonizers. The gateway to the St. Lawrence and Quebec, as well as an easy boat trip away from the populous British colonies of the east coast, it was contested in wars that prevailed well into the eighteenth century. Under the Treaty of Utrecht of 1713, the British officially assumed control, but their hegemony continued to be challenged. Whereas the French had co-existed relatively peacefully with the Mi'kmaq, the British did not. When Halifax was founded in 1749, its first governor, Edward Cornwallis, stole Mi'kmaw lands and offered rewards for Mi'kmaw scalps. A few years later, the British turned on the French, expelling thousands of Acadians from the Atlantic region between 1755 and 1762. That strategy provoked anger among the province's French Canadians and Mi'kmaq that persists into the twenty-first century.

As a result of the American Revolutionary War, more than thirty-five thousand Loyalists, among them free and enslaved Blacks, sparked Nova Scotia's division into three colonies in 1784: the western mainland became New Brunswick, Cape Breton became a separate colony (it rejoined Nova Scotia five decades later), and the eastern mainland peninsula became a smaller Nova Scotia. Scottish and Irish immigrants also arrived to take free, fertile land. The French Revolutionary and Napoleonic Wars from 1789 to 1814 (which include the War of 1812, fought on North American soil) increased Nova Scotia's commercial importance.

The arrival of Scottish Highlander, Irish, African American, and returning Acadian immigrants tripled the population from 65,000 in 1807 to over 200,000 in 1837. These settlers strengthened already diversified primary economies of agriculture, fishing, and forestry; created world-class shipbuilding and transportation industries; and staffed a burgeoning coal industry. Tertiary industries developed, including banks, mail service, and railways, and European-style socio-cultural and political maturity was epitomized by three colleges, several newspapers, an abolitionist society, the success of professional artists such as Maria Morris Miller (1813–75), and the implementation of responsible government in 1847. Progress was not total. Legislators restricted voting eligibility by making property requirements more onerous and by formally excluding women: the franchise was more than ever a privilege meant for white men who had proven their value through owing property. In the decades leading up to the Confederation era, Nova Scotia, although primarily agricultural and therefore sparsely settled with a population of 123,630 in 1827, was relatively flourishing. It could not compare, however, with Lower Canada (present-day Quebec) at a population of almost half a million or with the northeastern United States at approximately 5 million.

What would be coined the "Blue Nose" province stood at the centre of the region's pre-Confederation golden age, with booming shipbuilding, shipping, and coal mining. Nonetheless, the gains were not spread evenly. Roughly two thousand Mi'kmaq and eight thousand African Nova Scotians, alongside many thousands of Irish Catholic urban workers and Acadians, experienced racism and poverty. Slavery remained legal until 1833, and until 1826, Nova Scotia legislation disenfranchised otherwise qualified Catholics who refused to take an oath in support of Protestantism and against the pope. Women of any class or ethnicity lacked most rights and were treated as the property of their fathers or husbands, and racialized women were that much worse off; only single women with property had a legal presence.

In 1864, an invitation to the three Maritime colonies to confederate with the larger United Province of Canada, comprising today's Ontario and Quebec, reset politics. A fractious debate, occurring against the backdrop of the American Civil War (1861–65), emerged between defenders of the status quo and optimistic champions of a bigger canvas for ambitions. The latter prevailed:

with the United Province of Canada, Nova Scotia (and New Brunswick) entered Confederation in July 1867.

Criticism persisted, however, with secessionists pointing to unfavourable tariff and transportation costs. By the mid-1880s, the previously robust production of nails, confectionary, wool, leather, and glass was collapsing. Only iron and steel manufacturing remained lucrative but without local ownership. Nova Scotia businessmen and politicians assailed national policies – protectionist tariffs, western immigration schemes, and railway expansion – as unfair. Despairing Maritime youth, a significant number of them women, left for New England, where they became factory and domestic workers. Outmigration slowed Nova Scotia's population growth from nearly 20 percent (1851 to 1861) to just 2 percent (1881 to 1891).

Not only had Nova Scotia failed to integrate economically with Canada, it also remained socially and culturally connected to Britain and the Boston States by kin, transportation, and cultural ties. The largest ethnic minority group, the Acadians, blossomed due to lower rates of outmigration, higher rates of natural increase, and strengthened cultural awareness. In fact, the Acadian Renaissance of the late nineteenth century provides another example of the rejection of a Canadian identity for a local Maritime one. Frustration with Ottawa and nostalgia for the pre-Confederation era in the face of federal charges of backwardness poisoned the political environment even as Nova Scotian suffragists attempted to shift hearts and minds.

FAITH-BASED WOMEN'S ORGANIZATIONS

Suffrage arose from inspirational conversations, including among members of church-based reform societies, advocates of women's access to higher education and the professions, and legal reformers who targeted deserted wives' acts and married women's property acts. Baptist and Methodist churches increasingly produced female members who were impatient with the state of society and who transformed many generations of faith-based work into more secular (non-denominational) activism. A very early initiative was the Halifax Wesleyan Female Benevolent Society that formed in 1816 in the aftermath of the Napoleonic wars to address women's vulnerability when several thousand soldiers, sailors, and prisoners of war were "let loose in a little town of less than 10 thousand inhabitants."

Baptist women turned to missionary societies. One well-known missionary, Hannah Maria Norris (1842–1919), who served in Burma and India during the 1870s, founded the first Canadian woman's missionary society, which established thirty-eight provincial branches. Such initiatives gradually encouraged respect for female faith and capacity. By the late nineteenth century, many Protestants had shifted from an emphasis on personal salvation toward social reforms, such as providing food and clothing to impoverished families and aid to unmarried female domestics. Widespread racism forced Black Baptist women to conduct social reform work through the African United Baptist Association, formed in 1854, while white Protestant women turned to more secular solutions than they had in the past.

The first group to link religious reformers with enfranchisement was the Woman's Christian Temperance Union (WCTU). Founded in the United States in 1873 by Frances Willard (1839–98), it quickly established several Nova Scotia branches in that decade, as well as the Maritime WCTU in 1878. Though temperance societies had existed much earlier, the non-denominational (but Protestant) WCTU soon became Nova Scotia's largest women's group. In 1890, the same year it hosted the touring Frances Willard and her secretary, Anna Gordon (1853–1931), the Maritime WCTU set up a franchise department, the region's first administrative entity devoted to obtaining the vote for women. The inaugural director, Edith Archibald of New Glasgow, became a long-serving and effective suffragist. Convincing other pro-suffrage WCTU members that provincial franchise departments would be more effective than one regional one, Archibald transitioned into the superintendent role of the newly formed Nova Scotia WCTU franchise department in 1895. She was followed in that role by the equally capable Mary Russell Chesley who served more than two decades.

WCTU members took up the franchise for two broad reasons – because it was both a basic human right and a tool for reform. Their large numbers throughout the province were a force to be reckoned with. Meetings trained members in organizational leadership and public speaking. Soon enough, modelling themselves on Frances Willard, many moved well beyond calling for temperance. Tens of thousands of signatures on WCTU petitions to the Nova Scotia House of Assembly in the late nineteenth century inspired and enraged politicians. An 1878 petition from Hantsport, a rural shipbuilding town, signalled ambitions: "We, the undersigned Petitioners, residents of Nova Scotia, declare our belief that the need, as well as the spirit of the times, demands the political enfranchisement of women as an act of justice, and as a means for promoting the prosperity of the State, the Home, and the Individual."

Historians have sometimes stressed the middle-class elitism of the WCTU and its desire to control the working class through temperance, but some members, such as Mary Chesley, represent another inspiration, that of equal rights and pacifism: the vote was a human right. As a well-educated Nova Scotian who lived in Lunenburg, Chesley was living proof that the appeal of the Great Cause extended beyond Halifax. She also exemplified the steadfast high-mindedness that kept the WCTU at the suffrage forefront. In fact, for an activist outside an urban centre, the WCTU was Chesley's only opportunity to engage with other reformers; its various departments mimicked umbrella organizations representing a variety of reforms and interests beyond temperance.

HIGHER EDUCATION

As with faith-based women's societies, the campaign for women's admission to higher education intersected with demands for the vote. Both relied on intelligence and rationality, which is just where opponents insisted that women fell short. Mid-nineteenth-century Nova Scotia supported five institutions of higher learning: King's (1789), Dalhousie (1818), Horton, later called Acadia (1838), St. Mary's (1841), and St. Francis Xavier (1853). Their early establishment linked higher education firmly to progress. All were denominational and none accepted women. In 1860, however, Acadia founded a separate ladies' college (seminary) and dormitory. As at Mount Allison Ladies Academy in New Brunswick, the request of female students to take occasional college courses seemed natural, although they were told not to "consider [themselves] as members of the College." The shift was all the easier because the Baptist-affiliated institution was often in close contact with the denomination's female missionaries and preachers. Higher education was justified on the same terms as religious callings: women had divine gifts. By the 1870s, influential schools in New England, such as Mount Holyoke and Smith College, and New Brunswick's Mount Allison College, offered courses to the province's ambitious young women. When Clara Bell Marshall earned the top mark in history at Acadia in 1884, there was no public effort to deny her degree, as had been the case at Mount Allison a decade before. And in 1889, Acadia graduated the first Black woman in the region, New Brunswicker Lalia Halfkenny (1870–96), a remarkable and exceptional achievement given the barriers to the education of Black girls. Only two other women earned degrees at Acadia in the next few years, but between 1893 and 1900, their numbers increased to forty-five.

Dalhousie implemented women's admission with little opposition. The university paper, the *Gazette*, advocated coeducation, as did the *Presbyterian Witness,* the organ of the church that sponsored Dalhousie. Whereas Acadia boasted a ladies' seminary as a foundation for its initiative, Dalhousie started from scratch. Because its charter did not specifically deny them admission, interested women were told to apply. When some did in 1881, the senate passed a resolution "that female students shall hereafter be entitled to attend lectures ... and to compete for and take all such prizes, honours and exhibitions and Bursaries as are now open to male students, so that hereafter there shall be no distinction in regard to college work or degrees between male and female students." Two candidates were admitted a few months later. In the next two decades, almost four hundred women attended, composing almost one-quarter of the student body, though far fewer completed degrees. The resolution stated that there would be no distinction regarding college degrees, but the program remained tailored to men, and the gymnasium and reading room were off limits to female students. Coeds nevertheless disproportionately captured academic prizes more than twenty times between 1881 and 1921, including the top graduating award, which upset many male students and faculty.

Dalhousie and Acadia were Protestant strongholds. Nova Scotia's first Catholic institution to accept women was St. Francis Xavier, located in the Scottish Catholic area of Antigonish. Catholics may have worried that female students might draw young men away from the priesthood. The possibility of sexual temptation prompted many bishops to reject coeds. However, in Antigonish, two successive bishops showed sympathy for separate higher education. In the early 1880s, the nuns of Montreal's Congregation of Notre-Dame accepted an invitation to run a provincially funded girls' academy on the St. Francis Xavier campus. Mount Saint Bernard, named after the congregation's first mother superior, opened in 1883, with eighty female day students and four boarders. Within a decade, it offered college courses, and in 1894 it affiliated with St. Francis Xavier University, making it the first Catholic university in North America to provide courses for women leading to a bachelor's degree. Four graduated in 1897. Another Catholic university, Saint Mary's, rejected women until the 1960s, succumbing only due to financial necessity. Until then, Halifax had Mount Saint Vincent College, Canada's only independent degree-granting post-secondary institution for women and a leader in the second-wave feminist movement of Atlantic Canada.

THE PROFESSIONS

The settler women of Nova Scotia may have had a greater choice of universities than those in other provinces, but they faced a fierce fight for professional degrees and entry into the professions. The Halifax Medical School operated separately from Dalhousie between 1875 and 1889. After its reintegration, women were never formally excluded, although neither were they encouraged to enrol. In 1894, Annie Isabel Hamilton (1866–1941) became its first female graduate. In 1905, four of fifteen medical students were women. Their victory came in the face of bitter opposition from male students and professors, and within the profession. Hamilton was typically harassed about her looks. Dalhousie was never the only alternative. Nineteen-year-old Maria Angwin (1849–98) of Dartmouth graduated from New York's Women's Medical College Infirmary for Women and Children in 1882. After practising in Boston and London, she returned to Halifax to become the province's first licensed female doctor, with a practice focused on the poor. She might have preferred a different clientele, but few Haligonians would have chosen a female doctor.

Law proved a similar struggle. Frances Lilian Fish (1888–1975), a native of Miramichi, New Brunswick, became the first woman to earn a law degree from Dalhousie. She was called to the provincial bar in 1918. Like Angwin some quarter of a century earlier, she suffered continued abuse. As with many later graduates, Fish proved unable immediately to pursue a legal career. Working-class and ethnic minority women, who still remain underrepresented in universities and the professions, had far fewer opportunities.

THE LAW

Even as women demanded educational and professional advances, they sought legislative redress, particularly changes to the British common law principle that wives were politically, economically, and legally represented by their husbands. This cornerstone of Nova Scotia law underpinned voting qualifications. In 1832, Judge Beamish Murdock defended it, rationalizing that families' property and wages formed a collective fund to the benefit of all members. He stressed that husbands were responsible for family well-being and debts, including those incurred by wives. Many Nova Scotians knew full well that this ideal often failed in practice, leaving women vulnerable. Critics initially focused on the property rights of deserted wives, but eventually they evaluated the rights of wives in intact marriages. Because the franchise depended on property, that shift informed the suffrage story.

Married women's property law was a particular source of grievance for women. Enforced in colonial Nova Scotia, the English Dower Act of 1833 left a wife's property unprotected during the lifetime of her husband and restricted dower to property held at his death, although it protected widows from eviction by male heirs. Because there was no divorce law, deserted wives had few options when an absent husband claimed their earnings and very little way of acquiring financial support from him. Virtuous women raising children on their own could be held financially responsible for the debts of deserted husbands – a fact that angered middle-class politicians and reformers who feared dissolute sons- or brothers-in-law.

The first attempts at a married women's property law in Nova Scotia, intended to limit vulnerability in extreme circumstances, came in the 1850s and 1860s. The initial reforms targeted drunken absconders. The obvious next step, a modest 1855 bill modelled on the 1848 New York Married Women's Property Law, failed. Others similarly miscarried until a truncated version of the 1855 bill passed in 1866. Its very title, An Act for the Protection of Married Women in Certain Cases, signalled its limits. Deserted wives had to prove desertion to male judges, which only six women attempted between 1866 and 1884. Although the 1866 act was weak, at least it inspired later reform. Less positively, it reflected deep hostility to women's rights, including enfranchisement, and was considerably weaker than acts in other provinces. Women had two other options for protecting property. The first was a marriage settlement, a remedy whose costs deterred all but the relatively well-to-do. The second allowed the very limited group whose husbands were confined to Dartmouth's Grove Inebriate Asylum to be named guardians of family property.

In 1884, the married women's property law was finally amended significantly. Spurred by a revised English women's property law of two years earlier, the amendment boasted one hundred clauses on rights and responsibilities. Most foundational was the women's right to control the property they brought into marriage. In addition, they could insure their own lives; deposit or withdraw money from banks; and control their own wages, which were not subject to their husbands' creditors. Many provisions nevertheless required the written consent of the husband and maintained patriarchal oversight. Lacking direct access to the tools for revising legislation, women sometimes advocated for their own property rights by lobbying influential male relatives and friends.

THE MUNICIPAL FRANCHISE

"Rights talk" was pervasive in the 1887 discussion of the first municipal suffrage bill presented to the Nova Scotia House of Assembly. Property-owning single women were the first beneficiaries of this initiative. As one Liberal MLA argued, "it was pure justice" that a taxpayer who did not have a husband to represent her should have a voice in choosing the governments that set the taxation rate. Opponents countered by asserting that too few women wanted the right and that no respectable MLA would want his wife, sister, or daughter "insulted by the crowd around a polling booth." Anti-suffrage MLAs proposed to adjourn the 1887 vote for three months. At the final committee stage, one legislator made a last-ditch sortie in defence of the "old maids" who had not yet abandoned their hopes for matrimony. As he explained, their chances at marriage would be better if "husbands could vote on the property they held." Though that sophistry was at best comic, he correctly foresaw that "greater concessions" would follow. In the end, the committee unanimously approved the Act to Confer upon Female Ratepayers the Right to Vote at Civic and Municipal Elections, enfranchising all widows and unmarried women who owned sufficient property. The act also enfranchised *some* property-owning married women whose husbands were not qualified to vote – women who were under "protection orders" because of their husband's cruelty, abandonment, lunacy, incarceration for a criminal offence, or "minor status." Similarly significant was the provision, at least in theory, that a woman aged twenty-one or more who brought property into the marriage and whose husband was under twenty-one could vote until he reached the age of majority, after which he could vote on the basis of her property.

In short, for the first time since their exclusion in 1851, some women had the franchise. White settlers were the chief beneficiaries, but at least one African Nova Scotian, shopkeeper Louisa Ann Johnson, also profited. Although the new voters encompassed fewer than 5 percent of all Nova Scotia women aged twenty-one and over, they were joined a year later by their counterparts in New Brunswick and Prince Edward Island. Gaining the municipal franchise spurred demand for more.

EARLY SUFFRAGE BILLS

Following the 1887 advance, suffragists quickly turned to the provincial franchise. The 1890s produced Nova Scotia's strongest agitation. Grassroots support and sustained legislative interest, peaking in 1893 when a suffrage bill passed its second reading, exceeded those of most Canadian provinces. Nova Scotia could have become the first jurisdiction in the world, even before New Zealand, to grant the vote to qualified women. Although skullduggery at the committee level torpedoed the initiative, its near success suggested changing times.

The WCTU Franchise Department led Nova Scotia's early 1890s campaign, sending hundreds of petitions to the legislature from branches across the province. As its superintendent, Mary Russell Chesley is considered the province's "pioneer worker for women's suffrage." In 1895 alone, she led in organizing thirty-four petitions with ten thousand signatures. Evident enthusiasm spurred the progression of five suffrage bills through second reading in 1891, 1893, 1894, 1895, and 1897. The 1893 bill passed third reading, and those of 1894 and 1895 lost by only one vote at second reading. No other province matched that record in that decade.

The first four suffrage bills were introduced by Albert Hemeon, a merchant, justice of the peace, and Liberal MLA for Queen's County. Of German and Loyalist heritage, he was first elected in 1887 at age forty-four. His motives for introducing the bills remain unknown. Neither he nor his wife was a prominent temperance or reform advocate. After voting for the 1887 women's municipal enfranchisement act, Hemeon led efforts to extend eligibility to propertied single women in provincial elections. He and the seconder of the bill, MLA Charles Smith (1845–1905), justified this measure on the basis of municipal success and no taxation without representation.

Hemeon's first provincial suffrage bill entered second reading in May 1891, when twenty-nine Liberals had been in power for a

An international peace activist, **Mary Russell Chesley** *(1847–1923) stood apart from other Nova Scotia suffragists. Her American grandparents were pacifist Quakers who left the States during the American Revolution. Raised in Dartmouth, she moved to Lunenburg with her lawyer husband and fellow Mount Allison graduate, Samuel Chesley. As superintendent of the WCTU Franchise Department, she was the catalyst behind the thousands of signatures on WCTU petitions from the 1890s until 1918. (See Figure 1.1) She remained active in suffrage and peace movements almost until her death, a commitment all the more remarkable given the death of two of her children in the mid-1890s. According to historian Sharon MacDonald, Mary and Samuel "subsumed their grief in service to the church and public life," as well as in care for their last child. In* The Canadian Men and Women of the Time *(1898), James Morgan lists Chesley as a "controversialist" for her advocacy of suffrage and her beliefs in the "settlement of national difficulties by arbitration, and cooperation as opposed to competition."*

year against nine Conservatives. The main opponent of that bill and the four that followed was also a Liberal – Attorney General J.W. Longley – who used the ploy of skilful oratory to highlight what he termed "the best interest of the ladies." He equated voting with "political warfare," which would reduce women "in the affection and esteem of mankind." Equally dangerously, masculine traits would replace feminine ones, leaving women the losers. Other foes insisted that women would not be mature enough to vote until they reached the age of forty. The division of thirteen for and twenty-two against did not follow party lines. Suffragists could only take heart in glimpsing progress.

Two years later, Hemeon's next suffrage bill was considerably more ambitious. It proposed amending the Election Act of 1885, deleting the word "male," enfranchising women – married and single – with the same qualifications as men. Wives whose husbands held double the minimum property value requirement of $250 could also share the household vote. In the 1893 debate, Hemeon appealed to his reform-minded colleagues on behalf of married women: "Surely, if ... she had a family of sons and daughters ... she was not less affected by the good government of the land ... than when [she had been] a single woman." Others invoked class or status, condemning the fact that uneducated men were automatically enfranchised, whereas educated women were not.

Opponents, however, challenged a bill that had "too many sweeping provisions." Longley again marshalled the major arguments based on the sanctity of separate spheres (the notion that women belonged in the domestic sphere and men in the public sphere) and the need to protect women from the baseness of politics. MLA William Law (1833–1901) retorted that "a woman could not receive any more harm from depositing a ballot in the ballot-box than she could receive from dropping a letter in the post office." In the end, the 1893 measure passed second reading by nineteen for and seventeen against. While "passing in principle," on second reading, it still had to go to the law amendments committee for review, where the chairman, the recalcitrant Longley, stood firm. On 19 April, he reported that the majority voted to delay consideration for three months.

Hemeon urged assemblymen instead to refer the matter to the committee of the whole House, in other words to the same group that had already approved it. Another suffragist, MLA F.A. Laurence, challenged Longley, asking how a bill that had passed

WOMAN'S SUFFRAGE.

A. M. Hemeon's Bill to Enfranchise Nova Scotia's Women Passes Its Second Reading and is Referred to Committee.

The bill to enfranchise women on exactly the same qualifications as men passed a second reading by a vote of 19 to 17 in the house of assembly last evening, after a lengthy discussion. The vote stood as follows:

For—Tupper, Cameron, McKinnon, Clarke, Welton, Hatfield, Roche, Law, Laurence, Webster, Grant, Oxley, A. F. Cameron, Morrow, Hunt, McPherson, Hemeon, Fraser.

Against—Fielding, Longley, Church, Johnston, McNeil, McIsaac, Drysdale, Chisholm, McGregor, Munro, Cahan, Wm. Cameron, Bethune, Forrest, McDonald, LeBlanc, Matheson.

The bill was referred to the committee on law amendments and the general opinion is that its terms will be considerably modified before it passes the final stages.

"Woman's Suffrage," *Halifax Herald,* 11 April 1893. All members present in the House of Assembly voted at a bill's second reading. The third reading was usually handled by a subcommittee of MLAs who normally rubber-stamped the second reading's decision. For Premier Longley, as chair of this subcommittee, to ignore the second reading's positive decision was considered inappropriate interference and even dishonest.

second reading could be delayed. After more debate, Hemeon's amendment passed by seventeen to sixteen, but the Speaker of the Assembly ruled that the committee's refusal to recommend passage was "regular." Even as the legislature met until the end of its spring sitting, MLAs worked alongside suffrage supporters across the province to present petitions to embarrass Longley and contradict his claim that only educated Halifax women wanted suffrage. He refused to budge.

Undeterred, Hemeon introduced additional suffrage bills in 1894 and 1895. In 1894, he made a concession, narrowing his request to propertied, unmarried women. What he did not anticipate was the entrenchment of the opposition. Longley and his allies were determined to refuse any opening, and the bill failed by seventeen to sixteen. Twelve months later, Hemeon introduced the most limited of his suffrage bills, which would apply only to the widows and spinsters who met the property qualifications. Unsurprisingly dejected, he explained that "he could not conceive of a more restricted measure." Its limitations probably did not matter to the opposition. Longley presented his standard argument – women should "not be permitted to destroy themselves or be destroyed." He demanded an amendment to Hemeon's bill in language that was more patronizing and insulting than ever. The petitions with ten thousand signatures – male and female – were dismissed as more about temperance than suffrage. Furthermore, only about five thousand men had signed them. Longley considered the women's signatures of no value, incontrovertibly proving the suffragist claim that women needed the vote! His ninety-minute speech quoted an anti-suffrage poem:

> Rock-a-by baby, your mother is gone;
> She's out at the caucus and will be 'til dawn;
> She wore Papa's trousers and in them looked queer;
> Then hush-a-by baby, your papa is near.

Longley then successfully introduced a motion to defer the vote, which passed by seventeen to sixteen.

SUFFRAGISTS TAKE THE LEAD

The increasing condescension and virulence of Longley and his allies catapulted suffragists into action. Mary Chesley, then superintendent of the Nova Scotia WCTU Franchise Department, published her scathing attack on Longley at this time. A further public condemnation of government inaction came from the Halifax LCW, Nova Scotia women's second-most prominent reform association. By the 1890s, many of its members were leading suffragists. Created in 1894, through an invitation from Lady Aberdeen (1857–1939), wife of the governor general and president of the newly established National Council of Women, the LCW mobilized a women's network to tackle contemporary problems. In a clear rebuke to Longley, representatives of forty-three organizations attended the founding of the Halifax LCW. In addition to nineteen church groups, there were twenty-four nondenominational (but implicitly Christian) reform, charitable, and hobby associations, including the Halifax School for the Blind, the Protestant Orphans' Home, the Halifax Sketch Club, and the South End Tennis Club. Overall, these bodies demonstrated women's contributions to many realms. Many Halifax LCW founders such as Ella, Mary, and Eliza Ritchie, Anna Leonowens, and Edith Archibald, championed rights for women through the LCW franchise subcommittee, although like its national body, the local council avoided direct endorsement of suffrage until 1910.

In her first Council address, held at Government House in spring 1895, the founding president of the Halifax LCW, Emma MacKintosh (1845–?), offered a sturdy rejection of Longley's patronizing comments. Like many other suffragists in the British Empire, MacKintosh, who was married to former Halifax mayor and YMCA supporter James Crosskill MacKintosh (1839–1924), cited Queen Victoria as the ultimate example of female capacity for governing. Here was "a true helpmate and co-worker, instead of a servant and plaything of man." With many local dignitaries in attendance, including the Catholic archbishop, MacKintosh implied that only a backward nation would fail to see the logic that female citizens should participate in public life. The times themselves demanded their contribution:

As a result of the wonderful inventions of the age in which we live, the railway, steamship, electric telegraph, telephone, and the unlimited development of machinery, the pressure on the life of men makes far greater demands on their time and energies than in the past ... and it would seem to be an *imperative necessity* for women who are not so deeply absorbed in the rough struggle ... to try to make the world better.

Early LCW meetings and presentations drew large audiences thanks to the capable orators involved, including Anna Leonowens. In Halifax to supervise her grandchildren's education, Leonowens, former governess to the king of Siam's many children, claimed to be a the member of a distinguished British family, adding to the appeal of the causes she favoured. Her descriptions of Siam, including her condemnation of "human bondage and servitude," played well to white audiences everywhere, with a lesson that moral depravity loomed where middle-class activists failed. Although she left Halifax in 1897 without realizing her hopes for suffrage, stronger truancy laws, or a home for truant boys, she helped set up the Victoria School of Art, which later became the Anna Leonowens Art Gallery at the Nova Scotia School of Art and Design.

Even though most of the Halifax LCW executive stood for suffrage, the viciousness of the 1890s debates demanded caution, nuanced strategy, and an emphasis on more palatable reforms for the protection of women and children. Halifax LCW projects demonstrated women's leadership and ability to benefit all citizens. As it campaigned for a police matron, a kindergarten for the blind, improved factory conditions for women, an end to impure literature, a curfew bell for children under fourteen, and a covered patrol wagon, it strengthened the network of female reformers. Suffrage took a back seat as it focused on building capacity.

Rewards were slow, as the Halifax LCW met endless opposition from politicians and bureaucrats. Feminist capacity for collective action was also hobbled by ideological differences and insensitivity to relative privilege among the activists themselves. Many naively assumed that respectability and good intentions would deter misogyny. Moreover, the agendas of individual members became, cumulatively, too broad to support the common voice that had been the founding goal. For example, two prominent members, Edith Archibald and Eliza Ritchie, differed sharply over

---

Edith Archibald (1854–1936) came from a privileged background; her father, Edward Archibald, served as a lawyer, then as chief clerk and registrar of the Supreme Court of Newfoundland, and British consul to New York City. Like him, Edith remained an imperialist, a commitment evident in her reform work. She married her second cousin, Charles Archibald, when she was twenty, and they moved to Cow Bay, Nova Scotia, where he managed one of several mines his father owned. During their twenty years in Cape Breton, they raised four children, and Edith was active in the WCTU, becoming Maritime president in 1892. When the couple moved to Halifax in 1894, she became a founding member of its LCW, first representing the WCTU and then serving as president from 1896 to 1905. Her presidency has been described as "erratic and contentious" in part due to her "Protestant bigotry." Her main LCW interests included campaigning for women's appointment to school boards, improving the skills of domestic servants, and caring for (and controlling) the "feeble-minded." She epitomized the maternal feminist, whose participation in politics, whether as school commissioner or voter, sought to bring about moral and practical reforms. In many ways, she was the ideological opposite of her secular feminist critic Eliza Ritchie.

domestic service issues and whether meetings should begin with silent or audible prayer (this may now sound arcane, but the choice pitted many evangelical Protestants against others). Though both women depended on live-in servants to handle their everyday needs and thus free up their time for reform commitment, Ritchie called for guarantees of fair pay and standard hours, whereas Archibald emphasized better training for servants and overseas recruitment. Ritchie also dismissed the much more evangelical Archibald's insistence on reciting the Lord's Prayer at meetings.

THE END OF EARLY SUFFRAGE AGITATION

Chesley's public rebuke of Longley and the advocacy of the LCW and the WCTU could not defeat mounting anti-suffrage sentiment in the Nova Scotia legislature. The 1897 bill prompted the least debate and had the least support of the five 1890s suffrage bills. After its presenter, MLA Firman McClure (1861–1901) spoke for thirty minutes in favour, Longley countered in a confident fifteen-minute rebuke, leaving the bill to die, twenty-six to six. No further assault on the legislature would occur for two decades. The definitive 1897 defeat ended the first phase of the province's suffrage campaign.

Both the Halifax LCW and the WCTU Franchise Department lost motivation and momentum. By 1903, the former had lost two-thirds of its original affiliate organizations and discontinued its monthly meetings. The minutes of its February meeting show that it was contemplating dissolution: "We have not taken a very active part in affairs lately ... There is work to be done, shall we do it, or shall we sink into oblivion?" Its members elected to continue, but immediate success eluded them. In 1905, fearing low attendance, it ended its practice of having speakers at its annual general meeting.

The provincial WCTU entered a similar hiatus in the late 1890s. Having just split into three provincial organizations in 1896 to better mobilize, its energies were dispersed at the time of the 1897 legislative defeat. The franchise department's planned launch of a suffrage newspaper failed; insufficient capital was the official explanation, but disillusionment and fatigue were the more likely ones. In 1897, Mary Chesley, the provincial body's new president, expressed her impatience with the slow advance of political equality, but her determination was debilitated by the recent accidental deaths of two of her three children.

THE FINAL PUSH FOR THE VOTE

After a breather, Nova Scotian suffrage efforts rallied in the early 1910s in what became the final push for enfranchisement. Chesley reported greater sales of pamphlets, regular debates, and positive votes. Her annual updates on progress in the United States and Britain, some composed by travelling WCTU members, were well received. Optimism rose. In 1913, the WCTU president in the small community of Robert's Island, Yarmouth County, reported, "Last year I mentioned the fact that very few of our women were in favour of votes for women ... Now I can say that a change has taken place. A vote on the subject at a recent meeting showed all present, but with one exception, in favour." We will never know precise motivations, but the shift in twelve months from little to nearly unanimous support for the cause is noteworthy. By 1914, Chesley was confident: "I cannot think of any other reform, in regard to which there is so great cause for encouragement." A letter to the *Halifax Chronicle* affirmed the new state of affairs, hailing the WCTU as "one of the great forces that are making the world better."

The Halifax LCW was similarly rejuvenated in what was sometimes dubbed the "Woman's Century." New affiliates, such as the YWCA, the Ladies' Musical Club, and the Girls Friendly Society of St. George's Anglican Church, attested to enthusiasm, although public health and "city beautiful" initiatives, including campaigns around food safety, installing window boxes, and planting flower seeds, often drew more attention than political equality. In a still more conservative spirit, several meetings considered "feeble-mindedness," which, even more than the familiar preoccupation with the "servant problem," aimed at social control.

The Halifax LCW marked its renewal by hosting the annual national convention of the National Council of Women of Canada in the summer of 1910. That critical meeting endorsed official support for enfranchisement by seventy-one to fifty-one votes. The strong minority revealed that neither the Halifax nor the national council was entirely on board. Ritchie placated opponents, justifying the resolution as simply proof of the importance of the subject. The Halifax LCW failure to follow suit with its own endorsement confirmed resistance, or at least caution. Instead, it chose to emphasize reform, highlighting the betterment of women and children.

THE CAMPAIGN FOR WOMEN ON SCHOOL BOARDS

Simultaneously with the 1910 meeting, the Halifax LCW revived campaigns to appoint women as municipal school board commissioners, a right held by rural women since 1881. Describing it as a "matter of social justice and consistency, and especially for the well-being of the children," the Halifax LCW prepared an "exhaustive report" on female school board appointees, struck a committee, and lobbied politicians in 1911. It sent a circular to well-known and respected community members, asking for their opinion on women's suitability for school boards, and published the positive results in local newspapers. The responses were carefully chosen to depict school commissioner roles as safely within the women's sphere. One school board chairman stressed that, despite his opposition to their "participating in public life, ... he believed women had practical knowledge of the nature and needs of children from which the school board could benefit."

Midway through its school trustee campaign, the Halifax LCW retreated. Apparently, anticipating defeat of a bill on the appointment of female school board commissioners, it hoped to avoid repeating the backlash churned up by the 1890s suffrage bill failures. Its leaders decided to refrain from launching additional petitions "until further public opinion has been elicited." In the same vein, Eliza Ritchie convinced it to cancel a Mock Parliament. Only in 1917 did women win the right to be appointed school board commissioners, and none realized the opportunity until 1935. Discretion, not valour, was also in play when Ritchie vetoed publishing reports of Halifax LCW meetings in the local paper despite a request from the national council to do so. The provincial government's failures in connection with suffrage and female school commissioners contrasted with the approach of Nova Scotia's Anglican diocese, which endorsed suffrage in 1914.

THE NOVA SCOTIA EQUAL SUFFRAGE ASSOCIATION

By June 1914, a few Halifax LCW members were so frustrated that they formed their own suffrage association presided over by journalist Ella Murray, who had recently returned from living in the United States. Although the executive of the Halifax LCW had failed to promote suffrage "before the time was ripe," it disliked others taking the lead and promptly formed the Nova Scotia Equal Suffrage Association, with Eliza Ritchie as president and Murray relegated to librarian. Of the two groups, only the latter took root. Murray later defended her initiative, arguing "one should not wait for the time to be ripe, but to hasten the ripening." On the eve of the First World War, Nova Scotia finally had a group devoted to the vote, but broader campaign leadership remained precarious. Rural WCTU branches collectively persisted as the greatest force in the provincial movement, considerably more confident and effective than any urban rivals.

Ella Murray *(1874–1949). Becoming aware of the suffrage movement through her mother's involvement with the WCTU, she participated in suffrage activities during her time in New York (1905–13). She returned to Halifax to edit the* Halifax Evening Echo, *a job she held for twenty-three years. The first female editorial writer on a Canadian mainstream newspaper, she showed clear feminist sympathies. The fact that she was the only prominent member of the Halifax LCW who worked for a living, and her involvement in American suffrage circles, may help explain her differences with other members, whom she judged conservative. After her suffrage advocacy, Murray became a strong critic of the post–First World War taxes, which, she complained, hit middle-class women disproportionately. As Catherine Cleverdon's chief informant from Atlantic Canada, Murray encouraged her emphasis on the conservatism of Nova Scotia.*

THE FIRST WORLD WAR

When war was declared on 28 July 1914, most Nova Scotia suffrage advocates suspended but did not forget their earlier campaigns. Although nearly all reformers committed themselves 100 percent to the war effort, the pacifist Mary Russell Chesley was an exception, even though she curbed her opinions. Wartime Halifax, as a naval centre and the main staging area for overseas convoys, had an insatiable need for volunteers. The Halifax LCW stood out for its quick response to the crisis. One day after Britain (and thus Canada) declared war, Agnes Dennis (1859–1947) – former teacher, prominent member of the Halifax LCW, president of the local Victorian Order of Nurses, and wife of senator and *Halifax Herald* owner William Dennis (1856–1920) – invited city women to mobilize volunteers. She and the other main organizers chose to work through the Red Cross, and soon the Halifax LCW and the Nova Scotia Red Cross executives were barely distinguishable. Dennis became the Halifax Red Cross president and Edith Archibald (long-time Halifax LCW president) its vice-president.

Within months, over one thousand Haligonians volunteered for four hundred local Red Cross branches and other affiliated groups around the province. The LCW headquarters on Young Avenue became the main Red Cross staging centre for all supplies going overseas. Nurses were similarly organized and soldier recruitment encouraged. Halifax LCW member, women's technical education advocate, and Red Cross organizer May Sexton (1880–1923) gave demonstrations across the province on preparing surgical dressings, clothing, and other war supplies. Support for prisoners of war was especially visible since the Red Cross was the only organization that was able to work with the German military.

THE SUFFRAGE CAMPAIGN TAKES OFF

As the war dragged on, interest in suffrage resurfaced. Early in 1917, one of the younger members of the Halifax LCW, Ella Murray, lamented that Nova Scotia was falling behind. Manitoba, Alberta, and Saskatchewan had all granted qualified women the vote in 1916, and British Columbia and Ontario were primed to do the same. Veteran suffragists needed no more encouragement to return to the fray in the midst of their war work. The Halifax LCW, now representing 3,500 Halifax women in forty-one affiliates, voted unanimously to resurrect its 1910 statement in support of suffrage. Early in 1917, it called upon legislators to immediately grant women the vote on the same basis as men, lobbied individual politicians, and distributed two thousand suffrage pamphlets.

Simultaneously, the WCTU set a goal of obtaining forty thousand signatures on petitions. Allied reformers in the respected Social Service Congress and elsewhere publicly endorsed the cause, and some towns, including Wolfville, held special meetings in support.

Notably, and in keeping with significant racial segregation in society, Black women founded their own reform organization at this time, the Ladies Auxiliary of the Associated Baptist Alliance, but it did not become directly involved in suffrage. The auxiliary, whose founding president Maude E. Sparks (1878–?) served thirty-six years starting in 1917, hired an organizer in 1918 and supported community initiatives, including the Nova Scotia Home for Coloured Children when it opened in 1921. But neither it nor any individual African Nova Scotia woman became affiliated with the Halifax LCW or penetrated the suffrage movement. We do not know whether any Black men or women were among the tens of thousands who signed enfranchisement petitions. Suffrage leaders never appeared to consider the vote for Black women, even though enfranchisement had been a hot issue for African Nova Scotians since the 1840 colonial election, when Black men protested being left off the voters list because of unclear land titles. Reformer Joseph Howe did remove some voting restrictions for Black men in time for the 1843 election, but the validity of some land grants continued to be questioned into the twenty-first century.

Enthusiasm grew with scenes of enfranchisement around the world and women's wartime contributions as volunteers, nurses, war industry workers, and relatives of men serving overseas. Local newspapers circulated mostly positive reports of suffrage debates in the United States, Britain, and Canada, and depictions of the responsible behaviour of new voters in American states such as Wyoming, Utah, and Colorado. Unfortunately, no Nova Scotia newspapers carried a regular pro-suffrage women's column as in the West, where Francis Benyon (1884–1951) wrote for the *Grain*

Growers' Guide and Cora Hind (1861–1942) was agricultural editor of the *Manitoba Free Press*. Ella Murray had become an editor of the *Halifax Evening Echo* in 1913, but her support for suffrage was not yet apparent in her journalism.

Even though no Nova Scotia pro-suffrage organization or newspaper was radical by British or American standards, and no women journalists carried the torch as in other regions, demands for change had become widespread by 1917. The Halifax LCW spearheaded the drafting of a suffrage bill. At its request, Judge Benjamin Russell (1844–1915), Mary Russell Chesley's brother and a long-time suffrage supporter, prepared a thirteen-clause bill titled To Amend the Nova Scotia Franchise Act, and MLA Robert Graham of Pictou presented it to the legislature on 15 March 1917. Even with unprecedented support, its passage was not certain. The *Halifax Chronicle* warned that most governing Liberals were still opposed. Anticipation nevertheless built. Suffrage enthusiasts gathered in the legislature gallery on 20 March for the second reading but had to wait until the next day, although they remained for a legislative amendment that allowed women to study law and apply to the Nova Scotia bar. During the second reading on 21 March, opposition vanished. Graham insisted that there was no justifiable reason why women should not have the vote, and the bill passed unanimously, without debate, to go directly to the committee on law amendments.

The unanimity encouraged many to take heart. Few could imagine defeat. The International Women's Suffrage Alliance was apprised of the victory and the National Equal Union, a group formed in 1916 to campaign for federal enfranchisement, sent its congratulations, which were published in the *Halifax Chronicle*. When formal approval seemed tardy, eight high-profile Nova Scotia suffragists, including Eliza Ritchie, Edith Archibald, Mary Russell Chesley, and Mary Fletcher, addressed the law amendments committee in mid-April 1917. Fletcher scored the quotation of the day: "All women are not heroines, neither are all men heroes, but the ordinary woman is not so stupid as some men would affect to believe." The dauntless Archibald tackled the elephant in the room: "I scorn to think that [the law amendments committee] would slay this bill after having allowed it to reach the present stage without a word against it." Hardly reassuring was a promise from Attorney General Orlando Daniels (1860–1927) that the committee would give the matter its "most careful consideration." The eight recognized the familiar pattern of stalling as the legislative session came to a close.

On 21 April, the *Halifax Chronicle* warned that the attorney general was not likely to let the bill pass. Seven weeks after the unanimous second reading, the law amendments committee "gave it the hoist," insisting that time was insufficient to complete necessary revisions to the draft presented in the legislature. Long-term premier George Murray (1861–1929), a known opponent of suffrage, fatuously explained that it "would serve no useful purpose [at this time]." The Liberal government's resistance contradicted its own voting record, suggesting both duplicity and misogyny. Its determined opposition confirmed the pessimism of Eliza Ritchie, who had long been at odds with advocates of greater militancy. But after the 1917 treachery, Ritchie was not silent. When a letter to the *Halifax Chronicle* defended the government refusal, she pushed back hard. The author of the letter, W.E. MacLellan, had insisted that every legislator approved in principle and would gladly have voted for a "well-considered and properly-framed" suffrage amendment, but that "no intelligent and patriotic member" could support the bill that the Halifax LCW had engaged Justice Russell to draft. He concluded with the time-worn argument that too few women wanted the vote. Ritchie set him straight. Women had been "asking in good faith and earnestness for their fair share in the rights and duties of citizenship." Rejecting his advice to seek counsel from "a few well-informed and trustworthy men," she countered that counsel had been sought and would continue to be sought from Nova Scotia women, "whose mental powers, wealth of information, and force of character" equalled those of men. Other suffragists must have been similarly seething, but no further public denunciations appeared.

To some extent, the campaign focus next shifted to the Wartime Elections Act, implemented by Prime Minister Robert Borden to guarantee that his Union government won the 17 December 1917 election. This legislation disenfranchised pacifists and citizens who had emigrated from enemy countries after 1902, while enfranchising military nurses and women with serving brothers, husbands, and sons. Nova Scotian suffragists were largely unimpressed by this development. Women deserved the vote on their own merits, not because of their relationships with men.

As of 7 December 1917, however, concern shifted to the Halifax Explosion, the largest man-made detonation to that point in history. A Belgian relief ship, the *Imo,* collided with the *Mont Blanc,* a French munitions ship, setting off an explosion that killed nearly two thousand, injured nine thousand, blinded nine hundred, and left twenty-five thousand homeless. Activists rushed to help. As women volunteers laboured and the Red Cross became still more respected, anti-suffragists had to admit that women were full citizens. At long last, the tide had turned.

Heroism might have triumphed, but mean-spiritedness was not vanquished. The 1918 franchise bill became more restrictive than earlier bills. Earlier resistance to suffrage had focused on the breadth of eligibility, especially in relation to property. That anti-democratic viewpoint was taken up by Eliza Ritchie's old foe W.E. MacLellan, who favoured extending "the franchise to the better women elements without letting in a flood of the frivolous, ignorant, undesirable and dangerous ... It has already been extended much too widely to men." Suffrage advocates had to make an ugly decision. Should they insist on the right of all women to vote and therefore risk another failure, or should they accept a limited franchise as the best possible deal? In Britain, suffragists chose the latter approach; in January 1918, women thirty and over had gained the franchise. Only in 1928 was the requirement lowered to twenty-one, the same as for men. In 1918, the drafters of the Nova Scotia suffrage bill made a similar decision.

THE SUFFRAGE BILL

In February 1918, the Government of Nova Scotia promised women the same voting rights as men. That subsequent bill, introduced on 1 March 1918, was not for universal suffrage. It included property and race requirements for both women and men. Reserve-based First Nations women (and men) were not included in Nova Scotia (neither provincially nor federally) until 1960, and many African Nova Scotians of both sexes struggled to prove property ownership. There were some exceptions; for example, fishermen could count their gear as property. However, women

WIVES AND HUSBANDS TO BE ENTERED ON VOTERS' LIST.

Under Clause (g) of Sec. 3 (3).

Which entitled (wife or husband) Name of husband.	Name of wife.	Value of Real Property owned or occupied as yearly tenant.	Value of Personal Property.	By whom Property owned or occupied.	Number of Polling District in which Real Property is situated.	Number of Polling District in which Personal Property is	Residence of Husband and Wife.	Amount of income.

This 1918 form was used to record information about the assets of a husband and wife, confirming that both were eligible for the franchise. Capturing details of real estate ownership, personal property, and income, it created a financial snapshot of the couple and ensured that only the well-heeled could vote.

SONS AND DAUGHTERS TO BE ENTERED ON VOTERS' LIST.

Name of Parents alive.	By which Parent qualified.	Value of Real Property owned or occupied by Parent as yearly tenant.	Value of Personal Property.	Number of Polling District in which Personal Property is situated.	Number of Polling District in which Real Property is.	Residence of Parents or Parent.	Number of sons qualified to vote.	Number of daughters qualified to vote.	Names of sons and, or daughters qualified.
A. B.........	Father	$450 00	$ 0 00	Nine	Eleven		Two	Two	E.F. G.H. H.I. J.K.
C. D. (widow)		0 00	600 00	Eleven	Nine		Two	One	

Dependent children who were twenty-one or older and who had
no income of their own could vote if a parent possessed sufficient
property to enfranchise them. This 1918 form establishes their
eligibility by recording the real and personal property of their
parents. This was especially important in intergenerational farm
families, where the land was held in just one person's name.

required $150 in property – or proof that they were ratepayers –
to vote. A married couple needed twice as much – $300 for both to
vote. A son or daughter aged twenty-one who lived with the parents was entitled to vote if the family owned three or more times
the property requirement. The bill passed easily at both second
and third readings, but this victory was overshadowed by the recent Halifax Explosion.

Exclusions were of little interest to most early-twentieth-
century suffragists, who were overwhelmingly middle class and
British or European in descent. Their indifference was often
matched by exhaustion from decades of campaigns and gut-
draining war efforts. In many cases, the same women who founded
the Halifax LCW in 1894 and the WCTU Franchise Department in

1890 were still soldiering on in the second decade of the twentieth century. Mary Russell Chesley was seventy-one, Edith Archibald was sixty-four, and Eliza Ritchie was sixty-two. Anna Leonowens died in 1915 at age eighty-four. With the exception of Ella Murray, a succeeding feminist generation was much less visible.

How can we expect the country to turn toward anything moral and right when such [vulgar] men are sent as representatives and framers of its laws ... Such men may well dread the vote of every pure-minded woman.

– ELLA HATHEWAY,
NEW BRUNSWICK SOCIALIST AND REFORMER, 1912

THREE

NEW BRUNSWICK: EARLY PROMISE, SHARP OPPOSITION

A socialist activist, Ella Hatheway tirelessly advocated for women's labour and suffrage causes in Saint John. The photo was taken around 1885, a few years before she began her decades-long involvement in the Saint John Women's Enfranchisement Association.

THE APPEARANCE OF AN extraordinary Acadian woman in 1890s New Brunswick suffrage debates illuminates the 25 percent of the provincial population who spoke French as a first language. Émilie LeBlanc (1863–1935) was born in southeastern New Brunswick, educated in Memramcook by nuns and in Fredericton (where she attended Normal School), and taught for a time in Weymouth, Nova Scotia. Between 1895 and 1898, she wrote under the pen name Marichette to challenge the male political establishment in thirteen satirical letters to *L'Évangeline,* the Maritime liberal Acadian newspaper, then published in Weymouth. Her literary persona was a little-educated, overworked, resourceful mother of many children, tied to a lazy, uneducated husband. A precursor of the better known Antonine Maillet (1929–), author of the 1971 play *La Sagouine,* Marichette used colloquial language, satire, puns, and plain speaking to expose social, political, and economic injustices suffered by Acadians, especially Acadian women. In her first letter, Marichette addressed enfranchisement and how tired Acadian women were of waiting for the vote: "We want to get to the polls so we can show our men how to vote." With so few Acadian women publicly involved in the suffrage movement, in part because the Catholic Church condemned it, LeBlanc's voice spoke volumes.

Interest in improving women's rights – primarily those of middle-class women – emerged in New Brunswick before Confederation and was expressed most clearly in 1851, in the earliest

Married Women's Property Act in British North America, decades earlier than those of Nova Scotia or the United Province of Canada. Furthermore, the province saw the earliest granting of a bachelor's degree in the British Empire, to a Mount Allison woman in 1875. Leadership continued within temperance and other social reform organizations, and with the establishment of a Saint John branch of the Local Council of Women (LCW) in the late nineteenth century. The most influential and long-term suffrage leaders, including labour reformer and teacher Emma Fiske (1852–1914), businesswoman and internationally known playground advocate Mabel Peters (1861–1914), and socialist activist Ella Hatheway (1853–1931), collaborated in the Saint John Women's Enfranchisement Association. The association insisted that voting was a human right to which all adults were entitled, but early pro-suffrage politicians such as Alfred Stockton (1842–1907) and Amasa Killam (1834–1922) took a less radical, if more strategic approach – that female property holders deserved the vote because entitlement to it depended on ownership, not gender. Although a series of suffrage debates inspired several close votes in the legislature between 1885 and 1899, the detractors' main argument – that not enough women were supporters – flourished. Conservative premier Andrew Blair (1844–1907) always led the anti-suffrage charge, winged by Edward Wetmore (1841–1922) and John Sievewright (1846–98), with their swift and venomous motions of deferral. Worn-out suffragists withdrew from public agitation between 1899 and 1907. The 1908 election to the legislature of Frank Hatheway (1850–1923), Saint John progressive businessman and husband of Ella Hatheway, re-energized the campaign. For years, his equal rights arguments dogged the recalcitrant premier Blair. Only the First World War changed the outcome. New Brunswick passed a suffrage bill in 1919, and once again Indigenous women were excluded both federally and provincially until 1960 and 1963 respectfully.

DEMOGRAPHIC, ECONOMIC, AND POLITICAL
CONTEXTS OF SUFFRAGE

New Brunswick's status as Canada's only officially bilingual province as of 1969 belies a long history of ethnic conflict and inequality. The suffrage story was no exception. The colony was carved out of Nova Scotia partly because Loyalists fleeing the revolutionary United States demanded government appointments and large land grants. Some Loyalists – including several who eventually held the highest elected and appointed positions in the new colony – brought slaves, adding to the Black enslaved population established in the area in 1690. Female Loyalists joined male petitioners for compensation, laying a foundation for women's petitions, including for suffrage, in the following century. Free Black Loyalists were not provided with the land and rights they were promised, and many departed for better conditions, including in Sierra Leone. The accommodation of white Loyalist demands set the stage for future privileging of anglophone, white, British Protestants over racialized and ethnic minorities. Even in the twenty-first century, Saint John boasts its "Loyalist City" heritage, ignoring the privileging of appointed British administrators and fourteen thousand Loyalists over the Mi'kmaq, Wolastoqiyik, and Peskotomuhkati who had, for millennia, occupied the same land; the Acadians, who arrived from France in the early seventeenth century; and Black New Brunswickers, who were denied the vote even after slavery ended in 1833.

The Indigenous population diminished as new settlers sought lands and resources, introduced diseases, and set up assimilationist schools for Indigenous children. By the 1840s, the Mi'kmaq and Wolastoqiyik numbered fewer than fifteen hundred – less than 1 percent of the entire population.

The Acadians met a different fate. After 1764, they were allowed to rejoin some two thousand who had escaped capture during the deportation, particularly in northern New Brunswick. By 1803, nearly four thousand Acadians lived in the colony, primarily in northern and eastern coastal communities, where they depended on the fishery or the timber industry, as the best agricultural land had already been taken by the Loyalists. Prejudice against Acadians persisted, even as they established a degree-granting college and the region's first Acadian newspaper in the 1860s, and increased to 25 percent of the provincial population at the turn of the twentieth century. Not until the 1960s did an Acadian premier, Louis J. Robichaud, create the Program of Equal Opportunity, which, in seeking minimum standards of social, economic, educational, and cultural opportunities for all New Brunswickers, raise the living standards of many Acadians.

The Irish composed the largest ethnic minority group. During the eighteenth century, primarily Protestant Irish immigrants were drawn to the promise of free agricultural land and the lucrative timber trade. Irish arrivals increased in the 1820s and 1830s. More were Catholic, urban, and unskilled labourers, especially during the famine years (1844–51), when Saint John became a significant port of entry, industrial centre, and the third-largest British North American city after Montreal and Quebec City. Most, coming with few resources and too late for free land, were forced into unskilled labour with poor working conditions, including in the colony's main industry, logging. Timber sales drove immigration, the economy, and politics. Its barons were regularly elected to government, where they protected their own interests.

Property requirements for voting eligibility upheld and fostered ethnic and class differences. As compensation for their loyalty to Britain, white Loyalists received free land grants, and with this the franchise. Free Black Loyalists received smaller grants of less arable land, and, along with Black immigrants freed for fighting in the War of 1812,, were disenfranchised despite their property. In contrast, Irish immigrants and returning Acadians had to purchase their land but could vote when they did so.

New Brunswick maintained British North America's second-highest qualifications for voting, next to Quebec, and was the last jurisdiction to remove the male property requirement. The governing elite – largely Loyalists – increased already high property requirements for election to the House of Assembly. These rules disenfranchised the large population of Saint John's labourers (mostly Irish Catholics), who, as ratepayers, would have had the vote had they lived in Prince Edward Island or Nova Scotia. This is not to say that the rules were always effective. Common practice allowed occupiers of land to vote without question. In one 1825 election, some 30 percent of male occupiers of property cast their ballots. Saint John, the largest city, added to the complicated story by enfranchising so-called freemen, or non-propertied white men licensed to work in the city who could pay £5 for the franchise. The fee was later dropped, but Black men remained excluded until 1848, making New Brunswick the only Atlantic colony to specifically disenfranchise them.

Although it used the masculine pronoun, the original colonial legislation did not specify the sex of electors. Evidence reveals that some property-holding women did vote, but the proportion is unknown because records survive only from contested elections. They are nevertheless suggestive. At least forty-four King's County women voted in the 1827 election, and thirty-nine Sudbury County women did so in 1839. No details are available on the Sudbury contest, but twenty-five of the King's County women voted for the winner and nineteen for his opponent. Either single or widowed, all the women met the land and age requirements. Presumably, they believed that owning property made their actions legitimate. The House of Assembly disagreed. Unlike in Nova Scotia, with its contested elections involving women, New Brunswick disqualified all the women's votes in both counties and within five years formally restricted the ballot to qualified "male persons." This exclusion occurred seven years after Prince Edward Island and eight years before Nova Scotia did the same. As far as can be seen, no public outcry criticized the clarification. Indeed, the acceptance that female property owners had a stake in the community was effectively forgotten until the province's suffrage history was subject to close examination in the late twentieth century.

Confederation was a contentious issue. The government of teetotalling premier Leonard Tilley (1818–96) supported it, but it was toppled in 1865. He ran for office again fifteen months later, weeks after the Fenian Brotherhood, pro-Irish American Civil War veterans, raided Campobello, a New Brunswick island adjacent to Maine. The unsuccessful raid helped Tilley win the 1866 election and secure federal union. Yet many vocal Saint John businesses feared that their interests would be subsumed by central Canadians.

And thus in 1867, New Brunswick joined with Ontario, Quebec, and Nova Scotia. With a population of just over 200,000 and only 15 allotted seats in the House of Commons (out of a total of 181), it would be dwarfed. Some diehard anti-confederates called for continued British governance or annexation to the United States. In the 1870s and 1880s, the national tariff policy boosted some manufacturing (brass, nails, lumber, and machinery), whereas the old industries such as shipbuilding, shipping, and community-based artisan employment dwindled. Even Alexander "Boss" Gibson (1819–1913), who employed two thousand in his company town and had become one of Canada's wealthiest late-nineteenth-century industrialists, succumbed to a Montreal conglomerate. Women, like men, could not escape the consequences of massive outmigration and economic despair and resentment. In the 1850s, New Brunswick had had the highest population growth rate of any Atlantic colony at 30 percent during that decade. In the 1880s, however, it had no population growth whatsoever, as industrialism waned through the consolidation of Montreal businesses and the closing of many factories.

The backdrop to the 1880s launch of the New Brunswick suffrage movement included continued privilege of Loyalist ancestors, ethnic and religious conflict, a shaken economy, few positive socio-economic relationships with central Canada or the West, serious concern about outmigration, and a great nostalgia for the golden age of sail, timber, and lucrative free trade with the United States. Cultural and familial links were mainly southward and eastward, with the United States and Britain, especially Ireland. Not surprisingly, when New Brunswick suffrage leaders needed advice, they looked toward Britain and the United States, where they had more established ties, rather than to central Canada. Just as the new national economic policy was not national, there was no national suffrage movement.

MARRIED WOMEN'S PROPERTY LAW

As in the other Maritime provinces, New Brunswick's suffrage movement built on nineteenth-century social and human rights reforms. Earlier legal gains, especially in married women's property rights, were crucial. The colony's close link between property holding and enfranchisement triggered British North America's earliest married women's property law. By the mid-nineteenth century, a governing elite largely comprised of second- and third-generation Loyalists remained determined to uphold the pre-eminence of property in the franchise. Despite the implementation of universal male suffrage in many North American and European jurisdictions, New Brunswick extended the vote only to men over twenty-one with annual incomes or combined personal and real property of a minimum of £100. Even this cautious initiative in 1855, which enfranchised "tradesmen, professionals, and senior clerks," generated outrage. MLA James Ryan (1821–92) insisted that voting must remain "in the hands of those who have a stake in the country." Like many politicians, he strove to preserve the power of the landed elite by raising the property requirements.

This determination set the context for New Brunswick's first major women's rights reform. In 1851, New Brunswick became the first British North American colony to implement a robust married women's property law. Modelled on New York's Married Women's Property Law of 1848, it preserved aspects of Britain's 1787 and 1791 dower laws: the first requiring a wife's permission to sell more than two-thirds of the couple's combined property and the second requiring her consent to any revision to the dower. Assets held by a woman before marriage, or that she acquired during it, remained her own "separate property," not to be disposed of by her husband or by his creditors. Her "full consent and concurrence" was required to sell it, unless she had been in debt before her marriage. The intent was to ensure that widows with property would not be penniless if husbands left nothing but debts.

Compared with other Canadian colonies, which passed laws offering limited protection only to deserted wives, New Brunswick was relatively progressive. Later amendments excluded property given to wives by husbands who intended to shield it from creditors. But what did the 1851 law really mean? In New Brunswick, where the Loyalist legacy focused on landownership, fathers and brothers worried about the fate of the real estate that their daughters and sisters took with them into marriage. Would their new husband sell it? Thus, the families of the wives, as much as the women themselves, received protection under the Married Women's Property Act. Regardless, its introduction set the stage for granting single female taxpayers the municipal franchise or the right to vote or hold office in school trustee elections, just as the passage of the 1848 Married Women's Property Law in nearby New York state was tied to the Seneca Falls convention, which passed twelve resolutions on the rights of women and launched the American suffrage movement.

HIGHER EDUCATION

Another New Brunswick first – the conferral of the first bachelor's degree in the British Commonwealth upon a woman – similarly paved the way for suffrage. Mount Allison College, a private Methodist college in Sackville, opened a Ladies' College in 1854 and enrolled a strong contingent of primarily rural New Brunswick and Nova Scotia women. Its founding chief preceptress, Mary Electa Adams (1823–98), stressed an academic over an ornamental curriculum. In 1872, partly in response to financial need, Mount Allison allowed students from the Ladies' College to take courses occasionally that contributed to a degree. Three years later, Grace Annie Lockhart (1855–1916) earned a bachelor of science and English literature. Eleven years later, Harriet Starr

GRACE ANNIE LOCKHART
(1855–1916)

CANADA

Grace Annie Lockhart was the first woman to earn a university degree in the British Empire. Founded exclusively for the education of men, universities in the 19th century gradually began opening their doors to women. Mount Allison College became co-educational in 1872. This change built on the pioneering commitment to female education of the associated Mount Allison Ladies' Academy and of denominational schools in the United States. Lockhart, a student at the Ladies' Academy, took courses at the College, formally enrolled in 1874 and graduated with a degree of Bachelor of Science and English Literature on 25 May 1875.

Grace Annie Lockhart fut la première femme de l'Empire britannique à recevoir un diplôme universitaire. Réservées aux hommes, les universités du XIXᵉ siècle ouvrirent peu à peu leurs portes aux femmes. Le collège Mount Allison devint mixte en 1872 dans la foulée de l'engagement novateur à instruire les femmes, pris par la Mount Allison Ladies' Academy, qui lui était affiliée, et par les écoles confessionnelles des États-Unis. Étudiante à la Ladies' Academy, Grace Annie Lockhart suivit des cours au collège, s'y inscrivit officiellement en 1874 et obtint un baccalauréat en sciences et en littérature anglaise le 25 mai 1875.

Historic Sites and Monuments Board of Canada
Commission des lieux et monuments historiques du Canada

Government of Canada · Gouvernement du Canada

(1822–93) became the first woman in Canada to earn a bachelor of arts degree, also at Mount Allison.

The University of New Brunswick was unmoved. Impetus for it to accept women came instead from Mary K. Tibbets (1870–1951) who, despite earning the second-highest grade on its matriculation examination in 1886, was refused admission. Saint John Liberal MLA John Ellis (1835–1913) questioned why a provincially sponsored university did not grant women the same privileges as men. Most MLAs were of the same mind, so they passed a bill to produce that result. When the university senate proved

Grace Annie Lockhart (1855–1916) was raised in Saint John by her father, three older sisters, and the family housekeeper after her mother died when she was less than a year old. In 1871, she followed in her sisters' footsteps, enrolling at Mount Allison Ladies' College. Unlike her sisters, who each attended for one year, Lockhart earned her mistress in liberal arts after two years and then enrolled as a college student and obtained her bachelor of science and English literature in 1875. In keeping with the founding objective of the Ladies' College to extend education for women beyond the ornamental arts, female Mount Allison students could receive degrees on the same terms as men beginning in 1872. Before then, whereas men's programs were four years long, women's diplomas took three years, with less focus on classical subjects – Greek-language literature was specifically excluded – and career-related subjects, such as political economy and minerology. In 1888, Lockhart married her 1875 graduating classmate, Methodist minister John Dawson, and raised three sons. She was a member of the WCTU and a supporter of suffrage, though she does not seem to have taken a public role.

obstinate, the government threatened to cut funding. Nowhere else in Atlantic Canada did a government demand women's inclusion. Two decades later, the University of New Brunswick graduated its first Black woman, Mary Matilda Winslow (1885–1963), although another Black New Brunswick woman, Lalia Halfkenny, had graduated from a Nova Scotia university considerably earlier. Both Halfpenny and Winslow were forced to move to the United States to find suitable employment connected to their education. For Acadian women, several women's religious congregations from Quebec, Saint John, and Halifax opened francophone boarding and day schools during the 1870s and 1880s. Only in 1949 were women first offered French-language college courses and degrees, as well as teachers' and nurses' training at the Collège Maillet at Saint-Basile, which evolved into the Edmonston campus of the Université de Moncton in the 1970s.

WOMAN'S CHRISTIAN TEMPERANCE UNION

The long involvement of New Brunswick women in missionary and religious reform groups fostered the creation of early local WCTU branches in Moncton (1875), Fredericton (1877), Saint John (1877), Woodstock (1878), and St. Stephen (1879), as well as a provincial federation in 1879. By the early 1880s, many branches had expanded their original anti-drink agenda to endorse the vote as a "cornerstone of women's equality." This shift met resistance. In 1884, the Fredericton press refused to publish news about the local WCTU branch. Particularly in small communities, the WCTU was more successful than other groups in gathering thousands of names on suffrage petitions during the 1880s and 1890s to present to the New Brunswick government. In 1894 alone, it took more than ten thousand signatures to Premier Blair.

The New Brunswick WCTU contingent also regularly led the regional and national organizations. In 1890, Julia Turnbull (1828–1906) of Saint John captained the Maritime WCTU as it established a franchise department. As she explained, "Men and women should stand side by side in all moral reform; stand just as the creator placed them at the beginning, to work together for mutual health and comfort." The following year, Saint John hosted the massive WCTU convention that marked the national body's shift away from evangelical arguments with maternal feminist rationales for home protection to demands for equal rights. Fredericton native Emma Jane (Turnbull) Steadman (1834-?) presided over the event. Following the convention, the national WCTU went to Prime Minister Wilfrid Laurier with nearly twenty thousand signatures, arguing that

> in mental and in moral power, educational attainments, and industrial effort, the average woman equals the average man, and in all that constitutes true and natural citizenship, viz. intelligence, industry, love of home, country, the power to produce wealth, and to share the national burden the average woman has proved herself equal to man ... The test of sex in citizenship is a gross injustice to half the people and a direct violation of the principal of Representation by Population.

New Brunswick WCTU members also joined other Canadians in celebrating global ties, notably with the American WCTU and its charismatic founder and suffragist Frances Willard.

1880S AND 1890S PROVINCIAL SUFFRAGE BILLS

Advances in property law and education, and other forays into public life, set the stage for New Brunswick to introduce the region's first suffrage legislation. In 1885, Premier Andrew Blair presented a bill that proposed expanding the franchise to include tenants, owners of land, farmers' sons, and single propertied women because all had a stake in society, as embodied in their possession of land and/or personal property. A supporter challenged a naysayer: "Don't you think all property should be represented?" Another asserted that the result was the enfranchisement of "industrious men," as well as women with property, and excluded only "loafers." The bill's easy passage with twenty to six in favour confirmed that a "stake in society" could make voters of both sexes. But the smooth sailing was torpedoed by the Legislative Council (the upper house). When so many other jurisdictions were implementing universal male suffrage, it worried lest *all* New Brunswick women might benefit from the bill. The prospect so disturbed Premier Blair that he quickly accepted its rejection by the upper house and soon became the province's leading anti-suffragist. For Blair, only wealthy women mattered.

Not all politicians were craven. When a bill to allow propertied unmarried women and widows to vote in school board elections was proposed, William Pugsley, lawyer, businessman, and recently elected Liberal MLA for Saint John County, used the occasion to applaud a similar "tendency everywhere." He also singled out the "ladies" who organized the Saint John library as evidence of their concern for the young and capacity for good results. Another Liberal, John Ellis from Saint John City, added that married women should be permitted to vote in school board elections since they "were better judges of children" than were spinsters. Only York County MLA Edward Wetmore, who had helped defeat the 1885 franchise bill, dissented, claiming that "ladies had their own sphere of usefulness," that school meetings were too rowdy for them, and that granting them this vote would serve as a precedent for allowing them "certain other powers." Ultimately, legislators decided that, as no law actually barred female voters, no new bill was required to add them. Married women remained ineligible, no matter how wealthy they were or whether they had children. Nonetheless, this advance for single propertied women was easily won, especially when compared to that of Nova Scotia.

Still more importantly, the school trustee elections sustained momentum for suffragists. Although Wetmore's speech introduced three persistent anti-suffrage arguments – women's separate sphere, their indifference, and the prospect of further concessions – the broader gain was real. Responding in part to six petitions, John Ellis soon introduced a bill favouring propertied single women voters in civic elections. It passed easily and quickly. Since most female adults were married, this development benefitted probably fewer than 5 percent of Saint John women, but because property was recognized as the key to enfranchisement, it was another toehold. Fredericton's initiative in requiring the provincial university to admit coeds and in introducing a limited municipal and school board franchise for women in 1886 occurred in the context of an imminent provincial election, in April of that year. The popularity of reform causes such as temperance was an obvious incentive for Liberals, anxious to harness their energy, to make such gestures. Whatever their calculations, they handily won thirty-three of forty-one seats.

Passage of three women's rights bills in 1886 encouraged local WCTU members and others to circulate the first petitions for the Great Cause, which they presented to the government in 1887–88. Momentum continued when Westmorland County Liberal MLA and railway entrepreneur Amasa Killam championed propertied spinsters in 1888. The next year produced the first bill proposing to enfranchise both single and married women with property.

In 1889, the Blair government, in the fourth year of a strong mandate, proposed to eliminate landownership as a condition of male suffrage. Saint John MLA and legal expert Alfred Stockton, who had recently crossed the floor from the Liberals to the Conservatives, further proposed to include propertied widows and spinsters. The debate quickly distinguished New Brunswick from other Atlantic provinces. MLAs who had consistently supported propertied women's enfranchisement insisted that it was illogical to enfranchise unpropertied men when women *with* property went unrecognized. One Liberal MLA displayed commonplace racism, calling out Conservatives James Phinney (1844–1915) and Daniel Hanington (1835–1909) for supporting (male) "Indian" voters but not intelligent women. Liberal MLA Henry Emmerson (1853–1914) added, "This bill provides a vote for the man who may not know the multiplication tables but denies it to the woman no matter how learned she may be in literature and science." Prominent Orangeman and York County Liberal MLA William Wilson (1845–1921) took another tack but was similarly preoccupied with the middle class: "Women actually require the vote more than men because they are physically weaker and need protection from the law." References to the relative merits of

Henry Emmerson (1853–1914) was a leading nineteenth-century supporter of propertied women's suffrage in the New Brunswick House of Assembly. After the early death of his father, a Baptist minister, Emmerson and his three siblings were raised by their single mother. While attending law school in Boston during the 1870s, he earned a prize for his essay on the legal status of married women. In addition to success as a business-man and lawyer, he served as a Liberal MLA in 1888–90 and 1892–1900, including a term as premier, 1897–1900. He also held regional and national leadership posts in the Baptist Church in 1899 and 1900. From 1900 to 1914, he was a federal MP, becoming Laurier's minister of railways. Despite such success, he was considered a heavy drinker and womanizer. In 1907, when Laurier asked for his resignation from cabinet, Emmerson sued a Fredericton newspaper for dubbing him an "intolerable reprobate." How this squared with his support for women's rights is unknown.

educated and fragile, effectively middle-class, women in contrast to uneducated and racialized men replayed arguments used by provincial suffragists.

Premier Andrew Blair, normally the most vocal suffrage opponent, stayed out of the 1889 debate except to warn that the addition of property-holding women would scuttle the universal suffrage bill. Men's rights trumped those of women. Thus cautioned, the leading pro-suffragist Alfred Stockton withdrew his amendment, but he introduced a stronger resolution to qualify widows and spinsters with property. Supported by Wilson, Emmerson, Silas Alward, George Baird, Dr. Marcus Atkinson, George Hibbard, and Killam, he identified intelligence and residence, as well as property, as appropriate criteria for voting. Conservative MLA James Phinney professed himself newly converted by increasing public demand, precedents in New Zealand, Colorado, and local municipalities, and the reassurance that despite violent agitators, more "gentle, home loving women ... [were] daily giving the subject more attention, while they are much better informed on general political topics."

Opponents offered equally sentimental reflections on women's supposed lack of interest and separate sphere. The premier suggested that all widows and spinsters were merely in a "state of transition" before marriage and did not need the vote. The debate continued for one month, perhaps stoked by Alfred Stockton's recent shift to the Conservatives as co-leader. Now the province's most virulent anti- and pro-suffrage politicians stood nose-to-nose. Although enfranchisement had not been an entirely partisan cause, Liberals had generally been more sympathetic. That trend was broken with the two party leaders. In the final count, 40 percent of MLAs came out as supporters. However, their enthusiasm could not stop the bill from being deferred, which passed by twenty-one to eighteen. For all their promise, the 1880s ended without advances at the provincial level. Despite this disappointment, women's zest for suffrage and public life persisted in WCTU suffrage campaigns, the founding of the Saint John Women's Enfranchisement Association and the Saint John LCW, progress in revising married women's property law, the emergence of an Acadian activist, and the visit to Saint John by one of the most famous suffragettes of the day, Julia Ward Howe.

In 1888, the Eastern New Brunswick WCTU, comprising the counties of Westmorland, Kent, and Albert, presented nine petitions to the government, becoming the first regional WCTU group to call for suffrage, one year before Nova Scotia called for it. Two years later, the Maritime WCTU established its franchise department, although it did not formally endorse the vote. Local WCTU branches could show initiative, as when thirty-one Carleton County women signed a petition in spring 1891. The same year, another petition, drafted at the national convention in Saint John, secured almost twenty thousand signatures. It argued that "in mental and in moral power, educational attainments, and individual effort, the average woman equals the average man" and that "the rights of citizenship shall not be abridged or denied on account of sex." As Frederictonian Emma Steadman, national president of the WCTU, explained,

At first we asked for the ballot to declare ourselves against the liquor traffic, but now most of us can't see why we would not be able to vote as intelligently on all questions as our brothers, and so we have stepped out on the platform of equal rights … Miss Willard [founder of the WCTU] says that the greatest discovery of the age is woman's discovery of herself. To come to consciousness is evermore to come to power; and so, in the light of this knowledge, we ask for the ballot, the justice and needs of the demand daily becoming more apparent.

Even where local WCTU branches hesitated, their sympathy was evident. Although members of the Sackville WCTU decided against launching a pro-suffrage petition in 1894 lest it be "unpopular among the male constituents of their community," its secretary, Mary E. Humphrey, insisted that stopping the liquor traffic would require enfranchising women, even if men were offended. Several New Brunswick women joined the cause at the regional, national, and even international level. In 1895, the provincial WCTU formally came out in support of female enfranchisement.

SAINT JOHN WOMEN'S ENFRANCHISEMENT ASSOCIATION

In 1894, Atlantic Canada's only long-running suffrage organization was founded in Saint John. On 11 March, eighteen women met to plan, and within a month, fifty-six had signed up. Some,

Ella Bertha (Marven) Hatheway (1853–1931) was a founder of the Saint John Women's Enfranchisement Association, serving as its secretary for most of its existence. She worked tirelessly but preferred to remain in the background. Ella and her businessman husband, W. Franklin (Frank) Hatheway (1850–1923), were a prominent and effective Saint John reform couple who advocated for free daycare for working mothers, child factory labour laws, and women's suffrage. Nearly a century after they donated land to the city's trade unions, Frank was honoured in the naming of a permanent Saint John labour exhibit in 2007. Five years later, due to the efforts of a University of New Brunswick student, Susan McAdam, Ella's name was added to the exhibit. Ella and Frank had two daughters, Miriam (b. 1884) and Grace (b. 1885). The latter shared her parents' interest in socialism and became an activist and author after studying for her bachelor of arts at Oberlin College and her master of arts at Bryn Mawr.

such as founding executive members Sarah Manning (1839–1919), Mary Manning Skinner (1856–1915), and Ella Hatheway, were upper class, with family connections to the New Brunswick business and political elite and spare time that allowed an agenda of good work. A roughly equal number (including some of the same individuals, as well as women wage earners) appeared to be motivated by personal experiences of gender-based discrimination. Many advocates made a clear connection between political and economic oppression, and sympathized with the struggle for large-scale structural change.

Roughly half of Saint John Women's Enfranchisement Association founders were unmarried, and many depended on wages. The chair of the first meeting, Emma Fiske, sister to the first vice-president, Mary Manning Skinner, had been widowed at the age of twenty-five after only one year of marriage and subsequently made a living by teaching high school French and literature. Another, Mabel Peters (1861–1914), owned and operated a hotel with her sister. Helen Hanington (1865–1946) and Kate Sutherland (1861–?) ran a commercial school that trained female office workers. Some early members of the association were stenographers. Not surprisingly, wage parity figured in the goals of the association. During their first year, in addition to organizing a suffrage petition, its members discussed female teachers' right to equal pay and women's work in the home as equal in importance to men's wage earning outside. They familiarized themselves with taxation and property law and read the famous eighteenth-century economist Adam Smith. Prohibition was notably absent from their discussions, as it was judged too far from their core mandate. They did, however, send a suffragist delegate to the 1894 Maritime WCTU convention.

Although the enfranchisement association's chief focus was local politics, it was affiliated with the Dominion Women's Enfranchisement Association, founded in 1889 in Toronto, and it adopted a constitution that demanded for "the women citizens of Canada their right to vote at all elections." Emma Fiske served on the Dominion Women's Enfranchisement Association as its vice-president for the Maritime provinces, but ties lapsed during the 1890s. Members did, however, continue to seek external advice. While studying at Oberlin College, Grace Hatheway (1885–1936), daughter of Ella, appeared influenced by meeting American feminist activist Charlotte Perkins Gilman, who advocated for women's involvement in public life and the lifting of economic, social, legal, and political barriers against them. The second annual public meeting of the enfranchisement association, held at the Mechanics Institute on 14 September 1896, hosted high-profile American suffragist speaker Julia Ward Howe (1819–1910). She had shared the leadership of the American Woman Suffrage Association beginning in 1869 and remained engaged in demands for political equality and education. A report noted excellent attendance and frequent applause. Except for British suffragette Sylvia Pankhurst, who came to New Brunswick in 1912, Howe was the most prominent international feminist speaker to visit the province.

The goals of the enfranchisement association aligned with the vastly improved married women's property law passed in 1895. Its revisions extended the right of women to enter into contracts on their own, which meant they could sue and be sued; acquire, keep, or dispose of property; and retain their wages as long as their work was not shared with husbands (as was usually the case in farming, for example). A husband's debts did not affect their property, which could not be disposed of without their consent. Any land dispute between a husband and wife could be brought by either party before a judge. These amendments recognized the independent legal capacity and powers of women, and acknowledged their needs. Whereas mid-nineteenth-century married women's property acts usually focused on protecting nuclear families, later initiatives in New Brunswick were more interested in asserting women's rights as individual citizens.

SAINT JOHN LOCAL COUNCIL OF WOMEN

Just five months after the birth of the Saint John Women's Enfranchisement Association, some of its members participated in founding another prominent reform initiative, the Saint John LCW. As happened in Halifax ten days later, these women took up Lady Aberdeen's invitation to organize a local council to affiliate with the National Council of Women. She and her husband, the governor general, were on an official visit to Saint John, staying with Lieutenant Governor Leonard Tilley and Alice Starr Tilley (1843–1921). The latter advertised the invitation for the gathering, which was held at the Mechanics Institute, and Lady Aberdeen emphasized the council's role in uniting and amplifying the efforts of independent charities. Eleven Saint John groups immediately accepted her invitation; within a year, the local council had twenty-one affiliates, including several WCTU chapters, the Seaman's Mission, and the Saint John Women's Enfranchisement Association. Lady Tilley, with a history of reform work, particularly in health care, served as president for the first five years and as National Council of Women vice-president. At Aberdeen's urging, she also encouraged the creation of an LCW in Fredericton, but women in the capital appeared wary. Perhaps the affiliation of the Saint John Women's Enfranchisement Association put them off, or perhaps Aberdeen's personal support for suffrage was responsible, even though the national council remained uncommitted. Lady Tilley claimed that the LCW was more closely aligned with the WCTU than with suffrage, but her reassurance did not move Fredericton to found a LCW.

Such hesitancy may have foreshadowed the future conflict between the enfranchisement association and the Saint John LCW. Ultimately, some association members felt that the LCW was too conservative, whereas the LCW felt that the association was too radical. Only two more New Brunswick local councils were established in the next four decades: in Sackville in 1918 and Moncton in 1920. In contrast, Nova Scotia founded LCWs in New Glasgow in 1899, in Truro in 1912, and in several other places immediately after the First World War. In any case, the Saint John LCW remained conservative. Members of the enfranchisement association were nonetheless highly visible. Businesswoman Mabel Peters, who belonged to both groups, championed suffrage and the installation and safe operation of playgrounds. Louisa Donald Thompson (1844–1915) became national council president from 1902 to 1906, even as she maintained membership in the enfranchisement association. The 1979 official history of the Saint John LCW nevertheless revealed tension when it referred to the "rabid enthusiasm for suffrage displayed by the Enfranchisement Association," while simultaneously portraying the LCW as a rational "channel of education and influence."

As in other provinces, the initial projects of the Saint John LCW featured areas of consensus among female activists, including support for the arts and children's literacy, improvements in public health, and advocacy for a police matron. The Victorian Order of Nurses (VON), which Lady Aberdeen founded to bring medical services to both urban and remote areas, was another beneficiary of its efforts. Lady Tilley became VON president in 1899, and some members, including Mary Ellis (1841–1922), promoted the VON, the LCW, and the enfranchisement association. As in Halifax, gains proved harder to achieve than anticipated. In 1896, the City of Saint John only reluctantly funded the operation of a horse-drawn ambulance and three smaller field ambulances, which the LCW had donated. The LCW raised public interest in social issues, succeeded in fundraising, and demonstrated female talent. Its official history defended its caution on suffrage: had it permitted the divisive issue to dominate its deliberations, it might well have collapsed; it would most certainly have failed to achieve many of the signal accomplishments of its first three decades.

PARTICIPATION OF ACADIAN WOMEN

The WCTU, the enfranchisement association, and the Saint John LCW overwhelmingly attracted anglophone women. As noted previously, Émilie LeBlanc promoted rights for Acadian women in the 1890s under the pen name Marichette. Her anger with men was palpable. She declared that no man had the courage to write in *L'Évangeline* to stand up for Acadian women's rights: "You know, men are good for talking, but when it comes to acting, well, that is quite another song." She damned male politicians for buying votes with whisky, and men, including her own husband, for succumbing; ultimately, women were morally superior. Although this assault resembled the early WCTU argument that women were needed in politics to counteract male corruption, Marichette's perspective was distinctly Acadian and closely tied to her championing of the Acadian Renaissance of the late nineteenth century. When she was writing, one in four New Brunswickers was Acadian, but they had fewer educational and economic opportunities than their English counterparts. Outmigration of both women and men to urban areas of the Maritimes and to the Boston States – one of the many causes of the decline of Acadian culture decried by Marichette – was extensive in northeastern New Brunswick.

Since most Acadian, Catholic, and female voices went unrecorded, Marichette's successful insertion into the public debates on both suffrage and Acadian culture is extraordinary. Her enthusiasm was challenged by the Catholic Church, with its insistence on marriage and religious life as the natural vocation of women, opposition to their involvement in public life, and claim that it alone guarded Acadian culture. Good Acadian women – and other Catholic women – apparently could not be suffragists. Indeed, no recognizably Acadian surnames appeared among the founding members of the LCW, the Saint John Women's Enfranchisement Association, or the WCTU Franchise Department. Although Catholic temperance societies existed, none followed the WCTU in promoting suffrage. At least one politician exploited that stance. In 1895, Peter Venoit (1862–1936), Acadian and Liberal MLA from Bathurst, rejected women's enfranchisement in the New Brunswick House of Assembly. He argued that the WCTU "has no authority to speak on behalf of all women," implying that his constituency was hostile or indifferent. Marichette was a lone voice, one whose credibility was undermined by criticisms of her ungrammatical and crude French, despite that being her intentional strategy. LeBlanc's skill in producing correct idiomatic French was unacknowledged. She created an unforgettable character, who used the language of ordinary people to capture the experience of Acadian women. *Le Moniteur Acadian,* the conservative Acadian newspaper based in Shediac, New Brunswick, rejected her submissions. After three years, *L'Évangeline* would print no more of her letters, and suffrage disappeared from its pages. The one outlet for Acadian feminists was lost.

1890S SUFFRAGE DEBATES, RESOLUTIONS, AND BILLS

In the 1890s, the WCTU shift to emphasize suffrage as an equal rights cause, the creation of prominent anglophone women's reform groups, the appearance of Marichette, and the attainment of a stronger married women's property law all contributed to a sense of renewed opportunity. Dozens of suffrage petitions signed by thousands of New Brunswickers and the succession of suffrage resolutions and bills in the House of Assembly between 1894 and 1899 all sent the same message. In the face of this rising tide, Saint John MLA and leader of the opposition Conservative Party, Alfred Stockton, moved a suffrage resolution in the House on 17 April

1894. It was not, however, a straightforward declaration of support but an effort, he argued, to assess "the full expression of opinions on the general principle." During the debates on the municipal franchise in 1885 and the provincial franchise in 1889, he had tied rights to property. Now, he declared his determination to discover how "a subsequent bill might be formed in a way that would pass." Such an attempt to gauge support occurred nowhere else in Atlantic Canada.

Stockton refuted the 1889 naysayers, observing that thousands of women had petitioned for enfranchisement, and none had petitioned against it. He returned to the priority-of-property principle, asking, "Why should an ignorant footman have a vote, while the lady he drives, who is educated, intelligent and has property of her own, has none?" His colleague from Westmorland County, Amasa Killam, lent his support: women "would add the brightest gem to the electoral lists." Others pointed to the growing popular approval for suffrage, the injustice of taxation without representation, women's increasing participation in higher education, and much else. Supporter William Howe (1835–?) claimed that the "exercise of the franchise was one of the most potent and most sacred privileges of mankind." In addition to previous assembly supporters, such as Henry Emmerson, the pro-suffrage side benefitted from a valuable new ally, Kent County lawyer and Conservative James Phinney.

Five assemblymen, led by the persuasive premier Blair, declared themselves in opposition. Blair accused Stockton of deceptiveness for using a resolution in an attempt to verify the assembly's level of support. He was backed by Richibucto lawyer and MLA Henry Powell (1855–1930), who eulogized "the glory of Roman manhood and womanhood," and praised the Roman period as a time when "woman played no part in the political history of the nation." Newcomer MLA John Sievewright, a former school principal elected only that month in a by-election, proposed an amendment to delay

Stockton's resolution. That favourite strategy of antis in every province passed by twenty-one to fourteen. Stockton's resolution did not advance, but the pro-suffragists took heart from the 40 percent of MLAs who ostensibly favoured some form of female enfranchisement.

Stockton was optimistic enough to introduce an 1895 bill that was tied to a Saint John Women's Enfranchisement Association petition, but he proved unprepared for the increasing resistance. Sievewright pounced again, proposing delay even before Stockton acted. Subsequent MLAs who spoke disagreed on women's best interests, the imminence of their enfranchisement elsewhere, the importance of property, and the merits of various voters. A telling exchange occurred between Stockton and Sievewright; the former stressed a recent petition that bore more than ten thousand signatures, whereas the latter insisted that the MLAs themselves represented public opinion. Pro-suffragist MLA Marcus Atkinson asked why, "when we give the vote to the Indian and the savage shall we deny it to the wife and mother?" In fact, few Indigenous men were enfranchised and no women were. Convert James Phinney envisioned an electorate, whether male or female, that was restricted to the knowledgeable and educated. Others assumed that white women's votes would shore up the respectable middle class. Restigouche lawyer William Mott (1864–1911) rejected all such justifications, insisting that whereas male suffrage "was an extension in the way of liberty ... to that class of people who were recognized as being entitled to vote," female voters would negatively affect the natural order.

After a day of intense debate, Sievewright's amendment to delay was lost by seventeen to eighteen, but Stockton's bill was also defeated. Six members left the House before the suffrage bill vote. When criticized by the *Saint John Telegraph,* one of the deserters, Liberal MLA Marcus Atkinson, explained that he had been obliged to leave for health reasons, but he had paired up with an anti-suffrage MLA, Carleton County Conservative James Diblee. Some absconders clearly just wanted to dodge the controversy associated with a private member's bill, on which members voted according to their conscience. In the end, Liberals, Conservatives, and the descendants of Loyalists ranged themselves both for and against. Although their stances are not entirely clear, Acadians and other Catholics appear to have been solidly opposed. Whatever their motivations, pro- and anti-suffrage politicians were quite evenly matched in number.

Suffragists were not happy with this turn of events. They spent seventy-two hours lobbying opponents and finally convinced Conservative James Mitchell (1843–97), who had voted anti-suffrage on 22 February, to give notice on 25 February (first reading) for another bill to amend the New Brunswick Elections Act of 1889. At the same time, some MLAs (including two who had opposed suffrage three days earlier) presented pro-suffrage petitions from their constituents. Stockton and his allies hoped to triumph in another quick vote. Before a supporter could even speak, Premier Blair proposed to change the wording of the proposed bill to demand a "clear expression of public opinion," suggesting a referendum was needed before considering such a significant change. Eyeing an election, he urged both sides to wait, promising "suffrage sometime, just not now." Such sophistry did not prevent another full debate focusing on female capacity to vote intelligently and the extent to which women actually wanted the franchise. Blair denied the representativeness of twelve recent petitions from ten thousand supporters and stated that female voters would not benefit the country. Emmerson quickly retorted that "an acknowledged democratic principle [is] that the Government derives its just powers from the consent of the governed," that "taxation without representation is tyranny," and that "exclusion justified despotism." But his comments went unanswered. Blair held the line that every New Brunswicker was well represented in the legislature. Ultimately, his amendment to delay passed by nineteen to sixteen.

After the two close votes in 1895, suffragists took a different tack. Prompted by the Saint John Women's Enfranchisement Association, they concentrated on female school trustees. In February, Henry Emmerson proposed to amend the schools act. Premier Blair responded positively: the bill might quell agitation for the provincial franchise. The initiative for school trustees passed quickly.

Only in 1899, after an overwhelming election victory of forty to four over the Conservatives, did Henry Emmerson return to battle. Now the new premier, he suggested "that in the opinion of this House the time is now ripe for the enactment of a law providing that the rights of citizenship shall not be denied or abridged on account of sex, but that full franchise be granted to the women of this province on the same terms as men." Like Stockton in 1894, he hoped first of all to reaffirm the principle of female electors, "as there may be honourable members who might differ very materially with respect to the details." He invoked the enfranchisement association's concern for female breadwinners, citing the lower wages paid to women teachers. He argued that discrimination between married and unmarried women as voters "was not in the best interests of the country." In the debate, the usual arguments reappeared. Liberal William Pugsley, a Sussex lawyer and Saint John *Daily Telegraph* co-owner who had supported women's participation in school board elections, now emerged as the strongest anti-suffrage opponent, arguing that women had the protection they needed, namely a married women's property act. He ignored their desire to participate in government and the needs of those without property. Pugsley concluded, "Before a change so radical, so permanent and so far-reaching was adopted, the question should be submitted to the people." His colleague John Douglas Hazen (1860–1937) was more brutal: "Behind all legislation is physical force, and in the end the man must rule." Ultimately, the arguments were less nuanced than in 1894. In any case, an amendment to delay lost by thirty-two to eight, and the final vote lost by thirty-four to seven. Although a resolution and not a bill – meaning it measured MLAs support but would not proceed through the channels to become law – the situation resembled the 1899 vote in Nova Scotia that killed suffrage for a decade. No further resolutions or bills appeared in New Brunswick until 1909.

THE LULL

As elsewhere in Atlantic Canada, the New Brunswick suffrage campaign lost momentum, but the lull was comparatively short. In the immediate aftermath of legislative defeat, the provincial WCTU Franchise Department and the Saint John Women's Enfranchisement Association moved away from their suffrage work. WCTU petitions had no replacement. The enfranchisement association considered disbanding. Led by Ella Hatheway, whose businessman husband, Frank, and daughter Miriam showed similar sympathies, the province's only suffrage group began to study the British-based Fabian movement, which advocated a peaceful shift from capitalism to socialism. Topics of study included "Free and False Economy" and "Housework as a Profession," as well as Edward Bellamy's novel *Looking Backward* (1888), a runaway bestseller that portrayed the socialist utopia of the future. The shift from maternal feminism to an emphasis on broader human rights did not appeal to all members: meetings were less well attended, less regular, and less focused, as collectivism and Fabian socialism were discussed between 1900 and 1903.

As the enfranchisement association grew increasingly intolerant of conservatives, it inevitably clashed with the LCW. Frustration with the latter's refusal to endorse suffrage, failure to address class issues, and lack of support for reforms involving compulsory education, the creation of a Children's Aid society, and the city's almshouses, asylums, hospitals, and factories climaxed in

1901. The association declared, "The members of the Saint John Branch of the WEA feel keenly that on more than one occasion, and notably at their recent annual meeting, the attitude of the Women's Council toward them as affiliated members has been unjust and unkind. Therefore resolved that we sever our connection with the Women's Council." In the immediate aftermath of this resolution, the enfranchisement association temporarily disbanded, whereas the Saint John LCW hosted the National Council of Women's 1902 annual meeting. Its lack of commitment to suffrage would have been applauded by a key speaker at the convention, Adelaide Hoodless (1857–1910), the Ontario anti-suffragist and founder of the Women's Institute and the Canadian YWCA. The enfranchisement association nevertheless boasted its own luminaries. Mabel Peters had become Canada's best-known children's playground reformer, going on to serve as vice-president of the United States Playground Association.

The association's foray into Fabianism also offers a reminder that a few suffragists were prepared to tackle class injustice. Their advocacy of better factory conditions was rewarded by the 1904 appointment of a factory commission, with the association's own president, Emma Fiske, as its sole female member. A new factory act was passed the following year. That extensive statute forbade children under fourteen from working in factories (unless in "exceptional circumstances") and limited girls (aged fourteen to eighteen) and women to no more than ten hours a day or sixty hours a week, except for up to thirteen and a half hours a day or eighty-one hours a week for a maximum of thirty-six days a year. Such gains were hard-won, and perhaps the enfranchisement association took heart, as members regrouped and returned to the suffrage battle.

THE SUFFRAGE CAMPAIGN REIGNITES

Early in 1908, the Saint John Women's Enfranchisement Association reinstituted petitioning, composing suffrage bills, lobbying,

and encouraging public engagement. During the ensuing decade, despite bitter resistance, including the well-known persecution of British suffragettes, it found allies in the WCTU, politicians,
and even in the LCW. At moments between 1907 and 1917, triumph appeared imminent, a perception perhaps energized by developments in Britain and the United States.

Although MLAs Alfred Stockton and Henry Emmerson moved
on to federal politics, two Saint John MLAs, Liberal businessman
and social reformer Frank Hatheway, the husband of Ella, and
Independent John Edward Wilson (1861–1935), proved able and
energetic. Moreover, the pro-suffragists benefitted from the sur-
prise change of heart of William Pugsley, the Saint John Liberal
MLA and newly appointed attorney general. In 1906, he shep-
herded a bill allowing women to practise law. Three Saint John
newspapers endorsed the cause, further inspiring advocates.

The *Saint John Evening News* reprinted a published article in
1908 by American suffragist Rose Helmes. In a thinly veiled critique of the LCW, Mabel Peters, a member of the enfranchisement
association, had submitted the article, which condemned those
who prioritized their own prestige over the liberation of "the
great sisterhood of women." They were the "very same women ...
who ... are holding themselves up as examples of superior intelligence, moral integrity and religious devotion." A few months later,
the enfranchisement association organized a petition delivered
by four members to Premier Hazen. His response offered little
hope: only when a compelling number of women demonstrated
support would enfranchisement happen. He patronizingly suggested that they should keep to their own sphere and away from
"the public work of the country." Undeterred, if furious, the delegation returned in support of the 1909 suffrage bill, which had
been prepared by Mabel French (1881–1935), New Brunswick's first
female lawyer.

Even though the enfranchisement association and Frank
Hatheway, the MLA who presented the 1909 suffrage bill, were

firmly committed to suffrage regardless of marital status or property ownership, they were cautious. Anticipating that MLAs were most likely to accept a minor amendment to the Elections Act, the association, assisted by Mabel French, proposed enfranchising only single women who possessed property worth a minimum of four hundred dollars. This cohort of women already held the municipal franchise, so, if passed, the 1909 bill would enable them to vote provincially. Anti-suffragists, however, quickly offered an amendment to delay before Hatheway, or anyone else, could speak. Newly elected Acadian Conservative MLA Alphonse Sormany (1880–1943), a physician representing Gloucester, was particularly dismissive, describing suffragettes as "those masculine-feminine beings who had done very little to secure the rights of women, but much to impress upon the minds of people the deplorable conditions that would exist if women took part in politics." In response, Hatheway pointed to "the barest kind of justice to the many thousands of women holding property in the province." A member from the same party, Woodstock MLA James Flemming (1868–1927), agreed, explaining that taxation without representation was tyranny and that many women in business and education were making important contributions to society. In a long debate, Hatheway asked, "Would anyone say that there was no large and strong demand for the franchise for women when it lies at the base of the constitution of the WCTU?" Such common sense proved unavailing. Despite the bill's modesty, legislators voted twenty-four to fourteen to delay for three months.

Equally infuriating was the disrespect shown to Saint John Women's Enfranchisement Association lobbyists. When seven of them entered the House of Assembly viewing area, they were taunted by several MLAs, who yelled, "Help! Police!" Once the delay passed, some antis engaged in sexual innuendo by circulating a lurid drawing. Ella Hatheway, well known for her dignity and steadiness, waited three years to complain, lest she jeopardize the fight. Eventually, however, she could not contain her rage, asking in the sympathetic *Saint John Globe* in 1912, "How can we expect the country to turn toward anything moral and right when such men are sent as representatives and framers of its laws ... Such men may well dread the vote of every pure-minded woman."

In 1910, the enfranchisement association and the LCW reconciled when the latter followed the national council in formally endorsing suffrage. Over the next nine years, the LCW supported bills and petitions from the association. The united front undermined the charge of limited support. Another positive development was the enfranchisement association's affiliation with its renamed national counterpart, the National Suffrage Association. Previous indifference to the national suffrage movement – even while praising American accomplishments – disappeared. Reaffirming affiliation with Canada's National Suffrage Association widened networks and increased local credibility.

Outreach in Canada was accompanied by growing interest in Britain's militant suffragette movement, which was well covered in Canadian newspapers. The Women's Social and Political Union (WSPU) condemned the empty promises of male politicians and declared that the time had come for action rather than rhetoric. Sympathy for the charismatic Emmeline Pankhurst and her allies grew slowly, hindered by dismay and horror – stoked up by the antis – when the militants broke windows, set fires in postal boxes, and accosted politicians. In 1912, to much excitement, Sylvia Pankhurst (1882–1960), a leading figure in the WSPU and daughter of Emmeline, visited Saint John, her only stop in the Maritimes during her primarily American tour and an affirmation of the importance of the city and the enfranchisement association. One month before her visit, the association summed up the mixed response to militancy: "Let us withhold our judgment upon the window-smashers until the quiet comes after victory and not condemn what must seem rude and mistaken methods to

us who have no experience with old country politics, but remember what these English women are fighting for." In a powerful
two-hour address to a large audience at the Saint John Opera
House, Pankhurst covered a panoply of injustices, from unequal
pay to unequal moral standards between the sexes. Winning the
vote was the remedy. The Saint John *Telegraph and Sun* applauded
the seasoned and seductive activist: there "does not appear to be
anything militant about [Pankhurst] except her message."

The WSPU had other connections with the province. In 1912,
Welsford native Gertrude Harding moved to England, where she
became its key organizer.

1912 AND BEYOND: SUFFRAGE BILLS AND RESOLUTIONS

In 1912, following Pankhurst's speech, Conservative W.B. Dickson
(1847–1916) introduced yet another suffrage bill. During the debate that followed, advocates stressed that there was a demand for
enfranchisement, as demonstrated by five petitions and nearly a
dozen WCTU resolutions. After that bill failed on a technicality,
Woodstock Liberal MLA Donald Munro (1855–1939) tried again
the following year. That effort elicited the broadest backing of
any suffrage bill, with the Saint John Woman Suffrage Association
(formerly the enfranchisement association), the WCTU, and a
union of carpenters coming out in public support. Like the 1909
bill, the 1913 bill sought to extend the municipal franchise of
single, propertied women to the provincial one. Munro attempted
to navigate the slippery slope argument: further extensions of
the franchise were up to the future legislature. Women, Munro
argued, exhibited "just as strong patriotism ... and feeling for the
flag" as men, and were "just as well able, and in many cases better
able, to exercise the franchise if it were granted." Once again, opponents sought to discredit petitions, dismissing them as out of
date and signed by boys.

One of the strongest 1913 opponents was Saint John Conservative MLA Leonard Tilley (1871–1947), the son of MP Samuel Leonard Tilley, a Father of Confederation. He reiterated a common argument when he fabricated statistics to claim that 80 percent of New Brunswick women were opposed to suffrage and insisted that women's interests were already protected. They needed to stay at home to improve their children. Participation in politics would lose men's respect. The fate of the 1913 bill, a defeat of twenty-one to ten, was worse than in 1909. Since it had been a private member's bill, the split was not along party lines. Premier James Kidd Flemming, who had led the Conservatives to their largest ever majority, endorsed suffrage against his party majority.

The First World War and the deaths of two prominent Saint John suffrage leaders – Emma Fiske and Mabel Peters – followed on the heels of this defeat, and once again the cause shifted to the

*Although **Gertrude Harding** (1889–1977) had evinced no previous interest in the subject, after moving to England with her sister Nellie's family in 1912 at age twenty-two, she championed the suffrage cause. As she wrote in her memoir, "It was a completely unknown world to me, for I had never heard of such things as 'causes' or people who were willing to go to prison for them. It ... struck some kind of chord I didn't know I had." Her WSPU experience began with attending meetings and marches. As her organizational skills developed, she was assigned principal roles, including one after-hours smashing of orchids at Kew Gardens, an assignment that she and her working partner Lillian Lenton did with so much force that authorities blamed men.*

Harding became a paid organizer, contributing to the weekly union newspaper, Suffragette, *and becoming the founding*

sidelines. The next suffrage bill would not appear until 1917, but the Saint John Woman Suffrage Association made gains nonetheless. It successfully pushed for an April 1914 referendum to extend the municipal franchise to married women, though the relevant legislation would not see the light of day for two years. According to the *Saint John Telegraph,* 1,766 female taxpayers joined the already eligible 940 spinsters on the voters list. Even their combined number was small in comparison with more than 12,000 total electors. The suffrage association also gained ground in the labour movement. Ella Hatheway successfully appealed to the Trades and Labor Congress of Canada to endorse suffrage at its annual meeting in Saint John, where Leonora O'Reilly (1870–1927), American feminist union leader and guest speaker, called for an eight-hour workday and a living wage for female workers.

director of its bodyguard, a group trained in the martial arts to defend themselves and to protect suffrage leaders from police violence and protesters. After that eight-month-long assignment, which included organizing decoys for Emmeline Pankhurst's transportation, Harding was assigned to be Christabel Pankhurst's personal secretary during her exile in Paris. She became a primary writer and typesetter for the Suffragette, *of which Christabel Pankhurst (daughter of Emmeline) was editor. That a young rural woman would rise to such prominence in the WSPU suggests a strong latent suffragism in New Brunswick. Whereas Harding never convinced her family and did not advocate for suffrage in her letters home, her contributions to the British movement were significant.*

The recently founded New Brunswick Federation of Labour, one of the first provincial federations, already included a small number of female employees, although part of the rationale for their inclusion was to avoid unorganized women displacing men in employment. In 1916, the suffrage association also celebrated amendments to the Factory Act that required shop owners to provide chairs for their female staff.

In 1917, the suffrage cause took centre stage again. Saint John Liberal MLA William Roberts (1869–1938) introduced a bill to give women equal suffrage with men. Broader than the 1899, 1909, and 1913 versions, it extended to married and unmarried women, both propertied and unpropertied. As one local paper reported, the women did not want "half or three quarters of a loaf. No compromise is their motto." Roberts pointed out that the Prairie provinces had all granted women's suffrage in 1916, and England was about to follow. He argued, "A nation which holds women in servitude and ignorance is bound to remain low in the scale of civilization" and added that "just because some women don't want the vote doesn't mean none should have the right." For the first time in the House, women's war work was cited: "an indebtedness that time would never permit repayment."

As elsewhere in Atlantic Canada, the Great War attracted new allies and increased the credibility of suffragists. The connection between British women's war work and the vote was well covered in New Brunswick newspapers. A long-standing opponent, British Liberal prime minister Herbert Asquith, had finally admitted that wartime contributions made a difference. In New Brunswick, the Saint John Woman Suffrage Association joined other female volunteers. Like Asquith, MLA Leonard Tilley claimed a change of heart: female enfranchisement would now eradicate political corruption. On the Sunday before the legislative vote, Reverend H.A. Cody (1872–1948), the rector of Saint John's largest Anglican church, used his sermon to endorse the "justice and equity of the principle of equal suffrage." The suffrage association sent leaders on a speaking tour to towns around the province, including Newcastle, Chatham, Chipman, Perth, and Moncton. Nineteen branches of the WCTU, the LCW and twenty-five of its affiliates, and new supporters, including the female schoolteachers of Moncton, repeated the message. During the debate, eight delegations from various pro-suffrage women's groups stood on the steps of the legislature.

Despite this enthusiasm, the antis insisted that demand remained insufficient, that a referendum was needed, and that women aided the war effort because they wanted to help their families, not because they wanted the vote. Once again, the antis won their amendment to delay, twenty-four to fifteen. Even though both the premier and the leader of the Opposition were in their corner, suffragists were bitter and demoralized. This was perhaps the campaign's lowest moment. Slowly, however, activists rallied in response to a wave of suffrage victories elsewhere. In March 1918, Conservative Independent Kings County MLA James Murray (1864–1960) introduced a resolution, stressing that most jurisdictions had enfranchised women and that women's war work had "removed prejudice." Several other MLAs spoke positively, including – for the first time – an Acadian, the future premier Peter Venoit. The only negative voice came from Victoria County Liberal MLA Walter Foster, who wanted to perfect the wording of the resolution. Whereas a favourable resolution carried unanimously, a bill was required "in due time," as reported by the *Telegraph and Sun*.

SUCCESSFUL 1919 BILL

The bill was duly presented in spring 1919, at the next legislative session. Whereas suffragists had worked hard in service of the bills and resolutions presented between 1894 and 1917, they did little in connection with this one. Ella Hatheway was nevertheless quoted as saying that the legislature would be forced through shame to grant women the vote, which is basically what happened. The suffrage association remained uncomfortable with franchise as a reward for war work, but it recognized the conflict as an essential catalyst. A more cynical interpretation is that the politicians used the justification to save face as suffrage became pervasive. When asked by Catherine Cleverdon in 1944, Ella and Frank Hatheway's daughter, Miriam Hatheway Wood, agreed that women's war work was "the great contributing factor" because "men just did not have the nerve to refuse the vote to women who sacrificed their sons and themselves to the war."

In 1919, Walter Foster, now premier, introduced an anticlimactic measure that enfranchised women on the same basis as men and cited the war effort as its justification. In his words, "if one was given the franchise, all must have it, including Black and white." Despite this fine rhetoric, he paid no attention to possible non-white voters. Those of European descent remained the focus of legislative concern. Nor were women in fact equally treated. Unlike the other Atlantic provinces, New Brunswick did not include the right to run for public office with the right to vote. The former was withheld until 1934. As the *Telegraph and Sun* headline reported, "Women May Vote for Men but Not for Themselves." Moreover, the debate was infused with casual misogyny, such as when Moncton Liberal MLA Francis Sweeney mused, "with franchise extended to women an effort should be made to have elections take place in fine weather."

The simple amendment of the Electors Act in 1919 merely struck out "male person" and inserted "person whether male or female, married or unmarried." With its omission of a property requirement, this legislation enfranchised proportionately more women than did Nova Scotia's law, but much of the 1889 Elections Act remained intact. Prisoners who were serving time for a criminal offence, anyone receiving government aid, and inmates of charitable institutions were specifically excluded. Unlike most provinces, New Brunswick also deliberately named and excluded Indigenous people – "No person ... shall vote ... who is an Indian" – which confirmed existing federal law denying the federal or provincial franchise. As happened elsewhere, only in 1951 were Indigenous women living on reserves in New Brunswick even allowed to vote at the band council level, and only in 1963 could women (and men) living on reserves vote provincially or federally. Another significant lag occurred for all New Brunswick women at the municipal level. The property requirement for both single and married women persisted until 1966, leaving most unwaged women, including housewives, unenfranchised. After 1966, residency and age were the main requirements, and in 1971 the voting age was dropped from twenty-one to eighteen. In 2003, incarcerated New Brunswickers were finally permitted at the polls.

I feel assured that were the franchise extended [to women] not only in city affairs, but in local and dominion politics, their influence would be always on the side of civil and religious freedom.

– ANGUS B. MCKENZIE,
PRINCE EDWARD ISLAND MERCHANT AND MEMBER
OF THE LEGISLATIVE COUNCIL, 1888

FOUR

PRINCE EDWARD ISLAND: INFORMAL BUT CONSISTENT INTEREST

Elsie Inman (1891–1986), Mrs. Lou (Oliver) Pool,
and a man in a chef hat examining a box of Prince Edward Island
potatoes, ca. 1955. Inman co-founded the Women's Liberal Club
in 1916, lobbied the provincial government for women's
enfranchisement, and was appointed Prince Edward Island's
first woman senator in 1955, the year this photo was taken
in Winnipeg, serving until her death at the age of 95.

THE PRINCE EDWARD ISLAND legislature did not hold a suffrage debate until 1918, four decades later than the other Maritime provinces. Liberal MLA John Howatt Bell (1846–1929) championed PEI women's rights from the 1890s onward, but he failed to recruit sufficient followers inside the legislature until after he became premier in 1919. His political contemporaries preferred the status quo and accused Bell of being more interested in suffrage than women themselves were.

The history of Prince Edward Island is often portrayed as exceptional. Indeed, this characterization does have some truth, but it has been exaggerated with regard to suffrage. Although the island's size, culture, and history fostered unique political features, a focus on these alone obscures the lengthy evolution of feminism in PEI. This misunderstanding has been further exacerbated by conservative stereotypes and a shortage of documentation. Research suggests that PEI women have a long history of political engagement dating from the late eighteenth century, as both proponents and defenders of land tenure. Soon after representative government was established in 1773, it enacted protective legislation, including a 1781 dower law. During the Confederation era, new statutes granted propertied single women the vote in municipal elections and the right to serve as school trustees, and married women gained the right to hold property in their own names. As elsewhere, such initiatives favoured the middle class and ignored poor, racialized, and Indigenous women, notably the Mi'kmaq on the two reserves and women who lived in the Bog, Charlottetown's Black community.

Eighteenth- and early-nineteenth-century improvements to women's rights followed similar timelines to those in Nova Scotia and New Brunswick, and were achieved with minimal opposition. Not so the drive for provincial suffrage. The attention of the local press to campaigns in other provinces and countries and the suffrage petitions of the Woman's Christian Temperance Union (WCTU) in 1894 and 1913 kept the cause percolating, but there could be no success until suffrage bills were brought to the legislature. How are we to explain the absence of suffrage bills and debates in the 1890s, unlike in the other Maritime provinces? There are two possible reasons. First of all, PEI implemented a robust prohibition law in 1900, which weakened the key suffrage argument elsewhere that female voters were needed to bring in prohibition; and second, the province's small political circles made suffragists acutely aware of their prospects. Like Eliza Ritchie in mid-1910s Nova Scotia, they may have delayed because they saw no possibility of success before 1918. With the end of the First World War, their calculations shifted. A new Women's Liberal Club, founded in 1916, and the PEI Women's Institute, founded in 1911, were prepared to lobby. In 1922, the bill, as elsewhere, excluded Indigenous women living on reserves. They were obliged to wait until 1963 to cast their first ballot in PEI. Despite the appearance of tardiness, PEI's road to suffrage shared much with other jurisdictions. In the larger picture, the province cannot be dismissed as a conservative backwater.

DEMOGRAPHIC, ECONOMIC, AND POLITICAL CONTEXTS OF SUFFRAGE

Until 1767, European settlement in PEI differed little from that of Nova Scotia. Indigenous groups, ancestors of the Mi'kmaq, were its First Peoples, about whom too little is yet known regarding female authority. In the seventeenth century, the Acadians became the first European settlers on what they called Isle St. Jean. In 1758, the British expelled about three thousand Acadians as part of the deportation policy after the capture of Louisbourg, although a few hundred escaped detection. The colony briefly became part of colonial Nova Scotia. In 1767, London implemented a land settlement scheme, dividing the island into sixty-seven twenty-thousand-acre lots and giving them to ninety-eight men who resided in Britain, most of whom had ties to the British government. These owners, known as "proprietors," were obliged to find tenants to settle their property and to pay a land tax to the Crown. Only 1.5 percent of the land remained in the possession of the Crown. The Mi'kmaw and Acadian residents were displaced. Free land in neighbouring colonies, absentee landlords who did not fulfill their obligations to provide infrastructure but who refused to sell, and tenants who refused to pay their rents made the proprietorial land tenure system untenable, yet it was abolished only in 1875 in the agreement under which PEI entered Confederation. Presumably to encourage immigration, the colony passed a law in 1781 clarifying that slavery was legal – the only British North American colony to say so explicitly – and withdrew the statute in 1825, a few years ahead of the British Empire's final abolition of slavery. Perhaps not surprisingly, the Black population remained considerably smaller than in Nova Scotia and New Brunswick, even into the twenty-first century.

By 1799, when the colony was renamed Prince Edward Island, one-third of its lots were still uninhabited, and others were barely inhabited. The nearly four thousand settlers were mainly Highland Scots or Acadians; the rest were Loyalist, English, Mi'kmaq, and African American. Most of the five hundred Loyalists who attempted to settle on PEI quickly moved elsewhere. Frustrated white settlers who were unable to buy land outright resented having to pay rent. A political party advocating escheat – confiscating land from proprietors who failed to meet their obligations and selling it to tenants – attracted huge support on the island but never convinced the British. Settlement increased during the

1820s, and by 1841, two thousand of the total population of forty-seven thousand resided in the only significant urban area, Charlottetown, which never matched Saint John or Halifax as a city centre. Scottish, Irish, and English immigrants were the most numerous. In 1888, Lebanese Christian refugees escaping persecution began to arrive, joining the growing minority Acadian population and several hundred Mi'kmaq. Because its settlement period ended comparatively early, Prince Edward Island is less diverse than most provinces today.

Agriculture was by far the most common occupation, and it produced the most exports. Lobster and oysters eventually increased the importance of the fishery. Compared to its neighbours, PEI had little manufacturing. There was, however, small-scale production of shoes, tobacco products, furniture, sleighs, buggies, farm equipment, textiles, and alcohol. The first lobster canneries, employing many women, were established in the 1870s. Exports benefitted from the reciprocity agreement with the United States from 1855 to 1865. When reciprocity ended, exports to the States fell by 50 percent, a phenomenon often blamed on Confederation, as was the collapse of commercial shipbuilding after the 1860s.

Islanders were smug about resisting Confederation. Although the first Confederation talks were held in Charlottetown, PEI did not join the four original provinces in 1867. In 1873, it became the seventh colony to join. Their small population – vastly outnumbered by the new dominion's 3.5 million – combined with isolation during the regular freeze-up from December through March gave islanders no illusions about wielding power in a nation that aspired to reach from sea to sea. By the 1870s, rising debt and better terms made union more attractive. Many islanders came to condemn Ottawa's focus on the National Policy – which supported western settlement, a national railway, and the protection of manufacturing – as responsible for outward migration, especially of youth. Peaking in 1888 with nearly 110,000 residents, the population fell for almost a century, returning to that late-nineteenth-century high point only in 1971.

Next to that loss, alcohol and its associated evils – from violence to poverty and poor health – were the main social concern in late-nineteenth-century PEI. The late founding and brief existence of the Charlottetown branch of the Local Council of Women (LCW) meant that there was no infrastructure for a wider social reform movement, as in Halifax and Saint John. This may have encouraged a targeted focus on temperance. Seven local WCTU unions, forty-nine branches of the Sons of Temperance, several Blue Ribbon Reform Clubs, a PEI branch of the Dominion Alliance for the Total Suppression of Liquor Traffic, and the anti-Catholic Orange Lodge all demanded temperance and prohibition. Between 1880 and 1893, each of the province's three counties overwhelmingly voted for prohibition under the Scott Act, and annual per capita alcohol consumption dropped from 0.278 gallons to 0.122 gallons. Outside Charlottetown, islanders voted eight to one in favour of prohibition in Prime Minister Wilfrid Laurier's 1898 national prohibition plebiscite, and in 1900, PEI implemented five decades of prohibition, the longest in Canada by far. That result eliminated Canada's most popular justification for female suffrage.

Politically, PEI was effectively as democratic as other British colonies, introducing an elected assembly in 1773 and responsible government in 1851. It is impossible to determine whether any women voted in elections to the House of Assembly. Their legislative disenfranchisement in 1836 suggests, however, that the growth of a separate spheres ideology was mobilizing against women with political ambitions. Resentment of absentee landlords generated a broad male electorate, with PEI the only province to include road building as a means of enfranchisement for men. Such labour was deemed similar to property owning in demonstrating a stake in the community. Unlike in New Brunswick, Black men were not explicitly excluded from the franchise.

In 1862, an elected Legislative Council was created, whose elite members tried to offset the more liberal franchise of the House of Assembly by restricting its electorate to British male subjects who were thirty years of age and over, who had resided on PEI for at least five years, and who owned property valued at a minimum of £100. Elite power was further entrenched when property owning permitted votes in multiple constituencies until 1966. In 1893, PEI combined its elected houses and created fifteen constituencies, five per county, each electing both a legislative councillor and an assemblyman, an arrangement designed to encourage parties to nominate both Protestants and Catholics to deter religious conflict.

By the late nineteenth century, PEI possessed strong cultural identities in poetry, art, and song. On the literary side, Lucy Maud Montgomery began publishing short stories before the release of her bestselling *Anne of Green Gables* in 1908.

As the suffrage movement gained traction in the late nineteenth century, PEI had only recently joined Confederation but stood in contrast to the next two provinces to join, Saskatchewan and Alberta, both newly created upon entering in 1905. Whereas they symbolized Canada's youthful potential, PEI was generally regarded as backward and dependent, if perhaps idyllic. That assumption encouraged stereotypes about the reception of suffrage. Islanders, however, were anything but politically apathetic. The population of only some 100,000 at the end of the nineteenth century was deeply engaged in the choice of fifteen assemblymen, fifteen councillors, six federal MPs, and four senators. Small constituencies, slight margins of victory, and widespread vote buying made elections intense, with one historian labelling island politics "a blood sport." PEI's efficacy in introducing prohibition locally in 1880 and provincially from 1900 to 1948 demonstrates

Lucy Maud Montgomery (1874–1942) was raised by her maternal grandparents in Cavendish, PEI, after her mother's early death. From a young age, she kept a journal and wrote in several genres, publishing her first piece, a poem, at age seventeen. An advocate for higher education for women, Montgomery attended Prince of Wales College in Charlottetown and Dalhousie University, each for one year, claiming that she would have liked nothing more than to continue at Dalhousie studying for a bachelor's degree, but she lacked the means and her relatives considered it a waste for a woman. Her first and most famous novel, Anne of Green Gables, *became an international bestseller when published in 1908, and it continues to appear on lists of the best books of all time. In 1911, she married a Presbyterian minister, but the union was an unhappy one. Montgomery's diary describes the painful barriers she faced as a female writer, and most of the main female characters in her twenty-three novels mimic her critique of traditional gender role expectations of women, including those of ministers' wives. She is not known to have commented on suffrage, but she publicly defended broader women's rights.*

the same dedication. In the twenty-first century, islanders remain Canada's most enthusiastic voters, with turnouts of over 80 percent in all but one election since 1986.

LEGAL REFORMS FOR WOMEN

Prince Edward Island's premier pre-Confederation political issue, absentee landlords, dovetailed with women's rights because women mobilized on both sides. Although the original proprietors of 1767 were male, their heirs included major female landholders. In an exercise of power unusual for their sex, these off-islanders managed estates, contributed to educational and religious philanthropy, and fervently defended their class. When the land tenure system finally ended, thirty-five women held a quarter of the expropriated acreage. Women also stood out in violent protests against rent boycotts of landlords. That contest displayed a wide-ranging female agency and set the foundation for future political involvement. Prince Edward Island's legal history, including women's rights, remains relatively understudied. The emergence of legislative reform in the late nineteenth century nevertheless suggests concern for women's human rights. Protecting and extending the right of both single and married women to own and control property surfaced regularly on the political agenda. Dower laws giving widows a lifetime interest in (usually one-third of) their husbands' property were enacted in PEI in 1781 and remained intact into the Confederation era, unlike in the West, where women lacked dower protection. In 1860, PEI became one of the first colonies to pass a deserted wives' act, defending women from their husbands' creditors or claims to their wages or property. Though accepting the legal subordination of wives, it moved toward remedy. In the 1850s, legislative debates about the law of evidence and bastardy showed early awareness of women's sexual and economic vulnerability. The province's first seduction act was passed in 1876, advancing women's rights insofar as it allowed the female "victims" of seduction to sue for damages. Previously, this was reserved for their fathers. No one seems to have taken advantage of this option, but its presence admitted female vulnerability and the possibility of legal independence.

The dower, deserted wives, and seduction acts all involved financial protection or compensation from men who did not honour their financial responsibilities, but a broader campaign for married women's property rights began in the late nineteenth century, notably later than in Nova Scotia and New Brunswick. It was partly stimulated by the erosion of protection, as dower came to be regarded as cumbersome when land sales became an increasingly frequent and significant part of the economy – and legislators listened to the desires of heirs to control women's traditional one-third dower. The 1871 Act to Simplify the Mode of Extinguishing Dower allowed women to surrender dowable property by using a simple phrase of "release." In 1884, further legislation extended the permission to female non-residents who held PEI dower rights. There was no check on possible abuses.

MARRIED WOMEN'S PROPERTY LAW

Married women's property also attracted legislative attention. As in many provinces, the first legal changes focused on the capacity of wives for *selling* property. An 1880 Act to Facilitate the Conveyance of Real Estate by Married Women allowed them to convey, release, surrender, or disclaim land, just as if they were single. The requirement that their husbands must approve, with its abrogation of their independence, raised new questions. An 1881 amendment to the deserted wives' act, which protected husbands from the debts of their wives, also pointed toward greater legal autonomy for women.

In April 1895, PEI's first Married Women's Property Act came to the House of Assembly. It sparked a hasty petition with support from two Charlottetown physicians and Methodist social reformers, Richard Johnson (1831–1903) and Frank D. Beer, as well as Johnson's spouse and founding Charlottetown WCTU president Alice Johnson (1840–1921), along with others whose names have been lost. The three leaders approached Charlottetown assemblyman John Howatt Bell, who had presented the WCTU suffrage petition in the early 1890s, and who as premier would enact suffrage in 1922. Their initiative suggests an expectation of opposition, even though PEI lagged far behind other Maritime provinces in this legislation. Passed in 1896, the act removed the requirement that women must obtain permission from their husbands to buy or sell property and outlined how wives who had left marriages for cruelty and other justifiable offences, such as lunacy or drunkenness, could apply for protection against their husbands' debts. Such amendments assumed marriage to be permanent; PEI's divorce court heard its first case only in 1945.

In 1903, the married women's property statute was amended, a measure that a local newspaper hailed as a response to "the age of Women's Rights" in rejecting "the ancient idea that a woman by marriage loses her legal identity" and giving her "a new status with respect to the holding and disposing of her own property, personal and real, also of entering into any contract and of suing and being sued, in all respects as if she were *femme sole* (single woman)." The editor continued approvingly, "the wages, earnings etc., of the wife acquired in any employment, trade or occupation, or by the exercises of any literary, archaic, scientific skill or art, is her separate property. In short, there are full provisions to enable a married woman to have and dispose of her separate property independent of her husband." Women were moving "closer to the era of general emancipation." His use of both equal rights and maternalist arguments would have met the approval of the PEI WCTU, which had condemned the right of "a drunken reprobate [to] claim the hard earning of his working wife." The overlap of the implementation of married women's property law and prohibition suggests that politicians employed temperance and prohibition to protect women and families, and that feminist activists leveraged the same argument to advance women's rights. Second-wave island feminist Barbara Stetson proudly described the 1903 married women's property law as "a very liberal women's property act."

HIGHER EDUCATION

Access to higher education, as part of rights campaigns, was achieved in New Brunswick in 1875 and in Nova Scotia during the early 1880s. Until 1964, PEI had only one degree-granting university, the Catholic St. Dunstan's, which refused to accept coeds until 1939. Ambitious aspirants confronted the Catholic Church rather than the provincial government. Except for two requests in 1912 and 1916 by nuns for permission to study, little sign survives of public agitation for females to attend St. Dunstan's. Both nuns were refused; the university instead offered tutoring outside the classroom. Its encouragement of vocations to the priesthood may have fuelled fears of female intrusion.

In contrast, the broader history of PEI women's university attendance reveals a determination to extend boundaries. Many women completed the equivalent of the first two years of a university program at Prince of Wales, the island's junior college, and at least five hundred attended university off island between 1880 and 1942. The registers of Dalhousie, Acadia, McGill, Mount Allison, and St. Francis Xavier show that islander students were evenly split between urban (Charlottetown and Summerside) and rural communities. Large numbers of students from farm families suggests a significant motivation to earn degrees, all the more so as most lacked kin traditions of higher education. It has been suggested that PEI's pre-Confederation land tenure system, with its heavy emphasis on contracts, fostered appreciation of literacy and education. Whatever the case, PEI women faced prohibitive financial costs, as well as the commonplace fears that higher education diminished their suitability as wives.

They studied for various undergraduate, graduate, and professional degrees, and some won international distinction. Annie Marion MacLean (1870–1934), who was born in PEI and moved to Nova Scotia as a child, obtained a bachelor of arts degree from Acadia University and a PhD from the University of Chicago. In 1900, she was among the first North American women to earn a

PhD in sociology. Florence Murray (1894–1975) left PEI to study medicine at Dalhousie from 1914 to 1919 and worked as a medical missionary in Korea until 1969. Overall, island women attended university at rates similar to the national average. Independent PEI women, who might have contested the status quo at home, often chose to leave the island for education and jobs, much like their sisters in Quebec and elsewhere, who opted to take the veil.

Born in 1914 to a large PEI family, three of whom became nuns, Sister Bernice Cullen was the first woman to graduate from St. Dunstan's University, taking her bachelor of arts degree in 1941. In 1966, now Dr. Cullen, she joined the Religious Studies Department at St. Dunstan's and retired from university teaching in 1979. She and her sister Ellen Mary, who had also joined the Sisters of Martha, published a history of the order, titled *By the Flame of the Lantern*, in 2005, two years before her death at the age of ninety-two.

In 1917, the Sisters of Saint Martha became the only women's religious congregation formed in PEI. Created at the very height of the suffrage movement, it attracted recruits who may otherwise have contributed to the movement. Throughout the 1930s, its mother superior lobbied the bishop of Charlottetown to admit sisters to St. Dunstan's. Finally, in 1939, Sister Bernice Cullen (1914–2007) and Sister Ida Mary Coady (1900–1979) were accepted on the grounds that they needed bachelor's degrees to qualify to teach Grades 11 and 12 to PEI Catholic students. When Sister Bernice earned the highest marks in her graduating class at St. Dunstan's, it became very difficult not to accept secular female students. In 1942, women generally were admitted.

1880S AND 1890S SUFFRAGE AGITATION

As in Nova Scotia and New Brunswick, arguing for voting rights for propertied, *unmarried* women was one step in the larger project of emancipation. Unlike married women, who were represented in theory by their husbands under British common law, *femmes sole* represented themselves and paid taxes on property. Disallowing their vote contravened the principle of no taxation without representation, over which the American Revolution had been fought.

On PEI, the women's cause was taken up by Angus B. McKenzie (1838–1901), a Scottish-born Charlottetown merchant, member of the Legislative Council for First Queen's, and the island's earliest known public advocate for female enfranchisement. In 1888, he proposed to include propertied single women on the

Charlottetown voters list as a late amendment to an act incorporating the City of Charlottetown. Using self-deprecating humour to deflect controversy, McKenzie joked that, as he was the only bachelor on the council, it was not necessarily his place to champion women. He pronounced himself "astonished that honorable members who are married have so long neglected" the franchise. Pointing positively to the enfranchisement of single women in Toronto and several American cities, he raised the prospect of loyal voters: "Knowing the little I know about the ladies, I feel assured that were the franchise extended to them not only in city affairs, but in local and dominion politics, their influence would be always on the side of civil and religious freedom. I have no doubt they would all be true Grits if they had the franchise."

Suggesting advance collaboration, McKenzie's Liberal colleague Benjamin Rogers (1837–1923) from Alberton quickly seconded, playfully noting that he was rescuing the bachelor. His support focused on taxation without representation. Liberal John Scrimgeour (1842–1917) and Conservative Alexander Martin (1842–1921) chimed in that reform was overdue and was needed beyond the municipal level. Another colleague asked "if the amendment is not intended to make [McKenzie] popular with some particular lady?" In the end, the vote passed unanimously, although it squeaked through the Charlottetown City Council on a vote of only five to four. No *value* of property was specified, but the municipal requirements were the same for women and men, unlike in Newfoundland, which had universal male suffrage for St. John's city elections but maintained property qualifications for women when they began voting in the mid-1920s. In 1888, never married and widowed women voted in Charlottetown and Summerside, making them the first of their sex to cast a ballot since the colonial restrictions of 1836.

It is impossible to know what motivated McKenzie's interest in suffrage. A Sunday School superintendent at Charlottetown's Zion Presbyterian Church, McKenzie lived as a lodger in the 1880s and 1890s and did not seem to have any female kin on PEI. Neither has any record surfaced about why the four Charlottetown councillors objected to suffrage. Nor have women themselves been identified as agitating for the municipal vote or lobbying councillors. To be sure, they may have deliberately stayed in the background to avoid controversy. The swift passage and enactment of McKenzie's motion would have encouraged this strategy – effective for them but frustrating for historians!

Jurisdictions often follow each other's lead to avoid looking unprogressive. Such seems to have been the case with PEI's second-largest urban area, the town of Summerside, which amended its qualifications to include propertied single women in 1892. In 1886, that town had passed the same omnibus bill as Charlottetown would in 1888, to consolidate municipal bylaws, but it lacked an advocate such as McKenzie. In 1892, the municipal bill that enfranchised women came as a one-section act focusing solely on single property holders. It passed through both the House of Assembly and the Legislative Council without debate and with the same wording as Charlottetown's bill. Notably, it maintained distinctions between the sexes. Male residents who did not possess property valued at a hundred dollars could vote if they paid the one-dollar poll tax. Women lacked that option, an omission highlighting that men merited consideration as human beings, but women needed property. Not until 1927 could unmarried women without property pay a poll tax or married propertied women vote in Summerside. Wives without property waited until 1932.

For all that PEI's municipal amendments allowed qualified women to demonstrate their responsible use of the franchise, their numbers, with the exclusion of workers and non-British subjects, amounted to less than 1 percent of the population of Charlottetown and Summerside. The changes concentrated more power among municipal property holders just as men who did not own property were flooding the voters lists because of universal suffrage. The retention of common law notions of the husband representing *his* wife (read: his property) had the same effect.

LEADERSHIP OF THE WOMAN'S CHRISTIAN TEMPERANCE UNION

The same impulse to control the island's less respectable elements encouraged its particularly strong temperance movement, which included seven local WCTU branches. When the Charlottetown WCTU petitioned the legislature for corporate status in 1894, members of the legislature insisted that its "good work" in promoting temperance and moral reform justified waiving the usual fee. A month later, Liberal MLA and future premier John Bell presented a petition on behalf of the Maritime WCTU and other PEI residents calling for full parliamentary suffrage for women. Though Charlottetown reformer Alice Johnson was not named, as local WCTU president and vice-president of the Maritime WCTU, she was surely an instigator. The petition did not lead to a debate, but it confirms sympathies. A rapid achievement of prohibition seemed to render further recognition unnecessary. A successful 1893 provincial prohibition plebiscite led to a 1900 teetotalling law and its strengthening in 1905. Although the province continued to grant medical exceptions for the consumption of liquor, strict regulation was the official policy. PEI women appeared to possess political agency without having the vote. The continuing suffragism of some WCTU members reflected a deeper commitment to equality.

FEMALE SCHOOL TRUSTEES

Within a decade of the revision of the municipal electorate in Charlottetown and Summerside, legislation allowed women to run for school trustee. Just as in New Brunswick, the relationship of public school education to religious faith engaged politicians, churches, communities, and families. Catholic and Protestant conflict often surfaced, as in the controversial Bible Question debate in which Catholics insisted that education and religion were inseparable. Fearing a threat to their children's faith, Catholic parents refused to allow Protestant classroom teachers to read from the Bible. When women sought to become school trustees, they involved themselves directly in the most contentious of island issues, even as they insisted on the appropriateness of their service as maternal trustees.

Unlike the municipal vote, advanced by a supportive MLA, the subject of school trusteeships was raised by women themselves through an LCW petition to the legislature. In 1899, the president of the Charlottetown LCW was Catherine Anderson (1839–?), a Scottish Presbyterian immigrant and mother of four grown children who was married to the principal of Prince of Wales College. She petitioned the legislature to appoint enough women to comprise one-third of the school board. Her petition was presented by Samuel Prowse (1835–1902), an English Methodist and seasoned Conservative politician from Murray Harbour. Prowse watered down the request and proposed merely making women *eligible* for appointment. This passed three readings in the House on three successive days. The only debate was occasioned by the lack of three signatures on the petition, a technicality that could have delayed passage, but the Speaker expressed his satisfaction. No one expressed disapproval of the measure. Perhaps opponents assumed they could prevent subsequent appointments. Unlike early colonial franchise legislation, educational acts never formally excluded women as trustees. As a result, An Act to Further Amend the Public Schools Act, 1877, supplied only clarification: "Nothing herein contained shall be construed to prevent the appointment by the Lieutenant Governor in Council, or by the City Council of Charlottetown, or the Town Council of Summerside, of women as Members of the Board of Trustees."

Eligibility as school trustees held more promise than the municipal franchise. Even one female member would wield more direct influence on a small board than a handful of voters in a

much larger electorate. Of 544 voters in the Summerside municipal election in 1901, only 19, well under 1 percent, were women.
The Charlottetown LCW was decades ahead of its Halifax counterpart in connection with school trustees. Its success was highlighted by recognition in the National Council of Women's annual
report for 1899 and dozens of local newspapers, including the
Charlottetown Guardian. Such congratulations portrayed PEI as just
as interested in women's rights as any other province.

CHARLOTTETOWN LOCAL COUNCIL OF WOMEN

Since the LCW was so successful regarding the appointment of
school trustees, the brevity of its survival as a voice for women's
issues is puzzling. It was established as an umbrella organization
of affiliated women's groups in the same decade as its Halifax and
Saint John counterparts. Its affiliates included four Protestant
church societies, the WCTU, the Imperial Order Daughters of the
Empire, and the Ladies Aid of both the YMCA and the Prince
County Hospital. (Unlike the Halifax LCW, the one in
Charlottetown did not affiliate with Catholic organizations.)
Although the LCW mounted a full slate of officers, newspaper reports fail to list their first names. Ten executive members were
married and three were single, one of whom was Helen Anderson
(1879–?), the daughter of Catherine Anderson, the president. They
targeted public health and moral reform; their projects included
advocating for tuberculosis prevention, lobbying the City of
Charlottetown for better street signage, and supporting the establishment of an institute for "feeble-minded women," a contemporary concept of mental illness, a goal shared with the Halifax
and Saint John's LCWs. The Charlottetown LCW appears to have
been active for only a decade, starting in 1899. The seeming loss of
its minute books leaves only spotty newspaper reporting to chart
its activities. Perhaps, like suffrage associations, it was little
needed in the island's informal politics.

1894 SUFFRAGE PETITION FAILS TO GAIN TRACTION

Certainly, the LCW took a distant second place to the WCTU. Its first suffrage petition was inspired by the national WCTU 1888 endorsement, in turn adopted by the Maritime WCTU in 1894. That same year, the PEI WCTU launched a petition, "praying that the Legislature enact a law providing full parliamentary suffrage be conferred on Women." This petition followed directly on the heels of an overwhelmingly successful prohibition plebiscite in 1893, despite concerns about the threat to government revenue

SCHOOLTEACHERS AND SCHOOL TRUSTEES

PEI artist Robert Harris's famous 1885 painting, A Meeting of the School Trustees, *features an assertive rural PEI teacher confronting trustees. According to the artist's biographer, Moncrieff Williamson, it was inspired by a conversation Harris had in August 1885 with Kate Henderson, whose name appears on the booklet at the lower left of the painting. A twenty-seven-year-old schoolmistress named Catherine Henderson does appear in the 1881 census for Lot 34, a community near Long Creek. A 1992 Heritage Minute animated the painting, portraying the teacher as bright and capable. The climax of the dramatization comes when the most hostile trustee admits that he cannot read, though the other three seem more respectful. That story was painted fourteen years before PEI women were eligible to become school trustees and sixty years before the first women, Helen MacDonald (1914–2005) and Dorothy Lantz (1904–94), were appointed in 1945. Competent female teachers can readily be seen as their legitimate precursors.*

caused by stopping the sale (and therefore the taxation) of alcohol in a jurisdiction that had so little Crown land and so few other sources of income. The WCTU asked Liberal John Bell to present the bill. A Scottish Presbyterian who had studied at Prince of Wales College before completing his bachelor's and master's of arts degrees at a small Ontario college, Bell studied law in Toronto and worked as a lawyer in Ottawa and then Manitoba before moving to practise in Summerside in 1884. In 1886, he obtained the Liberal seat for Fourth Prince in the House of Assembly as a well-

known prohibitionist, interrupted only by his temporary depar-
ture from provincial politics in 1896 to serve federally from 1898
to 1900. Bell pushed for provincial prohibition when the 1898 national plebiscite failed to result in federal prohibition legislation.
When he presented the 1894 WCTU suffrage petition to the House
of Assembly, he was apparently ruled out of order, leaving the bill
unread. The following year, he tried again and was mentioned in
the *Charlottetown Patriot* but fared no better. Unlike other Atlantic
provinces in the 1890s, PEI never saw a suffrage bill reach a vote.

Bell, however, appeared irrepressible. He was more successful
in presenting the 1895 petition for improved married women's
property rights that resulted in the robust 1896 property act. In
a province that was not known for reformers, he was once called
PEI's William E. Gladstone, a reference to the famous British prime
minister and reformer. Although the *Charlottetown Guardian* dismissed him as motivated by hopes of amassing voters, he remained loyal to both prohibition *and* suffrage throughout his
long political career. Ultimately, he had the honour of becoming
the suffrage premier. Unfortunately, the women who stood with
him cannot be similarly identified. We are left to presume that
his wife, Helen Howatt Bell (1845–?), the daughter of prominent
PEI anti-Confederate politician Cornelius Howatt, had suffragist
sympathies.

LULL, 1900–13

Compared to preceding decades on the island, the first decade of
the twentieth century brought little advance in women's rights.
Perhaps women were content with earlier gains, confident that,
as issues arose, they would secure additional reforms by partner-
ing with high-profile, supportive politicians. Perhaps an older
generation of women waited for the next one to take up the
cause. Perhaps PEI's small and overwhelmingly rural population
chose to focus on cultivating Women's Institutes, rural improve-

ment groups that first appeared on the island in 1912, and advocating for badly needed public health infrastructure, rather than channelling resources into an enfranchisement association such as in Saint John. Or perhaps PEI women were waiting for opposition to dissipate. All seem plausible explanations for so little public agitation for suffrage.

In contrast, island newspapers during these years reveal a sustained but not urgent interest in the subject. In 1904, a *Charlottetown Guardian* editorial forecast attainment of the vote as soon as enough interest was demonstrated. The editor pointed out that Prime Minister John A. Macdonald had been convinced by MPs in the 1880s to wait until the time was right. In time, advocates would "find their desires conceded." The *Guardian* itself kept readers abreast of suffrage legislation in other countries, particularly in New Zealand, where women got the vote in 1893 and outnumbered men on the voters lists, and in Australia, where, it was reported, they tended to vote for the Labour Party.

OPPOSITION INTENSIFIES

Suggestions of support were accompanied by increasingly vocal opposition. Explicit and implicit resistance, much of it imported from elsewhere, materialized regularly in the early decades of the twentieth century. McGill professor of medicine, PEI-born Andrew Macphail (1864–1938), often described as the island's most distinguished man of letters, weighed in during 1910, "showing little mercy for the woman who desires to vote." The local press found his opinions well worth reporting. In 1910, the *Charlottetown Guardian* offered a lengthy review of his *Essays in Fallacy*, which contained two anti-suffrage chapters. One of these, "The Psychology of the Suffragette," condemned "the mind of the suffragette" as possessing "a peculiar aptitude for that absurdity which makes a man impatient and finally contemptuous of all femininity, and resolute to his own ideal." From the perspective of a luminary whom the *Guardian* identified as a "trained, original, and exceedingly vigorous mind," assertive women loomed as unattractive, unlikeable, and unmarriageable. What feminists made of this is difficult to know. No letters to the editor commented on Macphail's anti-suffrage stance.

A second category of misogyny continued in the spirit of Macphail. Maritime newspapers regularly paraded reports on the militancy and "poor behaviour" of suffrage advocates. The clear message was that PEI women were to resist such contagion. Between 1910 and 1922, the *Guardian* referred to the more respectable "suffragists" 29 times and to the infamous "suffragettes" 134 times. Before 1920, none of its articles on suffrage referred to Canadian advocates. Given Western Canadian women's suffrage activity in the early 1910s, such an omission is astonishing. The press's colonial orientation to the Old Country made the tactics of British militants all the more newsworthy. In October 1913, the *Morning Guardian* mocked prominent suffrage leader Emmeline Pankhurst as "General Emmeline Pankhurst" and reminded readers that she and her daughter were imprisoned for inciting violence in 1907. A similar article, reprinted in November 1913, warned that enfranchising women was

> not a question of whether we should simply allow a few well-conducted, well-educated, self-respecting gentlewomen to quietly record their predilection for Liberalism or Conservatism, but whether we should let in the wider ... uneducated, unrestrained, irrational, and emotional womanhood to sweep the polls. What policies may become when women take part in it is shown by the conduct of militant suffragettes.

In comparison, long years of peaceful protest in the United Kingdom as elsewhere went largely unmarked.

RETURN TO SUFFRAGE ACTIVISM, 1913–23

In September 1913, at its annual meeting in Summerside, the Maritime WCTU petitioned each Maritime legislature for suffrage, arguing that female voters would secure prohibition and other needed moral reforms. PEI, of course, had already secured prohibition and would need only to maintain it. Indeed, the province's extensive and persisting prohibition owed something to women's political efficacy, both before and after enfranchisement. Whereas Quebec's prohibition act, instituted in 1919, survived for less than a year, and earlier legislation, enforced during the First World War in the other eight provinces, lasted only four to eleven years, the island initiated it more than a decade earlier than any other Canadian jurisdiction and kept it in effect for forty-eight years. As late as the 1960s, female voters were credited with maintaining prohibition and related laws, including the requirement of permits to buy alcohol. Perhaps the PEI WCTU foresaw that success when it expressed its support for the Great Cause.

During the second decade of the twentieth century, the stalwart WCTU and Women's Institutes were joined by a new organization, the Liberal Women's Club. Consisting of ninety members, it mobilized in Charlottetown in 1916, with Margaret Rogers Stewart (1869–1954) as president. Its vice-president was Elsie Inman (1891–1986), who would go on to become PEI's first female senator. Like the WCTU, the new group did not claim suffrage as its primary purpose. The speed of its endorsement, however, suggests that it was far from a new cause. Indeed, women could hardly avoid the discussion about political emancipation that had gone on in liberal ranks around the world for decades. The club soon sought advice from Prairie suffragists, including Nellie McClung, and British suffragettes, whose names it did not record. Ultimately, it agreed to educate as many women as possible and to lobby politicians provincially and federally. In the late 1970s, Elsie Inman reflected on its positive reception but admitted that the campaign was time consuming and, occasionally, ugly. Opponents objected that women did not understand relevant political issues and would be too easily influenced by gossip. When pressed to comment on interest among island women, Inman explained that PEI suffragists linked themselves to the broader suffrage movement in Western Canada and Britain, as they lobbied politicians and campaigned to have women eligible for election to school boards. Revealingly, no mention was made of Ontario or Quebec suffragist influences, perhaps due to hostility to central Canada that dated from Confederation.

The Liberal Women's Club immediately spurred new calls for women's eligibility to vote and be elected to school boards, which had been deemed implicitly eligible in 1899 but had still not occurred. Chief Superintendent of Education Robert H. Campbell (1864–?) urged an amendment to the School Act to explicitly allow the wives of ratepayers both to vote in and be eligible to run in school trustee elections. Once the amendment passed, Campbell continued lobbying, sending letters to every school district secretary and copied to every clergyman in the province "for support." The letters stated that the election of women as school trustees would provide much-needed "liberal support for teachers" in helping to raise their salaries at the district level, thus stemming their outmigration to other provinces for better pay. The assumption that women were the more liberal sex, and more likely to "do the right thing" by favouring the pay raise, mirrors pro-suffrage arguments that their moral superiority would boost politics generally.

IMPACT OF FIRST WORLD WAR

The First World War was formative for the second phase of the suffrage movement. Islanders were quick off the mark to support Canadian involvement overseas, with almost three hundred young men signing up to fight during the first three months, a government food pledge for soldiers, and generous civilian donations to the Patriotic Fund. The Red Cross coordinated with local Women's Institutes to contribute knitted gloves and socks, other clothing, and food parcels. More than one hundred PEI women served in the Canadian Army Medical Corps, the American forces, and small private and public contingents. They followed in the footsteps of Georgina Fane Pope (1862–1938), nicknamed the "Island's Florence Nightingale" for her service in the South African Boer War, for which she became the first Canadian to receive the Royal Red Cross. Although in her mid-fifties, Pope served in France in 1917–18. Rena McLean (1880–1918), from Souris, was the only islander chosen from dozens of volunteers to join the first nursing contingent in the Canadian Expeditionary Force. A graduate of Mount Allison Ladies' College and Halifax Ladies' College, McLean left her post as head nurse at a Massachusetts hospital for almost the whole length of the war. She died in June 1918, when the hospital ship the *Llandovery Castle* was torpedoed off Ireland while returning to England from Halifax.

As PEI was primarily an agricultural province, there was tension in its war effort. Despite the patriotic enthusiasm, its enlistment was lower than in every province except Quebec, as islander participation was limited by the need to retain male farm labour. Conscription was unpopular. In the notorious election of 1917, the island elected four Liberal MPs. But after the overseas ballots of soldiers and nurses were figured in, two of them were replaced by Conservatives, part of Prime Minister Borden's pro-conscription Union government. Borden's Wartime Elections Act, which enfranchised nurses overseas and women who had close male relatives in the military, seems to have raised his popularity in the province, yet PEI stood with Quebec as the only two provinces that did not give a majority to the Union government.

LEGISLATURE FINALLY CONSIDERS WOMEN'S SUFFRAGE, 1918

Late in the war – five years after the WCTU petition and two

Nursing Sister Rena McLean, the first PEI nurse to serve in the
First World War, holding the dog Rags, the hospital mascot, in
front of No. 2 Canadian Stationary Hospital, France, c. 1916.

years after the founding of the Liberal Women's Club – the PEI
legislature returned to the vote for women. In April 1918, the
Charlottetown Patriot described a suffrage debate that went un-
reported in the *Journals of the House of Assembly*. Two members
of the governing Conservative Party – John Dewar (1863–1945)
representing Third Kings and A.A. MacDonald (1864–1920) representing Second Kings – opened the debate, pointing to suffrage
success elsewhere. Their Conservative colleague Harvey MacEwan
(1860–1938), also representing Second Kings, waylaid the discussion with an attempt at humour. He was not *against* women

voting, but because they were likely to choose the best-looking candidate, he feared for his chances should he ever find himself running against "a young fellow with a two-inch collar and a mustache curled up at the corner." The only Liberal to speak in support was the steadfast John Bell, who concluded that women should get the vote to "safeguard their own interests for all time to come." Other speakers suggested that it be granted as a reward for wartime service. In summarizing, the *Patriot* noted that the debate had occupied much of the evening session, ending with the unanimous passage of the resolution in favour of enfranchising women. This proved a great anticlimax: the Conservative government, under the first Acadian premier of PEI, Aubin Arsenault (1870–1968), ignored the resolution without explanation.

A year later, facing an election, the Opposition Liberals proposed enfranchising PEI women who had served in the military overseas, primarily as nursing sisters. They had "risked their lives ... and did so much for the comfort for the soldiers and really helped as much as the men in the winning of the war." The question of whether veteran nurses should be given the vote had not come up in New Brunswick or Nova Scotia, because numerous debates and bills had considered suffrage as a human right long before the advent of the war, and the inclusion of military nurses was not an issue, as the war set the stage for enfranchisement. In contrast, PEI had still not given suffrage a real airing in the legislature. The May 1919 suffrage debate's acknowledgment of female veterans reflected the high-profile contributions of some one hundred island nurses, about 10 percent of whom were daughters of politicians – including fallen nurse Rena McLean, whose father was a Conservative MP from 1891 to 1896 and a senator from 1915 to 1936 – and two of whom were daughters of former premiers. Leveraging the anticipated enfranchisement of such deserving recipients, Liberal MLA Albert Saunders (1874–1943) went farther, perhaps too quickly suggesting that "if the franchise was

going to include any women it should include all." According to
the *Guardian,* his proposal met with silence, and "the matter was
accordingly dropped." Ultimately, the debate signalled that the
governing Conservatives opposed even the most limited franchise, whereas the Liberals preferred opening the door widely.

KEY SUPPORT FROM ISLAND PRESS

A few months later, in the 1919 election, the Liberals under John
Bell won an overwhelming majority – taking twenty-four of thirty
seats – and suffragists, particularly the Women's Liberal Club, expected the speedy passage of a franchise bill. But the government
let them down, showing the limits of even supposed legislative
sympathizers. In 1920, the local press stepped up, supporting suffrage in various ways, from comments on federal politics to jokes
and opinion pieces. In 1921, during the first federal election in
which most Canadian women voted, the politically independent
Guardian proved itself. An editorial claimed that, though women
did not have sufficient experience to evaluate tariff policies, they
were highly qualified on other matters, with "a deep interest in
the moral progress of the country and in the moral standing,
acts, and reputation of the political men of the country." The
Conservative *Guardian* also played up the incumbent prime minister Arthur Meighan's appeal to female voters, reminding readers
that his party had granted women the federal franchise three
years earlier and adding the exaggerated claim that this was done
"voluntarily and as a matter of justice."

The most significant assistance from the island press came in
printing an effective essay on women's rights written by eighteen-
year-old Gladys McCormack, a Catholic resident of Charlottetown.
Penned originally for her studies at Halifax's Mount Saint Vincent
Academy that fall, it was reprinted in a December 1920 issue
of the *Guardian.* A teenager, not a seasoned journalist or veteran
campaigner, highlighted the strides that women had made over

Gladys McCormack (1902–93). In 1920, when this yearbook
photo was taken, McCormack was an eighteen-year-old Grade 12
student at Mount Saint Vincent Academy. Her yearbook profile
reveals that she wrote a medal-winning essay on Canadian thrift,
always took top marks in bookkeeping exams, and played the
violin in the school orchestra.

the centuries, pointing out that their average intelligence was
"not less than men's," even as she reassured readers that women
should never forget their most important role as mothers, "for
unless we have good mothers, we shall have neither good legislatures nor good voters." Reasonable women far outweighed the
"few" militants, and she regretted "the shrill contempt heaped by
a few vehement women upon men." The fact that the *Guardian*
devoted so much space to McCormack suggests that at long last
it anticipated a sympathetic audience. A similar belief may have
been behind the inclusion of a joke in a May 1920 issue: at a

dinner party, a professor announces his support for suffrage to a woman, explaining, "My dear lady, I maintain that man and woman are equal in every way." To which the woman sweetly replies, "Oh Professor, now you are bragging."

PREMIER'S SUFFRAGE SUPPORT THWARTED

While the press kept suffrage hopes alive, the government caucus was in disarray. Despite a strong majority, Bell did not enjoy the confidence of every Liberal MLA. In March 1921, his colleague Edmund Higgs asked him about suffrage petitions from women and when the government would act. His intent, with his emphasis on the receipt of only one petition, was clearly hostile. Bushwhacked, Bell stalled, and Higgs got what he wanted, a public statement from the premier that suffrage would not be introduced without greater signs of interest.

This setback prompted suffragists to renew their efforts.

BOOST FROM WOMEN'S INSTITUTES

In the spring of 1921, the Women's Institute (WI), with its surging membership, endorsed suffrage. By 1920, PEI had thirty-one WI branches with six hundred members; within a year, this nearly doubled to sixty-one branches and thirteen hundred members, suggesting an untapped demand for greater organization. The WI focus on bettering rural schools and communities, as well as supporting agriculture, not only garnered respect for it but also helped it to develop networks with provincial, national, and international affiliates. Its high-profile partnership with the Red Cross, new paid public health nurse Amy MacMahon, and attempts to improve public health – especially in fighting the highest rates of tuberculosis in Canada – further burnished its reputation. Reports about the organization found a home in the dominant *Charlottetown Guardian,* a keen advocate:

Wherever a women's institute has been organized, its influence for good is to be seen in the school, in the social life, and in the farm home. Through their efforts, many schools have been made brighter, healthier, and in every way more helpful; social conditions have been improved and the standard of living for both men and women have been perceptibly elevated.

When local WI groups endorsed suffrage, politicians had to listen. The president linked political advocacy to the WI mandate: "Our motto – 'For Home and Country' allows us a large field and a great scope for our work and I am sure [the path] upon which we have entered will be productive with great results and far-reaching benefits in our Province." The demand of a primarily rural organization that was spread throughout every electoral district required a response. In contrast, the Liberal Women's Club went largely silent, embarrassed by the failure of the ruling Liberals.

FIRST AND ONLY SUFFRAGE BILL, 1922

In April 1922, Premier Bell moved, "Resolved: That it is expedient to introduce a bill to extend the vote to women: And that the qualifications of the male and female voter should be the same." Still fearing internal dissension, he tried to curtail debate by introducing the motion late in the session and insisting upon the urgency of a matter that had already been decided federally. He added that women's war work had *entitled* them to the franchise. J.J. Hughes (1856–1941) seconded the motion, as part of "the progressive spirit of the age." PEI should not be backward. Ultimately, of the thirty MLAs, only two resisted – one from each party. Liberal Stephen Hessain (1891–1962), the youngest elected member, repeated the objection that Edmund Higgs had made the year before – too few women wanted the vote – and further condemned the premier as the only true legislative proponent. The Conservative, Murdock Kennedy (1873–1950), charged all Liberals with chasing the votes of women who had endorsed them during the federal election. He capped his hostility with less than immortal words: "The wife's place and woman's place is in the home in the kitchen looking after home affairs ... Right here I say square and above board, you are taking the wrong stand."

Despite the attack, other Liberals stood behind Bell, speaking so enthusiastically that passage was never in doubt. Responding to MLA Hessain's criticism that the government had tried to ram the legislation through in the dog days of the session, Creelman MacArthur (1874–1943) pointed to the enfranchisement plank in the 1919 Liberal platform, arguing that the delay was intended to give "the women time to mull it over." Additional petitions meant that the time had come. Such explanations were hardly credible, but at long last the antis were outnumbered. When Murdock Kennedy invoked the Book of Genesis, asserting that woman was created from Adam's rib and should therefore be man's helpmate, *not* his equal, Frederick Nash (1862–1929) objected passionately and countered with the Book of Exodus. The greatest lawgiver of all time had been saved by a woman: "It was Pharaoh's daughter who discovered Moses in the bull rushes, and for that alone women should be entitled to vote." Nash ended his speech with the prediction that, one day, women would serve as MLAS, "even young women. And there would be nothing to prevent them from nursing their children while they pass the laws of the country." (Nearly a century would elapse before his prophecy was realized. In 2012, Quebec NDP MP Sana Hassainia brought her three-month-old son to a vote in the House of Commons. After initial consternation, she was told that babies were welcome.)

Following a debate of less than an hour, the suffrage bill easily passed first reading, by twenty-eight to two. The very next item in the House of Assembly – still on the morning of 26 April 1922 –

was the Election Act of 1922, which amended the previous act of 1913 to include female voters. The act was further reformed to make them eligible for election to the House of Assembly: "Any person shall be eligible to be elected as a member of the assembly who is a British subject, male or female, of the age of twenty-one years or upwards, unless he or she be disqualified as hereafter mentioned." The disqualifications were similar to those elsewhere: civil servants, "an Indian ordinarily resident on an Indian reservation," and non-British subjects were not entitled to vote.

One complication, peculiar to PEI, required women's incorporation into the multiple voting system of the province. Their eligibility for electing assemblymen was a simple matter because there was no property requirement, but voting for councilmen necessitated the possession of property with a minimum value of $325. No one questioned that single women with sufficient property could vote for a legislative councillor. The situation of married women was less clear, since property was held in the name of the husband. Were husbands and wives entitled to vote on the same property? Because PEI ridings were so small, elections were regularly won on fewer than ten votes. In the end, it was decided that women whose husbands qualified also qualified, and that they too could vote in as many ridings as they had sufficient property for. Female enfranchisement in 1922 underscored the irrationality of the electoral system: from 1918 until 1966, a married couple who owned property worth $4,875 divided among various ridings could conceivably cast sixty votes in a provincial election. Such couples reinforced and reproduced the PEI elite and kept politicians attentive.

Even with suffrage and election legislation, the island press – both the Liberal *Patriot* and the Conservative *Guardian* – remained vigilant, proving itself the most consistent and powerful supporter of votes for women. The *Guardian* had been bought by the Conservative Party in 1912 and was owned officially by Charles

Dalton (1850–1933), a wealthy businessman and prominent Conservative. Needing to recruit a new managing editor, he enlisted the aid of William Dennis (1856–1920), a fellow Conservative politician and owner of the *Halifax Herald.* Dennis chose James Robertson Burnett (1871–1952), a Scotsman, who was a progressive and pro-suffrage editor. Agnes Dennis (1859–1947), William's wife, was a prominent suffrage supporter and president of the Halifax LCW from 1905 to 1920, so the choice of Burnett may have been deliberate. In a 1922 editorial, Burnett pointed out,

> This promise [of suffrage] has been standing for three sessions. Last night we had the promise repeated, accompanied by a little curtain lecture to the women as to how they should exercise the franchise when they get it! We have still to see how that promise will be carried out. Very little has been done so far, and it appears to me that it will be very much like [Premier Bell's] other unfulfilled promises.

A letter to the editor in early May 1922 approved women playing "a great and worthy part" in public life, suggesting that they would increase the level of morality in public administration.

The Women's Liberal Club turned its attention to political education. In December 1922, it hosted a talk titled "What the Women Should Do with Their Vote." A month later, it hosted a partisan speech by the Liberal MP John Sinclair on federal politics. However, its members were not uncritical, and the *Guardian* noted that "many of the ladies were not quite as unsophisticated as Mr. Sinclair imagined." Female islanders first went to the provincial polls on 24 July 1923. During the election, both parties courted their vote. It had been assumed that they would favour "softer" issues such as moral reform and improved education, which were stressed by the party that had enfranchised them, but Bell's Liberals were trounced, reduced to just five seats. This result suggested that women voted much the same as did as their husbands, fathers, and brothers.

Evidence on just how many cast their ballots is unclear. According to Elsie Inman, the suffragist and co-founder of the Women's Liberal Club, the "majority of PEI husbands" forbade their wives to vote, and "most women" were too afraid to do so. Later studies estimated, however, that 50 percent of eligible women voted in 1923, with a rise in subsequent elections. Inman claimed that her own husband, a politician elected to the legislature in 1927, never revealed his position on suffrage while never stopping her from campaigning. Intimidation persisted, as demonstrated by her account of driving one wife to the polls in a disguise so as to avoid alerting an abusive husband. Inman herself served as a senator from 1955 until her death in 1986 at the age of ninety-five; she was most notable for opposing mandatory retirement for senators, rather than for feminist issues.

Permit her to do something in a legal and efficient manner to defend her home [and] her children ... The right to vote on the liquor question is in all justice, fairness, and common sense, due to the women.

– JESSIE OHMAN,
NEWFOUNDLAND NEWSPAPER EDITOR
AND TEMPERANCE ADVOCATE, 1892

FIVE

NEWFOUNDLAND: LONG AND FIERCE OPPOSITION

Julia Salter Earle campaigning during the 1925 St. John's municipal election. Twenty people ran for six council seats, Earle as a labour representative, and though 1,244 people cast their ballots for her, she lost by just 11 votes.

TEMPERANCE AND WOMEN'S suffrage were especially close-knit on Newfoundland; the St. John's branch of the Woman's Christian Temperance Union (WCTU) was founded in 1890, almost simultaneously with the 1891 endorsement of suffrage by the World's WCTU. Early Newfoundland WCTU members immediately introduced a petition campaign for female eligibility to vote in area plebiscites on whether to implement prohibition in their locale, commonly referred to as "local option." Six months later, fifty members of the St. John's WCTU, wearing white ribbons, presented twenty-six petitions with several thousand signatures to the Legislative Assembly. Although the immediate goal was to enfranchise women for the local option prohibition vote, public debate instantly turned to their right to vote more generally.

Having soundly rejected confederation with Canada in the 1860s and again in the 1890s, Newfoundland finally joined Canada in 1949 after two hard-fought referendums. Although Labrador has been considered part of Newfoundland since 1809, the province's name did not change to Newfoundland and Labrador until 2001. The long campaign for suffrage occurred while Newfoundland was a fairly autonomous colony of the United Kingdom. Although British influences were evident, its development had much more to do with local colonial circumstances. Newfoundland is set apart from the Maritimes, not only physically, but also culturally and economically. These distinctions, combined with ongoing economic crises, made its path different from those of Nova Scotia, New Brunswick, and Prince Edward Island. Its suffrage movement confirms its uniqueness.

The lack of research on higher education for women, the evolution of married women's property laws, and the Mi'kmaw, Innu, Chinese, and Labrador communities leaves substantial gaps in our understanding of women's rights in Newfoundland. Although the suffrage campaign started later than in the Maritimes, there were two surges in agitation. The first, 1891–93, was driven by a feisty, short-lived newspaper, the *Water Lily,* that combined suffrage and temperance. A steady and longer second phase beginning in 1909 saw the emergence of a new generation of suffragists, including Armine Nutting Gosling (1861–1942), Fannie Knowling McNeil (1869–1928), Antonia D'Alberti Hutton (1875–1961), and Julia Horwood (1872–1938); the founding of the Ladies Reading Room; the high-profile engagement of prominent suffragists in the dominion's impressive Women's Patriotic Association; and finally the post-war seven-year suffrage drive that produced a bill in 1925, albeit one with a discriminatory age requirement of twenty-five. Like Andrew Blair in New Brunswick, Liberal prime minister Richard Squires (1880–1940) led the anti-suffrage forces. Although most agitation originated with middle-class women in the capital, St. John's, other coastal communities, for the most part associated with the prevailing fishing economy and commonly referred to as outports, also produced demands for women's rights. Suffragists presented familiar arguments stressing female intellectual capacity and right to influence government, as well as Newfoundland's politicians' backwardness, especially as compared to Britain and Canada. Enfranchisement came with a brief Conservative government in 1925.

DEMOGRAPHIC, ECONOMIC, AND POLITICAL CONTEXTS OF SUFFRAGE

Indigenous peoples inhabited the land now known as Newfoundland and Labrador for many thousands of years. The inhospitable land and harsh climate challenged the ancestors of today's Innu and Inuit in Labrador and the Mi'kmaq in Newfoundland.

The experience of the Beothuk is tragic. Cut off from the sea by European fishers who controlled the shoreline, they starved and became extinct in 1829. The last known Beothuk, Shawnadithit (c. 1800–29), provided researchers with the history of her people.

The Norse set up several sod buildings on Newfoundland's northern tip, later named L'Anse aux Meadows, around 1000. Centuries later, migratory fishers from France, England, Portugal, and Spain rushed across the Atlantic to profit from cod and whale fisheries, setting up a resource extraction economy that influenced the socio-economic and political future of Newfoundland into the twenty-first century. The French solidified their hold on the western shore with a colony at Placentia in 1662. By the 1750s, the year-round British population had approximately ten thousand summer residents – mainly Irish Catholic labourers – but still only a few hundred year-round settlers. By the 1750s, the year-round English population had reached seven thousand, thanks to the continued steady stream of southeast Irish Catholic immigrants. Triangular trade between Europe, the Caribbean, and Newfoundland was highly lucrative, but Britain valued the island more as a pawn in its international trade relations than as a locale for serious development, granting France rights to the western shore in 1713 and repeatedly reaffirming them. Controversy over these shore rights preoccupied politicians as late as the first surge of the suffrage campaign. The fishery workforce consisted largely of young Irish Catholic men, a situation that did not encourage the settlement of Euro-Canadian women and children, the development of a resident middle class, the presence of clergymen, the creation of a local newspaper, or any significant social institutions beyond the Benevolent Irish Society founded in 1806. Connections with the Indigenous population were rare.

In the late eighteenth and early nineteenth centuries, women became crucial in the fishery, as families replaced the migratory workers in producing dried cod exports. Women were critical in curing the fish and sustaining the family economy with berry picking and potato growing. At the insistence of locals, Britain implemented colonial status, with an appointed civilian governor, a five-member governing council, and a permanent supreme court in 1825. In 1832, it introduced representative government, late in comparison to Nova Scotia in 1758 and Prince Edward Island in 1773. More independence came with responsible government in 1855, but three areas still lacked political representation: the south coast west of Fortune Bay, the French Shore, and Labrador. Britain retained control over foreign affairs, and to the chagrin of Newfoundlanders, not only continued to renew French treaty rights on the northeast shore, but also New England's rights to fish outside a three-mile limit. By 1874, the French Shore (Notre Dame Bay area) boasted almost nine thousand residents, or 5 percent of the island's population, but was subject to French (rather than British) law and protected by the French navy. It paid no taxes.

Social, ethnic, and religious cleavages intensified during the mid-nineteenth century, widening the gulf between St. John's wealthy merchants and poor outport fishers. Church authorities were so deeply embedded in colonial politics that the Catholic bishop – who led the 45 percent of the population that was Catholic – was referred to as Newfoundland's most important politician. Economically, Newfoundland did not have a mid-nineteenth-century golden age, as the Maritimes did, because the free trade benefits of the reciprocity treaty between the United States and Britain (1854–66) were countered by competition from American fishers. At the same time, the seal fishery collapsed. Concern over unemployed young men flocking to St. John's and engaging in violence generated interest in temperance.

Despite their unhappiness with Britain, Newfoundlanders rejected Confederation with Canada and settled for remaining a self-governing colony within the empire. Although there was some interest in potential economic diversification, the main selling points of Confederation, including a coast-to-coast railway, were ultimately irrelevant to Newfoundland. As the nineteenth century closed, its fishery still employed 85 percent of the workforce and accounted for 95 percent of exports. Unlike in the Maritimes, where fishers could often supplement their income with agriculture when catches were poor or prices were low, Newfoundland fishing families were limited by little arable land. Small sawmilling and lumber manufacturing provided the only alternative industries outside the fishery. High unemployment caused outmigration in the late nineteenth century, though not to the extent of the Maritime provinces. The population grew slowly from nearly 160,000 in 1874 to almost 200,000 in 1891. A decade later, some 13 percent of the colony's population of 220,984 resided in the capital, which implemented municipal government in 1888.

Newfoundland was never very ethnically diverse. As late as 1945, 96 percent of its residents reported origins in the British Isles, with English heritage by far the most common, followed by Irish. The Indigenous community consisted of the Mi'kmaq, closely associated with communities in Nova Scotia, and the Innu, an Algonquin-speaking people who extended into Quebec. Both groups were smaller than Indigenous populations in the Maritime provinces. No nineteenth- or twentieth-century Indigenous reserves existed, but several almost exclusively Mi'kmaw communities were located on the southwest coast. Although people of Asian and African descent had lived in Newfoundland for decades, each group accounted for less than 1 percent of the population, even in 2016. Ethnic Chinese, most of whom were men employed in laundries and who were subject to a three-hundred-dollar head tax after 1906 (female Chinese immigrants were barred completely until 1927), were St. John's most visible non-European community until the Second World War.

EMERGENCE OF REFORMS RELATED TO SUFFRAGE

To understand the suffrage history of Newfoundland, we must take into account women's important roles in the fishery, the expansion of legal rights, and the temperance movement. Each emerged in the context of political and economic turmoil that limited other achievements, such as local access to higher education for women, attained in Nova Scotia and New Brunswick much earlier.

Newfoundland women and girls did not have precisely the same common law rights and opportunities as those in the United Kingdom. Although those who were married or below the age of majority were largely legally defined by their relationship to men, colonial legal practice was distinctive. Dower law, which guaranteed widows one-third of their deceased husbands' property and land, was often applied more generously than in Britain. Because female shore crews were so central to preparing the fish for export, women possessed a degree of power, including in inheritance practices. In the outports, matrilocal settlement patterns were common, with male immigrants often joining the fishing operations of their in-laws. Whereas nineteenth-century inheritance law in England favoured male primogeniture, Newfoundland inheritance law, like that of British North America generally, was more egalitarian. One of the earliest laws was the Chattels Real Act (1834), which sidestepped the common law tradition of primogeniture to affirm the decades-old practice in fishing communities of distributing the land of a deceased fisher, as well as his flakes, rooms, and wharf, among his wife and children. Classifying fishing property – both moveable (gear and temporary fixtures) and immoveable (real estate) – as chattels evaded the usual rules of primogeniture and partiability.

WOMEN AND PROPERTY LAWS

Nor did local judges necessarily bar married women from owning land or other fixed property. They could pass it on to the next generation. Though wives could supposedly own land separate from their husbands only after the colony's first married women's property law in 1876, the *practice* of married daughters controlling land and related fishing gear began at least a century earlier. This practice, like the dower laws that protected widows and the statutes that protected abandoned wives from the 1840s, may have muted demands to reform married women's property laws. Judges' greater intolerance of the abuse of women than in the law required, demonstrated in their crediting accusations of rape, may also have tempered demands for change. Far from being passive, unhappy women showed a willingness to employ violence, public shaming, or gossip to defend their property, motivate men into accepting fiscal responsibility (including for paternity), improve their moral standing, or smear the reputations of offenders.

Newfoundland nevertheless did make its own contribution to reforming married women's property laws in 1876, 1892, and 1895. Its 1876 act, based on the British Married Women's Property Act of 1870, gave wives *limited* rights to their own wages, access to bank accounts, and investments within capped amounts, and the possibility of separate proprietorship of business. Following a British amendment in 1880, Newfoundland stressed married women's equivalence with single women by giving wives unrestricted rights to their wages, bank accounts, and life insurance policies, as well as the right to sue and be sued, in 1884 and 1895.

A handful of Newfoundland women also informally sought broader reforms and rights, notably through the prohibition of alcohol sales. Outport fishers often flocked to St. John's taverns, a habit long associated with abuse and intemperance and widely condemned for family dissolution, illness, unemployment, and poverty. In 1851, Protestant women, especially Methodists, embraced the newly founded local branch of the Daughters of Temperance, which was closely allied to the Sons of Temperance and the predominantly male St. John's Total Abstinence Society.

Such awareness fuelled support for deserted wives' acts. The founding of the WCTU in St. John's in 1890 and its rapid spread to many outport communities mobilized still more activists whose networks created suffragists and legitimated a role for women in public debates.

1890S: THE FIRST SURGE OF SUFFRAGE AGITATION

As mentioned, because the WCTU came to Newfoundland later than in the Maritimes, it immediately engaged with suffrage, linking women's rights to guarding the home. This approach built on the sentiments that inspired earlier laws for the protection of deserted and widowed wives. Despite their restraint, temperance leaders met foes who charged them with unfeminine meddling in political affairs. The challenge of credibility was all the greater since the 1890s colonial government was predominantly Liberal, whereas the WCTU had Conservative ties. Its two leaders, Emma Peters (1839–1913) and Susanna Janetta (Milroy) Thorburn (1845–?), were both married to Conservative politicians: John E.P. Peters (1839–1919) and Sir Robert Thorburn (1836–1906) were elected members of the Protestant Reform (Conservative) Party.

As the introduction of the first suffrage bill in the House of Assembly drew near, the prominent and opinionated temperance paper the *Water Lily* – founded in 1892 – targeted prohibition obstructionists. Although the paper was not an official organ of the WCTU, its outspoken editor, Jessie Ohman (1856–1937), was secretary to the local branch and was affiliated with other similar groups. The paper inserted women into municipal and provincial politics as Christian wives, mothers, and daughters while remaining silent on their expanded roles. Readers could be reassured that traditional duties would be honoured. Eschewing political and denominational funding, the editor was free to name, shame, and blame opposition. In 1892, when St. John's Atlantic Hotel held a smoking concert, a form of musical entertainment and informal debate for men only, sponsored by the Cricket Association, the paper's criticism was typically sharp: "The idea of [the Atlantic Hotel] ... condescending to open its doors, and encouraging a species of drunken rivalry, under the guise of a 'smoking concert' for charitable purposes, is as undignified, unwarrantable, and inexcusable, as it is illegal and punishable." The next month, the *Water Lily* denounced a second infraction at the same location: "These license laws must be kept, or if those whose duty it is, fail to see them carried out, we shall in no uncertain way see that fish is not made of one, and flesh of another." When condemned for "meddling in politics," the editor justified its critique of the lack of liquor regulation, calmly asserted that the paper had little use if it did not hold politicians accountable.

The editor contended that prohibition had more relevance to the lives of Newfoundlanders than any other political issue. Nor

---

THE DRINK TRAFFIC COLLEGE, N.F.L.D.

FACULTY OF INSTRUCTION.

Principal : Professor Alcohol, Gra. A.Q.V. *Vice-Principals :* Thomas Rum, Gra. J.W.V.; Mons. Brandy, Gra. A. d V., Fr.; John Gin, Gra. Eng.; Alex. Patrick Whisky, Sc. and Ir. *Intermediate Department:* Misses Wine, Claret, Ale and Porter, Graduated Teachers. *Primary Eepartment:* Herr Von Beer, Bav., Bot. and Gard.

This College, with the above galaxy of illustrious professors and teachers, is under the distinguished patronage of His Excellency the Governor-in-Council. It is approved of by the highest officials in the land, namely, Honorables Sir William V. Whiteway, K.C.M.G., *Premier :* Robert Bond, *C.S. :* R. H. O'Dwyer, *R.G. ;* H. J. B. Woods, *S.G. ;* A. W. Harvey and E. P. Morris. It is also recognized by J. P. Thompson, Esq., E. R. Burgess, Esq., T. Paton, Esq., S. Blandford, Esq., D. C. Webber, Esq., E. White, Esq., W. Duff, Esq., W. H. Whiteley, Esq., Eli Dawe, Esq., J. A. Clift, Esq., E. Rothwell, Esq.,. J. S. Tait, Esq., M.D.; J. Murray, Esq., J. Studdy, Esq., &c., &c,, &c.

"The Drink Traffic College, N.F.L.D.," published in the February 1892 edition of the *Water Lily*. Suitably amended for an island location, the newspaper's title is a salute to an earlier and more famous temperance publication, the *Lily*, which was printed in New York from 1849 and 1856.

did the paper's temperance thunder abate in its "Drink Traffic College," an 1892 article in which it parodied faculty and curriculum at an easily identifiable St. John's Catholic college. Its staff were listed as "Principal: Professor Alcohol, Gra. A.Q.V.; Vice-Principals: Thomas Rum, Gra. J.W.V.; Mons. Brandy, Gra. A. d V., Fr.; John Gin, Gra. Eng.; Alex. Patrick Whisky, Sc. and Ir."

More pointedly still, the *Water Lily* named the government officials and prominent men whom it held responsible for the degeneracy of the college. The accusation that tax dollars were funding youth intemperance would have made Ohman a political target, which she would have understood, but she pressed ahead nevertheless. One editorial cartoon portrayed politicians keenly reading the *Water Lily.*

Cartoon published in the September 1893 edition of the *Water Lily*. Offering something for everyone, the *Water Lily* printed poetry, letters to the editor, short fiction with a hefty dose of Christian moralizing, temperance essays, snippets on current events, jokes, and the occasional cartoon, like this one. The subscription fee for the monthly publication was a dollar per year.

Editor Ohman was forthright in tying Newfoundland's political failings to women's lack of power. In March 1892, when the *Water Lily* first mentioned suffrage in its third editorial, it firmly tied women and children's vulnerability to the abuse of alcohol:

> If there be any enjoyment in a drunkard's career, or in the life of a man addicted to drink, there is absolutely none but grief, sorrow and misery, to the wife of such a man. The care of the children is thrown upon her. She has to keep them clean and tidy, see that they are fed and educated. She has to bear the frown of a cold world, whilst spending her strength and life to keep the wolf from the door. Her toil is unceasing. No slavery is so desperately hopeless as that of a drunkard's wife. Bound to her dissipated husband by ties as sacred as heaven, her only hope is in his reformation; and how can such a stupendous work be accomplished, with all the allurements and temptations which lie in his way.

The remedy was obvious:

> Raise her hopes; brighten her dismal lot in life, by permitting her to do something in a legal and efficient manner to defend her home, her children, and – if needs be – remove the temptation from her sons, brothers, or husband, as the case may be.
>
> The right to vote on the liquor question is in all justice, fairness, and common sense, due to the women.
>
> To withhold that right any longer is nothing less than continuing to propagate heathen principles, or barbarism.

Readers could hardly fail to get the point – that Newfoundland's first women's suffrage bill (to enable women to vote on implementing prohibition in their own local district), anticipated that session, merited their attention. The claims of women's intellectual equality *and* the necessity for prohibition constituted a carefully packaged approach to women's rights.

FIRST SUFFRAGE BILL

Despite WCTU ties to the Conservatives, Donald Morison (1857–1924), a Bonavista Bay lawyer and member of the Liberal (Reform) Party, introduced the first suffrage bill in the House of Assembly in March 1892. Opponents saw it as the thin edge of the wedge – permitting women to vote for prohibition would inevitably lead to their voting in dominion elections – and immediately presented it as a threat to male and female gender roles. Reflecting divisions within families, MLA James Murray (1843–1900), the brother of prominent prohibitionist Jessie Ohman, spoke resolutely against prohibition. His frustrated sister wryly noted that the best part of his speech was when he sat down. One can only imagine their private conversations! Catholic Frank Morris (1862–1947), Liberal MLA for Harbour Main, thundered that

> when a young man arrived at the age of twenty-one, he was then invested with the voting power, on his own account, as the potential head of a family. The female vote was thus merged with the male vote by the consent of both parties, and this could not be dissolved without at least the consent of one of the parties to it.

He urged Morison to prove that support for female enfranchisement was widespread and, in an exercise of hyperbole, demanded signatures from a majority of the approximately forty thousand Newfoundland women who were aged twenty-one and over. He next shifted to a religious objection: God had divided the human world into families, with men in charge of politics. The final 1892 vote was close: thirteen to ten against women voting in the local option for prohibition referendum. In some ways, this was not a bad showing, especially since seven members of the governing

Liberals crossed party lines to vote in the affirmative. Somewhat buoyed, the WCTU stepped up its agitation, especially for the broader women's rights agenda.

WATER LILY STOKES THE FIRE
Fulfilling her original promise that the *Water Lily* would praise the good and condemn the wrong, Ohman complimented supporters and berated opponents:

> Women of Newfoundland, think of this fact: that Sir W.V. Whiteway, Bond, Morris, O'Dwyer, Webber, Studdy, Clift, Murray, Fox, Shea, Murphy, Carty, and Woodward, refused to give women the right and the justice that belongs to them, while at the same time they hand over, as it were [through universal manhood suffrage granted in the Elections Act of 1888], the voting power to the besotted drunkard and the iniquitous liquor traffic ... We should think that any man on the island having a decent wife, or a loving mother, would be ashamed to vote at the next election for any of these men, who have placed the wives and mothers of our land on the same level with the idiot.

She mocked those antis, whose anthem, sung to the tune of "Yankee Doodle," was

> *Manhood suffrage for the clown,*
> *And fool, and knave, and dandy,*
> *But let us keep the women down,*
> *And gulp our gin and brandy.*

Ultimately, Ohman's points embodied three pro-suffrage arguments: "decent" women – meaning abstaining, morally upright Christian women – would be more responsible voters than the men who imbibed; denying women the franchise suggested that they were on a par with the male "idiots" and others who were barred; and exclusion was part of a political effort to suppress women and protect male immorality.

The *Water Lily* kept suffrage and prohibition on the front burner until the next legislative debate. In January 1893, Ohman reminded readers that the March 1892 bill had been "the most reasonable measure any assembly had ever been asked to give its assent to." The February issue bragged that its recent editorial on suffrage had "stirred up the sterner sex wonderfully." Moving the cause more firmly into the realm of equal rights, the March 1893 edition observed (incorrectly) that women could earn the highest degrees at Oxford and Cambridge, as well as elsewhere, and went on to assert that "until woman is politically the equal of man, until she has equal rights with her husband, her brothers, and her sons, she cannot be said to have gained the position which her intellectual and moral power warrants her to occupy." It also covered WCTU petitions and lobbying. On 19 April 1893, the biggest pro-suffrage meeting to date occurred at St. Mary's Anglican Church hall, with plenty of male pro-suffrage speakers, including three local clergy. J.O. Fraser, the dominion's postmaster general, argued that the pro-suffrage and pro-temperance women were "not seeking notoriety, but the well-being of mankind." Unfortunately, both St. John's newspapers, the *Evening Telegram* and the *Herald,* were unconverted. The editorial in the former was the most damning: "We have no word of sympathy or encouragement for those ladies who would voluntarily unsex themselves, and, for the sake of obtaining a little temporary notoriety, plunge into the troubled waters of party politics." Spirits must have sagged.

SECOND LEGISLATIVE DEBATE

In 1893, the House of Assembly returned to the fray with An Act to Extend the Privilege of the Franchise to Women in Elections Held under the Temperance Act of 1889. It proposed to enfranchise in any local option referendum women aged twenty-one and older who had lived in Newfoundland for at least a year. Both sides were better mobilized, the fight was nastier, and debate focused on the logic of broader women's suffrage even though only the local option was on the table. Again, Donald Morison introduced the bill, now framing his support practically: Newfoundland paid high costs for intemperance, and women's support for prohibition would save money. Conservative Alfred Morine (1857–1944), also from Bonavista, anticipated interest beyond women's input in local option prohibition by upholding the common rationale that female taxpayers should possess the vote. The anti-suffrage assault came mostly from Liberals, who insisted that since women could not join the military, they were not entitled to the franchise. Premier William Whiteway (1828–1908) argued that women would be torn from their domestic duties and would destroy the "peace of the house." Taking direct aim at Jessie Ohman's editorship of the *Water Lily*, he claimed that her paper's terrible lies and falsehoods "could not have been written by a woman." His defence of male "home comforts" was praised by the St. John's *Evening Telegram*. During this debate, the critique that enjoyed the most traction built on the *Telegram*'s earlier comment about unsexing. If they wanted equality, suffragists should try "going to the ice" as sealers, a job well known for its danger, hard physical work, and gore. In the face of such misogyny, the bill failed by seventeen to ten.

Ohman defended suffragists against Premier Whiteway's charges that women were deserting their proper sphere. As she explained, women, herself included, had tried the approved means of approaching the legislature through petitions, but he had been rude: "Had he been speaking to a drunken mob, he could not have used more appropriate language in the endeavour to elicit applause." Her attack accused the premier and his Liberal colleague Robert Bond of being drunk in the legislature, "a failure to do their job so great as to make the necessity of women's suffrage beyond a question." Whiteway, however, found many in agreement that unfeminine women threatened families, churches, and communities. Suffragists were condemned for unnaturally asserting themselves. The same timeless patriarchal tactic would later be employed in 1985 by another Newfoundland politician, Conservative MP John Crosbie, when he told Liberal MP Sheila Copps to "just quieten down, baby," in the House of Commons.

Since the Liberals proved especially obdurate, Ohman turned her attention to the upcoming election of 1893. Buoyed by promises of railway building and renegotiating fishing treaties, the Liberals remained in office, but corruption charges forced them to resign a year later. By then, the *Water Lily* was no more. The promoters of suffrage had been blamed for weakening the prohibition campaign, and the resulting environment had been too hostile for it to continue. Jessie Ohman and her family moved to Montreal a few years later. The suffrage issue was left to the mercies of an unsympathetic press and unchecked politicians. Equality was a long and bitter fight away.

HIGHER EDUCATION

Over the course of the next three decades, suffragists joined many campaigns, including for higher education for women, their entrance into the legal profession, the creation of a women's intellectual club and a trade union, and British, as well as local, suffrage. Although they were clear advocates of higher education, it was less closely tied to the cause than in either Nova Scotia or New Brunswick. In 1893, a *Water Lily* article counted as victories the acceptance of British women into St. Andrew's University and the Royal Geographical Society and was encouraged by progress toward admission into the British Medical Society. Such gains rightly recognized their intellectual capacity and equality "in the more practical affairs of life."

And as the second surge of suffrage agitation gained momentum during the First World War, the *Distaff,* the fundraising journal of the Women's Patriotic Association, ran a full-page tribute titled "Our University Girls." It featured Helen Fraser, who had just earned a bachelor of arts at McGill University, and Rose Carmichael, who received a master's degree at the University of Edinburgh. Ambitious students sought opportunities to study in Canada, Britain, and the United States. At least fifty-six young Newfoundland women attended New Brunswick's Mount Allison College between 1890 and 1925, and a further seventeen enrolled at Dalhousie University in Nova Scotia between 1920 and 1925. Their energies and enthusiasm might well have served the struggle for the vote in their new homes. Since Newfoundland did not establish Memorial University College until 1925, when it immediately became coed, the battles for educational equality that had mobilized student suffragists in many provinces did not occur. Mount Allison's best-known Newfoundland female graduate before 1925 was Helena Strong from Little Bay Island, who was rewarded with a mistress of liberal arts in 1902, before returning to teach school in Newfoundland for a few years and then marrying Richard Squires, who became its prime minister in 1905. Although she opposed suffrage in the 1910s and 1920s, she became the first woman to hold a seat in the Newfoundland House of Assembly, in 1930.

THE PROFESSIONS

Newfoundland did not have a provincial medical school until 1969, which meant that the early female physicians who contributed to feminist causes elsewhere were also largely absent from the island. The first Newfoundland-born woman to practise medicine, Edith Weeks Hooper (1882–1964), graduated from the University of Toronto in 1906. She spent most of her career in Vancouver and Asia. Her home province was less hospitable. Such absences were important when it came to the movement's ability to point to living exemplars of female talent and expertise.

Female lawyers, whose claims directly trespassed on male monopolies in public life, were also in short supply. Lobbying for the entrance of women into the Law Society of Newfoundland overlapped with that for the franchise. Many justifications were the same in both instances. Since early-twentieth-century legal practice came through apprenticeship rather than university courses, applicants had to convince the law society's male gatekeepers of their worthiness. When eighteen-year-old Janet Miller (1891–1946) applied to enter the law society as an articling clerk in 1909, she was told that it was open only to men. Like early candidates elsewhere, she turned to personal contacts for aid. Her uncle Donald Morison had presented the first two suffrage bills in the House of Assembly in 1892 and 1893 and had served on the Supreme Court of Newfoundland between 1898 and 1904. Demonstrating the power of elite family networks, he took up her cause. After failing to convince the law society to reconsider, he brought forward legislation to permit women to belong to it. As a result, in 1910, the law society and the House of Assembly debated admission almost concurrently, with the newspapers reporting on both. Just after the bill's first reading, the law society once more refused. Since it could overrule the society, the assembly continued its debate. During second reading on 11 March, assemblymen fought over the merits and threats of female lawyers. Morison himself, who was also minister of justice, introduced comprehensive legislation to admit women as clerks, students at law, solicitors, and barristers. He reassured his listeners that some of the oldest and most experienced lawyers in St. John's favoured accepting women "on the same terms as men." It would be "inequitable" not to do so, as they were able to enter other professions and indeed law in Canada, the United States, and Britain. Aiming perhaps to deter arguments about their proper place, he described the profession of law as "merely a competition of brain." In any case, approval was moot since any Newfoundland woman who was determined to practise could train elsewhere, and licensing agreements required the Law Society of Newfoundland to accept her application.

Other champions put the controversy in a larger context to suggest that opponents should logically challenge the higher education of women and the municipal enfranchisement of those who held property. One Conservative legislative councillor, John A. Robinson (1867–1929), went so far as to blame opponents for forcing women into "adopting methods that had shamed their womanhood." He predicted further conflict: "When we deliberately refuse the woman tax-payer, the woman breadwinner, the right of the franchise we were giving cause for agitation." The absence of arguments in the assembly that cited the law's unsuitability for the "gentle sex" signalled progress. The results were solid majorities: first reading passed by thirteen to eight, second reading by sixteen to four. After consideration by a committee of the whole, the law went into effect in 1910. Equally significant, the arguments for admission to law were ultimately indistinguishable from those in favour of suffrage. Both even included references to British militant suffragettes.

Janet Miller did not complete her legal training or become the first Newfoundland woman to qualify as a barrister and solicitor. She moved to Scotland when her fiancé, later husband, served in the First World War. When the now widowed Janet Ayre (later Janet Murray) returned to Newfoundland in 1920, she did not practise. In a testament to the value of female professionals to the movement, she immediately became a prominent member of the capital's suffrage movement. The first woman to work as a barrister and solicitor was Louise M. Saunders (1893–1969), who began as a legal secretary in the law practice of Richard Squires during the 1910s. Almost two decades later, she became an articling clerk. Called to the bar in 1933, she became a partner in Squires, Saunders, and Carew in 1951. Although not a known suffragist, Saunders was instrumental in the founding of the St. John's YWCA in 1925.

LADIES READING ROOM

Another example of the rights advocacy that bridged the first and second phases of the Newfoundland suffrage campaign was the establishment of the Ladies Reading Room and Current Events Club. It was founded in 1909, after women were excluded from a St. John's men's club for making caustic remarks during a speech. The timing is interesting, since their ejection coincided with local newspapers' graphic coverage of militant British suffragists. Such news, along with a defence of militants by Armine Nutting Gosling, an emerging St. John's reformer, may have led to their expulsion. The new group attracted 125 female members during its first few months. Spearheaded by Gosling and Julia Horwood, both members of the Church of England and multiple reform societies, and eight other St. John's women, it offered regular lectures and housed a well-stocked library. In the absence of a university, such opportunities were sought after. Like the Toronto Women's Literary Club, founded some thirty years earlier in 1876, the Ladies Reading Room met intellectual, cultural, and reform needs, became increasingly concentrated on enfranchisement, and was tied to offshoot suffrage groups.

The creation of the Ladies Reading Room marked the rise of a second generation of St. John's suffragists. Joining Gosling was Myra Campbell, a former teacher who had worked in a New England factory before marrying a railway supervisor and having five children. In 1913, her Ladies Reading Room lecture in support of equal rights centred on the lack of appreciation for women's work, which she referred to as the "slavery of the home." She also praised women who chose not to marry, went so far as to mention that men treated their mistresses better than their wives, and stated that the vote would be a good start in recognizing female merits. Such outspokenness appears to have upset the reading room executive, which suppressed publication of her talk for seven years as part of its careful management of women's rights agitation.

If elite suffragists exercised caution, working women – who were well represented in the expanding waged labour force of

St. John's and beyond – were restless. Like men, they contested low salaries, poor working conditions, and overly long hours. In August 1918, a notice published in the *Daily News* invited female workers to attend a meeting to organize a Ladies Branch of the Newfoundland Industrial Workers Association. Its all-female

Armine Nutting Gosling (1861–1942) grew up in a working-class home in Waterloo, Ontario, with an alcoholic father and a determined mother. In 1882, after obtaining her teaching certificate at McGill, she moved to Newfoundland to become principal of the Church of England Girls' School. Within a few years, she married William Gosling (1863–1930), a Bermuda native, merchant, and municipal councillor, with whom she raised four

executive was separate from the men's, with Julia Salter Earle (1878–1945), a city clerk, serving as its first president. The fact that four hundred women joined up in the next three months and engaged in strikes suggests pent-up demand for collective action. The first strike, over poor wages at a bread and biscuit

children. A reform couple, they were active in municipal public health, care for orphans and the elderly, and the prevention of cruelty to animals. Because William's business interests focused on importing rum, they were not involved in temperance. After Gosling volunteered for several charitable pursuits while her children were very young, her shift to greater prominence was marked by her response to a 1908 St. John's newspaper report on Britain's newly formed Women's National Anti-Suffrage League, which had gathered a lot of support from British aristocracy and politicians who applauded the status quo for women's roles. Historian Margot Duley identifies Gosling's fiery intervention , which outlined how women's suffrage was required to solve a wide array of world problems, as the first pro-suffrage public statement by a Newfoundland woman since WCTU efforts in the early 1890s. Reflecting on the success of the Ladies Reading Room, Gosling noted its importance in providing mental inspiration and demonstrating women's capacity to work "in peace and harmony ... without the least friction," a rebuttal of the common calumny that women readily succumbed to bickering. Termed the intellectual leader of the St. John's suffrage movement, Gosling spread the message of women's rights in local cultural groups, work in reform societies (such as the Church of England Orphanage, the Girl Guides, the Cowan Mission, the Women's Patriotic Association, and the YWCA), and the Women's Franchise League, which she founded in 1921.

factory, was unsuccessful, but the second, at a ropeworks factory, won the rehiring of a non-unionized employee. The Ladies Branch was also important because it offered opportunities to strategize outside the workplace. With its support, Earle emerged to help lead the second surge of suffrage agitation, beginning in 1920. Her practical orientation was evident in her suggestion that the rope-works factory commemorate wartime sacrifice with a club build-ing for employees, especially women.

THE WAR YEARS, 1914–18

Newfoundland women's many contributions to the Great War reinforced simmering feminism. Though the colony had been slowly increasing its autonomy, residents strongly identified with and threw their support behind Britain. Women's war work enabled both the pro- and anti-suffrage factions to reframe their arguments. As female leadership clearly benefitted the war effort, antis began a diplomatic about-face, claiming that women de-served the vote in recognition of their contributions to the war.

Newfoundland suffragists were encouraged by the British Dominions Women's Suffrage Union to count on patriotic endeav-ours as the route to political emancipation. Fundraising, clothing soldiers, supporting military families, and backing the Red Cross won applause from politicians and ordinary citizens. Early in the conflict, the Women's Patriotic Association, an arm of the Red Cross, founded branches across the island, often building on ex-isting networks. Soon, 1,500 women belonged to its 208 branches. In many communities, the association branch was indistinguish-able from the local Methodist Ladies Missionary Society or the Church of England women's group. The dominion executive over-lapped with the organizers of the Ladies Reading Room, includ-ing Armine Nutting Gosling, whose husband became mayor of St. John's in 1914, and Julia Horwood, whose husband, William Henry Horwood (1862–1945), served many decades in the House of Assembly, starting in 1894. Collectively, the branches of the

Women's Patriotic Association raised half a million dollars, provided tens of thousands of essential items to soldiers, and made hundreds of visits to their families. Their industrious production of socks for soldiers evoked responsible motherhood and inspired short stories and poetry, including *A Pair of Grey Socks,* a brief inspirational story written by association activist Tryphena Duley (1866–1940). It features Mary, a young unmarried resident of an outport community named Sweet Apple Cove, who, like all her female friends and relatives, knits grey socks for soldiers. At the urging of a friend, she slips her photograph inside one pair, writing a heartening message about bravery, as well as her first name and that of her small community, on the back. Stationed at Gallipoli, the young soldier who receives the socks falls in love with the sweet girl in the picture. Romantically, the two marry at war's end. Such results could only reassure those who feared the century's more modern women.

The leaders of the Women's Patriotic Association advertised their own work in two twenty-page fundraising editions of their newsletter, the *Distaff,* in 1916 and 1917. Like the *Water Lily* in the 1890s, it covered considerable ground, ranging from detailed descriptions of the Women's Patriotic Association and Red Cross work to travel adventures. Clearly championing a new post-war role for women in public life, it called for enfranchisement even as the work of making bandages, socks, and clothes, accomplished in the "Red Cross Room" at the association headquarters in Government House, demonstrated their efficiency and competence. Like a good business, the Red Cross Room was hailed as running "as if on oiled wheels."

A 1916 article *Distaff* article by Armine Nutting Gosling, who had a daughter driving ambulances in France and a son serving on the Eastern Front, justified enfranchisement on the grounds that women had performed labours from which they had previously been excluded and had demonstrated that society could not do without them. Since even former Liberal British prime minister

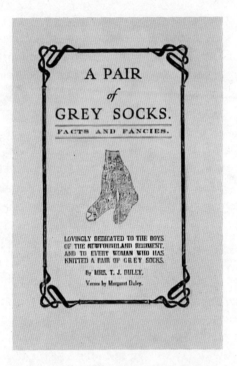

A PAIR
of
GREY SOCKS.
FACTS AND FANCIES.

LOVINGLY DEDICATED TO THE BOYS
OF THE NEWFOUNDLAND REGIMENT,
AND TO EVERY WOMAN WHO HAS
KNITTED A PAIR OF GREY SOCKS.

By MRS. T. J. DULEY.
Verses by Margaret Duley.

Cover of *A Pair of Grey Socks.* Co-written by Tryphena Duley and
her daughter Margaret, who supplied the concluding poem, *A Pair
of Grey Socks* was published in 1916. As it declares, the socks "are
a bond of unity between rich and poor, high and low, between all
mothers who have sons at the war, between all women who knit.
The grey sock has become the tie that binds."

H.H. Asquith had reversed his position, the dominion should not
be a laggard. In the *Distaff,* Gosling quoted the *London Daily
Telegraph* argument that "women have shown so much ability and
resource in adapting themselves to all sorts and conditions of
masculine employment that there is little to fear even if they take
the places of some of our overpaid MPs. Votes for women ... were
inevitable sooner or later and it is as well, perhaps, that they
should be granted sooner." The *Distaff* gave the final word to

another imperial male authority, Lord Derby, British secretary of state for war, who remarked that women "have given for two years a constant example of unselfish devotion to the National cause. They have helped largely in the success of our farms, and when the war is over they will ask for the vote. Shall we give it to them or shall we fight them? There can, I think, be but one answer." Newfoundlanders risked being backward, isolated, and uninformed if they failed to embrace change. Ultimately, the Women's Patriotic Association broadened and deepened the appeal of the suffrage movement, which had been closely tied to the WCTU and its Protestant supporters. In contrast, the new group crossed class, religious, and rural-urban boundaries. Old barriers fell, as any woman (or man) could knit for the Women's Patriotic Association, and any community could establish an association branch. This expansion generated a ready-made network for a reinvigorated suffrage movement in 1920.

Old activists nevertheless remained crucial. A rejuvenated WCTU stood side-by-side with the patriotic association. For many members, the war confirmed the dangers of alcohol. It handicapped recruiting, damaged home front efforts, and wasted money better spent patriotically elsewhere. Except for Quebec, every Canadian province instituted wartime prohibition. In 1915, one thousand WCTU members marched on the St. John's legislature, demanding that Newfoundland follow suit. Politicians listened. The resulting referendum narrowly achieved the required votes, and alcohol sales ended in 1917. Though many were exasperated by the need to beg, female activists had demonstrated their power.

By the end of the war, suffrage victories elsewhere simultaneously made Newfoundland conspicuous as an outlier and offered the option of a seemingly graceful retreat for former opponents. In 1920, the previously obdurate *Daily News* was forced to conclude that women had "shown their ability and influence in a manner that not the most confirmed misogynist dare dispute." The main newspapers of St. John's, the *Evening Telegram* and the

Daily News, justified their endorsement in the name of women's war work.

WOMEN'S FRANCHISE LEAGUE, 1920–25

Newfoundland had a combined death and casualty rate of more than 60 percent, higher than that of any other British dominion, which underscored its sacrifices for the war effort. The question remained: What had been the point of the war? Activists demanded that women share fully in the new world order that was confidently expected to dawn. In spring 1920, Armine Nutting Gosling and Anna Barnes Mitchell (1861–1946), members of both the Ladies Reading Room and the WCTU, founded Newfoundland's first group specifically dedicated to suffrage, the Women's Franchise League. Its creation highlighted the fact that except for South Africa, Newfoundland was the only British dominion that still denied women the vote. The franchise was optimistically anticipated as one legacy of a "just war." Gosling became the founding president of the league, Fannie McNeil its secretary, and the younger third-generation suffragist Agnes Ayre (1890–1940) its assistant secretary. Its remaining executive members consisted of Antonia D'Alberti Hutton, Helen Baird (1889–1965), Maud White Hutchings (1870–1961), May Kennedy Goodridge (1876–1974), Margaret Mulcahy Burke (1868–1963), Adelaide Browning (1875–1950), and Emilie Stirling Fraser (1868–1958). Notably, all were middle-class, educated St. John's women, connected to the elite merchant and governing class through their birth families and/or marriages.

As with most suffragists, each founding executive member brought organizational experience from a variety of local cultural, athletic, charitable, denominational, and reform societies. Most had been involved in the Women's Patriotic Association, and several belonged to the Ladies Reading Room, the Child Welfare Association, the Society of Art, Girl Guides, and the Ladies Avalon Curling Club. As there were proportionately more Catholics than usual in an anglophone suffrage society, several members had served presidencies of the Catholic Women's League, the Dorcas Society, and the Knights of Columbus Ladies Association. Many Methodist, Presbyterian, and Church of England women's groups were also represented.

The only league member who was not of British descent was Antonia D'Alberti Hutton. Her Spanish mother and Italian father had raised her and her two sisters in London, where all were well educated in sciences, languages, and music. She married Charles Hutton (1861–1949), a musician, businessman, and Liberal politician while he was studying in England and moved with him to St. John's. Her sister Lenora, who regularly visited Newfoundland, provided valuable international suffrage ties as founding editor of the London-based *Catholic Suffragist.* St. John's newspapers often strategically reprinted its articles to mitigate suffrage controversy for the Catholic community, which constituted nearly half of the highly sectarian dominion's population. Hutton was far from the only league member with international connections. Fully half of the executive had emigrated as adults from either Scotland or England and kept up kinship ties with visits, correspondence, and newspapers. Another three had studied in Ireland, England, or Wales. In other words, eight of the ten executive members had lived outside Newfoundland for a significant portion of their lives and were particularly invested in Britain's suffrage movement.

Backed by some one hundred recruits, the capable executive moved quickly to develop Women's Patriotic Association networks to firmly link the Great Cause to women's service for Newfoundland soldiers. It organized a multi-pronged publicity campaign: newspaper articles and letters to the editor, door-to-door canvassing, communication with suffragists in outport communities, and political lobbying. Within a month of the league's founding, the first suffrage bill since 1893 came before the House of Assembly. There, it encountered a seemingly immovable object in the fervently anti-suffrage prime minister, Sir Richard Squires

(1880–1940), who was in only his first year of office. He was already practising intimidation, having threatened government employees, including Fannie McNeil's husband, Hector, with dismissal if their wives supported suffrage.

Sure enough, during the spring 1920 debate in the House of Assembly, Squires attacked the bill's main advocate, Liberal Progressive Cyril Fox (1889–1946). His assault was vicious and duplicitous. Two members of Squires's Liberal (Reform) Party, F.P. Le Grow (1882–1961) and Harvey Small (1884–1965), were absent during second reading of the bill. Both were war veterans who had earlier tabled a suffrage petition with 1,700 signatures and thrown their support behind enfranchisement at both the municipal and government levels. When Fox reprimanded them for their absence, Squires seized his opportunity to sidestep the enfranchisement issue by going after him, condemning him as an elitist, selfish, highly educated city boy who had *not* fought in the war. Advocates vainly tried to bring the debate to a vote, repeatedly citing the wartime contributions of Newfoundland women, their unquestionable morality and intellectual capacity, and the merits of following the United Kingdom. All to no end. In a too-familiar ploy, the government secured a six-month delay, arguing that if democracy were to be practised, the outports needed to be consulted, not merely the effete residents of St. John's, as represented by Fox.

Frustrated with this obstructionism, the franchise league prepared heavily for the spring 1921 legislative session. To address the concern (disingenuous as it was) about support beyond St. John's, the league circulated a suffrage petition that employed both traditional and up-to-date arguments and addressed both middle- and working-class women:

Whereas we regard ourselves as partners in the responsible business of homekeeping which is so vital to the best interests of the Dominion; and

Whereas we are subject to all the laws and taxations which apply to men; and

Whereas many of us are workers helping to produce the wealth of the Dominion; and

Whereas in other parts of the British Empire women enjoy all the rights of the franchise and assume its responsibilities; and

Whereas the women of Newfoundland rose to every call made upon them during the Great War, and showed energy and executive ability in the organization of relief and other work, and that many of them served overseas as Nurses, V.A.D.s and Ambulance Drivers;

Your petitioners therefore humbly pray that your Honourable House will, during the present Session, pass a law by which there will be given to the Women of the Dominion the rights of the franchise on conditions similar to those commonly required of men.

In addition to preparing the petition, league members approached Prime Minister Squires, who assured them in mid-April that he would soon table a new suffrage bill. Stalling, however, continued. The league nevertheless wrote him regularly and kept lobbying others in government. Still, nothing happened in the House of Assembly. Appeals were followed by flimsy excuses, among the least convincing of which was a claim by Squires that, due to a printers' strike, he had been unable to send the league a copy of the bill he had composed.

Finally, the minister of justice, William Warren (1879–1927), fulfilled a 1920 promise to introduce a suffrage bill himself, if not actually to support it, in the 1921 legislative session. On 4 May 1921, he tabled league petitions from every district, with a total of 7,485 signatures, and concluded, "From this it will be seen by honorable members that the women have gained a strong foothold all over the Island." Upon being asked if his intention were to introduce a motion, Warren replied with a simple "no"! Other foes of equality denied that the entire population of Newfoundland had been sufficiently consulted. In response, Cyril Fox accused Warren of "prolonging the agony for these people who are demanding something that is not a favour, but merely a right entitling them to vote." His charge was in vain, as the bill died in committee.

Anticipating further intransigence from Squires, the franchise league published a comprehensive statement in the *Daily News* on 18 August 1921: "History of the Woman's Franchise Bill. Unparalleled Duplicity of the Prime Minister. Signed Statement on Behalf of the Women's Franchise League." The dense article, occupying two full columns and signed by eight members of the league executive, explained that they had taken Squires at his word, noting that their acceptance of additional conditions, including an age requirement of thirty years, signalled a definite deal. They quoted correspondence, including an 11 June 1921 letter from Fannie McNeil to Squires, which read, "Dear Sir ... you must have forgotten that you definitely promised to ensure the successful passing of our Bill this session by offering to introduce it as a Government measure yourself." Squires had not replied to the letter, so they had been driven to make an appointment with him. During this meeting, they were treated even more rudely:

> On being ushered into the Presence we found the self-contained arbiter of our destinies seated at the table with his back to us, smoking a cigar. He omitted to rise, or to greet us in any way, continuing to enjoy his cigar ... This attitude of the Prime Minister gave the women of the deputation just cause for indignation, and foundation for the belief that there had never been any intention on the part of the Premier to fulfil the pledges made by him.

The franchise league ended with a declaration of its unwavering determination.

A *Daily News* editorial of the same day applauded the league's efforts on behalf of ten thousand Newfoundland women (the updated number of signatures on the 1920 petition). It censored Squires: "The story ... is one of definite promises deliberately evaded; of unparalleled duplicity; cheap trickery; low-brow insults and clownish rudeness." At long last, anti-suffragists got a taste of their own poison. After years of charges that suffragists were unfeminine, the franchise league had shown that the prime minister was no gentleman, a weak specimen of masculinity who was unfit to govern Newfoundland.

MUNICIPAL VOTE

Advocates also turned their attention elsewhere. At the end of 1921, St. John's suffragists gained the municipal franchise for rate-paying women as part of a slate of municipal reforms promoted by city councillor William Gosling. This occurred much later than in the Maritime provinces, at least for single propertied women, but its terms were more inclusive, treating women on the same basis as men. Although the act remained unclear as to whether a household could cast more than one ballot, it seems to have been interpreted as enfranchising all female residents of a property on which taxes were paid, thereby including both mothers and adult daughters of male ratepayers.

Because this municipal achievement is buried among the 390 sections of a 120-page-long omnibus act, it has often been overlooked. The section on voting qualifications did not specifically add women. Instead, the act repeated the 1902 voters requirements using gender-inclusive language: "all British subjects" and "any such person or body corporate who resides in a taxed dwelling." Even the relevant St. John's Council minutes do not mention the unprecedented inclusion. The preamble to the act is clear:

"Words importing the masculine gender shall apply to females as well as to males." Eligibility for municipal office was implied. No woman ran for city council in 1921, but three did in 1925, one of whom was Julia Salter Earle.

THE FINAL PUSH

The franchise league's next legislative opportunity occurred with the 1922 sitting of the assembly. At this stage, it drew on its affiliation with the International Alliance of Women for Suffrage and Legal Citizenship, which had been founded in 1904 by the world's leading feminists, including Americans Carrie Chapman Catt and Susan B. Anthony, as well as British suffragist Millicent Fawcett. Its publication, *Jus Suffragii* (the right of suffrage), was well known to Canadian suffragists for charting the state of suffrage across the world, and its triennial congresses kept the pot boiling. By 1922, women in virtually all the English-speaking world had at least limited access to the vote.

In Newfoundland, the International Alliance of Women for Suffrage and Legal Citizenship provided high-profile and timely support. Kate Trounson, its secretary and a former British munitions inspector, addressed six meetings in St. John's during the spring of 1922, including a standing-room-only crowd at Methodist College Hall. Prime Minister Squires arranged for a secret report to be written on at least one. He counted himself lucky that Trounson summarized the state of women's rights in the world without focusing on the "local situation." She did, however, congratulate Newfoundland women for putting up a good fight and offered her organization's full endorsement. She trusted that Newfoundland would not allow itself to be "the last to deal with this important question." At least as valuable was the five-hundred-dollar donation to the franchise league that Trounson arranged with alliance president, Chapman Catt. The alliance pressed Squires with invitations to its international congress in Rome in 1923 and approached him on a visit to London's Savoy Hotel.

Executive members of the franchise league pored over *Jus Suffragii*, valuing the international support and discussing their options. Although the league could not send a representative to attend international meetings, it forwarded reports for publication and updates, circulated and cited International Alliance of Women for Suffrage and Legal Citizenship pamphlets and arguments, and benefitted from Antonia Hutton's sister Lenora's work as the Newfoundland correspondent for *Jus Suffragii*. These ties must have offered some consolation in the face of little visible progress in 1923 and 1924, despite the forced 1923 resignation of Richard Squires due to debts and scandals.

1925 SUFFRAGE BILL

In the 1924 election, which Squires did not contest, the winning coalition, the Liberal-Conservative Progressive Party, proved infinitely more receptive to suffrage. Led by Walter Stanley Monroe (1871–1952), it gave birth to a suffrage measure just nine months after taking office. The result was almost unanimous. The 1921 suffrage petition's final tally of twenty thousand signatures offered most previous dissenters a path to concession. In fact, most politicians, now that victory was in the air, lined up for to be thanked. Female voters could prove very useful to them. The only significant disagreement centred on the qualifying age. Monroe explained that Britain entitled women to vote at thirty and men at twenty-one because wartime losses and a longer life expectancy meant that female voters would otherwise outnumber male ones. A compromise of twenty-five years was accepted. Though unstated, the assumption remained that men had more responsibilities than women did and were thus more deserving.

A notable shift in principle nevertheless appeared in the rhetoric of the 1925 House of Assembly debate. For the first time, most supporters endorsed the franchise as a right for women as well as men, no longer simply as a reward, whether for war work or morality. It is difficult to know for sure, but perhaps labour activist

Julia Salter Earle and her allies had gained some ground in the trenches of the labour force. Since at least 1918, Earle had been urging politicians to remember women when they considered (or failed to consider) waged workers. The labour movement had declined in concert with the flagging post-war economy, but Earle continued writing to newspapers, lobbying politicians, and raising consciousness about workers' rights among members of the Ladies Reading Room. Her efforts may have influenced Prime Minister Monroe, who, during the 1925 debate, linked women's increasing power to their growing participation in paid employment. The colonial secretary, John Bennett (1866–1941), went so far as to state quite erroneously that their earning power now equalled that of men: "Families who formerly were in straightened circumstances because they had no breadwinner but a man are now in comfort through the industry of the young women and girls ... And why should they not have the vote?" Harbour Grace Liberal Reform MLA William Warren, who had served briefly as Newfoundland's prime minister in 1923–24, pushed the breadwinning rationale even farther, pointing to the irony that the taxes of unenfranchised female workers were helping old male voters on relief. By the time the bill passed in 1925, working-class women's breadwinning was routinely acknowledged alongside the wartime contributions of their sex.

On 3 April 1925, an act amending the Election Act of 1913 passed unanimously. For the first time, an enfranchised person included "every male British subject of the full age of twenty-one years and every female British subject of the full age of twenty-five years of sound understanding and resident in this Colony for two years preceding the day of [the election]." Women with an annual income of $480 or property that was valued at a minimum of $2,400 were now eligible to run for a seat in the House of Assembly on the same terms as men. Since the dominion had no Indian Act, First Nations citizens were included alongside naturalized ethnic Chinese citizens. *Jus Suffragii* ran a story to celebrate the victory, noting, "This decision calls for much rejoicing for it leaves but one place on the continent of North America between the northern border of Mexico and the north pole where women do not vote on fairly equal terms as men ... Quebec." The insertion of "fairly" reminded canny readers that the Atlantic dominion, like the United Kingdom, still discriminated against younger women. Inequality's odour remained. Newfoundland suffragists celebrated their victory with a large women-only banquet a month later, sponsored by the Women's Franchise League, which unveiled its transformation into a non-partisan League of Women Voters: "Though we differ in many things – in religion, in race, in politics – we shall be a unit in our demand of women's share of the privileges, opportunities, and responsibilities our country has to offer." With no press present at the event, suffragists were wise to recognize that their fight had not ended.

1925 MUNICIPAL ELECTION

After waiting so long to vote, Newfoundland women maintained high participation rates in city and dominion elections – and in St. John's in 1925, Fannie McNeil, May Kennedy, and Julia Salter Earle, all known suffragists, ran as municipal candidates. McNeil and Kennedy, both former executive members of the Women's Franchise League, were sponsored by the League of Women Voters, and Earle ran for labour. Earle placed most strongly, losing a council seat by just eleven votes, a near miss which the City of St. John's website now celebrates as women's progress toward equality. Earle provides one of the most important lessons of the Newfoundland suffrage campaign. Though the Women's Patriotic Association and the franchise league were vital in developing female networks, *sustained* interest from working-class women was invaluable. As her biographer argues, Earle stood out as more a labour leader than a suffragist. She would have confronted the ugly reality that the exploited female employees who were paid pitiful wages and who toiled in substandard conditions worked in

Julia Agnes Salter (1878–1945) was raised in a large St. John's family, attended the Newfoundland Methodist College, married Arthur Earle in 1903, and had six children. For thirty-five years, she worked as a clerk in the Newfoundland House of Assembly, which gave her valuable insight into the functioning of politics, government, and legislation. While preparing a bill for the House on cruelty to animals, she raged that factory girls were not similarly protected. During intense labour strife at the close of the First World War, Earle founded the autonomous Ladies Branch of the local Newfoundland Industrial Workers Association and supported its strikes. In letters to the press and in public speeches, she demanded safer working conditions, an end to child labour, and a living wage for women since many were

factories that belonged to the husbands of many of St. John's suffragist elite. Her candidacy for labour rather than the Women's Party demonstrates the competing urgencies of labour and gender in reform agendas.

In the first general election in which Newfoundland women could vote, on 29 October 1928, 52,343 cast their ballots, representing a 90 percent voter turnout rate. The electorate included Indigenous and Chinese voters, unlike in the Maritime provinces where Indigenous women who lived on a reserve remained disenfranchised because of stipulations in the Indian Act. (Racism abounded in other forms, including in the three-hundred-dollar head tax on Chinese immigrants until 1949.) Newfoundland was also the only jurisdiction in the region to elect a woman soon after her enfranchisement. Whereas Nova Scotia, New Brunswick, and Prince Edward Island elected women to their legislatures only in 1960, 1967, and 1970, respectively, Lady Helena (Strong) Squires *often the sole breadwinner for their families. She informed readers of the* Daily News *that a female factory worker needed a weekly wage of $8.50 – the average salary was less than half of that – to cover basic expenses. She challenged bosses to prove otherwise. Unlike most female reformers of her day, Earle held long-term employment. Although her biographer describes her as middle class, both she and her husband, a jeweller and fellow union leader, worked for wages all their lives. Like the suffragist seamstress and writer Flora MacDonald Denison in Toronto and dressmaker and union organizer Helena Gutteridge in Vancouver, Earle crossed class lines. In the Ladies Reading Room, she mingled with elite St. John's women. Unfortunately, no evidence has been found of their response to her politics.*

(1879–1959), became the first woman to sit in the Newfoundland House of Assembly, in 1930. As she was a known suffrage opponent who had a "frosty relationship with the League of Women Voters," her easy by-election win in the Liberal stronghold of Lewisporte after her husband, Richard, was re-elected prime minister in 1928 was a twist of fate. Unlike Lady Astor, the first woman to take a seat in the Commons at Westminster, Squires, a former student of Mount Allison and Boston's Emerson College of Oratory, never publicly repudiated her previous hostility to female enfranchisement, but rather explained her role as "mother" to her constituents. The sad fact of her near silence in the House of Assembly showed the limitations of democracy, although she interrupted it in 1931, when she spoke in favour of regulating shop closing hours: "I'm here for [the shop workers], to protect these people. That is what they elected me for."

[Sandra Lovelace], author of the communication dated 29 December 1977 and supplemented by letters of 17 April 1978, 28 November 1979 and 20 June 1980, is a 32-year-old woman, living in Canada. She was born and registered as "Maliseet Indian" but has lost her rights and status as an Indian in accordance with section 12 (1) (b) of the Indian Act, after having married a non-Indian on 23 May 1970 ... Accordingly, the Human Rights Committee, acting under article 5 (4) of the Optional Protocol to the International Covenant on Civil and Political Rights, is of the view that the facts of the present case, which establish that Sandra Lovelace has been denied the legal right to reside on the Tobique Reserve, disclose a breach by Canada of article 27 of the [International Covenant on Civil and Political Rights].

– FROM *SANDRA LOVELACE V. CANADA*

SIX

THE LEGACY OF SUFFRAGE IN ATLANTIC CANADA

PEI's Famous Five in 1993.
Back row, l to r, Nancy Guptill, Speaker of the House; Pat Mella, Leader of the Opposition; and Elizabeth Hubley, Deputy Speaker. *Front row, l to r,* Marion Reid, Lieutenant Governor; Catherine Callbeck, Premier. That year, the island's highest provincial government positions were all held by women.

SANDRA LOVELACE NICHOLAS (1948–), a Wolastoqi woman raised on the Tobique reserve (Neqotkuk) in New Brunswick, moved across the border to Maine in 1965 at age seventeen to work as a carpenter. When she was twenty-two, she married an American, moved back to California, and then had a child. She divorced and moved with her son to the Tobique reserve in the mid-1970s, but she was refused on-reserve housing or other support normally extended to Indigenous people. She and her son were forced to live in a tent. Under the terms of the 1876 Indian Act and its most recent 1951 version, when she married a non-Indigenous man she had permanently lost both her status as a "registered Indian" and her entitlement to any government aid. She mounted a campaign, accusing Ottawa of discrimination under the Indian Act because Indigenous *men* who "married out" did not lose their Indian status. In fact, their non-Indigenous wives actually *gained* it. In 1981, after the Canadian government had ignored the issue for years, Lovelace Nicholas took her complaint to the United Nations. In 1985, Bill C-31 amended the Indian Act, finally returning Indian status to her, approximately 114,000 other Indigenous women who had married out, and their children. This campaign demonstrates that, for Indigenous and other racialized women, the pathways and timelines toward sexual equality differed from those of their Euro-Canadian sisters. They were forced to contend with more layers of sexual discrimination.

The many motives, strategies, and blind spots of pro- and anti-suffragists produced long and contentious enfranchisement campaigns in Atlantic Canada. Persistence was key. But even after non-Indigenous women won this important symbol and tool of citizenship and democracy, much unfinished business remained, most of all for racialized and poor women who had never been a priority. This chapter focuses on the legacy of suffrage, including the ongoing shaping of the story, the slowness of electing female politicians, subsequent human rights campaigns – especially among racialized women – and some suggestions for further research.

Just as *We Shall Persist* addresses the stereotype of Atlantic Canadian women as passive and disinterested in suffrage, the companion volume in this series, *Ours by Every Law of Right and Justice,* by Sarah Carter, shows that stereotypes also skewed Prairie suffrage stories. Earlier historians ignored the race, ethnic, class, and gender hierarchies of settler society, most notably those that oppressed its Indigenous hosts, and therefore exaggerated nineteenth-century Prairie gender equality. Together, these volumes show how the myth of the progressive West amplified the stereotype of the conservative East. Interconnected suffrage stories evolved, "proven" by the earliness of western enfranchisement compared to its lateness in the east. In fact, the first Prairie province to gain suffrage was Manitiba in January 1916; the first in the Maritimes was Nova Scotia in April 1918, only a twenty-seven-month difference. Overemphasizing the lag fit regional myths not only of the suffrage era, but also of subsequent periods, as historians rewrote the suffrage story. In the same vein, assumptions that the Atlantic Canadians who were most unhappy with the status quo left the region and weakened its progressiveness are false. They contradict the reality that the poorest folk could not afford to leave and that the young single people who did go elsewhere in search of job opportunities, who made up the bulk of the outmigrants, were unlikely to be any more progressive than the parents and siblings they left behind.

THE CONTINUING CAMPAIGN FOR WOMEN'S
POLITICAL EQUALITY

Suffrage was largely the project of middle-class, educated white women, and that group continued throughout the twentieth century to progress toward equality at a faster pace than women from visible minorities and the working class. A new cohort of female professional social workers, including Jane Wisdom (1884–1975),

Raised by a family of strong Liberal supporters in Shediac, **Muriel McQueen** *(1899–1997) graduated from nearby Mount Allison College in 1921 and then apprenticed at and was briefly employed in her father's law office, passing her bar examination in 1924. In 1926, she married Aubrey Fergusson, a First World*

heavily influenced the Atlantic Canadian social reform agenda in the years following the First World War. The founding secretary of the Halifax Bureau of Social Service, she was the city's only trained social worker at the time of the Halifax Explosion. She distributed relief to hundreds of devastated families, while creating one of the country's first modern municipal social welfare systems. During and after the Second World War, women of all classes and

War veteran, taking over his law practice when he became ill in 1931. Soon afterward, she was appointed a probate judge, New Brunswick's first female justice. After her husband died, she moved her family to Saint John, where she was employed on the Saint John Wartime Prices and Trade board, and then to Fredericton, where she became the regional director of family allowances. Only men were permitted to apply for this bonus, but Fergusson's colleagues in the Canadian Federation of Business and Professional Women in Saint John successfully protested the discrimination. In Fredericton, she became politically active, petitioning for the right of all women to vote in municipal elections, and then being elected herself by acclamation to Fredericton City Council in 1952. From there, she became the first Atlantic Canadian woman to be appointed to the Senate, where she remained for the next twenty years, until her retirement in 1974 at age seventy-five. Though she never identified as a feminist, she was a progressive who advocated, especially in the Senate, that women and men should have the same career opportunities and equal pay for equal work. Throughout her long career in law, government, and politics, she belonged to many women's groups and valued women's networks for strategizing for change.

ethnicities joined the waged workforce in ever larger numbers, still mostly in domestic, teaching, nursing, clerical, retail, and factory work. Their entrance into non-traditional professions continued at a snail's pace. In all cases, they were paid considerably less than men, reflecting the long trend of their economic subordination, especially for racialized and working-class women.

Though feminism is often divided into waves – the suffrage era as the first, and the 1960s to 1980s women's movement as the second – women's activism was a constant. From the 1920s to the 1950s, Atlantic Canadian organizations such as the Local Councils of Women continued their earlier work; new groups such as Newfoundland's Jubilee Guilds (1935–68) emerged; more women entered the workforce; female municipal politicians such as Halifax's indefatigable Abbie Lane (1898–1965) and Fredericton's tenacious Muriel McQueen Fergusson exerted significant influence; and the peace movement grew. Traditional gender roles were nevertheless ubiquitous, as we see in a 1953 *Maclean's* description of Lane as a "well-corseted pleasant-looking woman" who had recently "trimmed to a hundred and fifty pounds."

Dissatisfaction with women's subservient status grew in the 1950s and exploded in the 1960s as part of a wider call for a less restrictive, more egalitarian society that valued women's participation in public life. "The personal is political" ideology – that the challenges of individual women were widespread and required the attention of politicians – propelled a broader agenda than the first wave. Alongside waged women's demands for pay equity, maternity leave benefits, and an end to sexual harassment, female university students and peace activists called to end patriarchy and the oppression of minority peoples. Women's university attendance outpaced that of men in the 1960s. In Halifax, Mount Saint Vincent University, the only degree-granting women's university in Canada, offered one of the earliest women's studies courses in the country, which grew into a minor and then a major, becoming a national "unprecedented experiment." Université de

Moncton, Acadia University, Memorial University of Newfoundland, and the University of New Brunswick soon added women's
studies to their curricula.

Women's leadership in the peace movement of the late 1950s
marked the start of second-wave feminism. In at least one Maritime family, international peace activism extended seamlessly
from the 1880s to the 1920s and 1930s, from mother Mary Russell
Chesley to daughter Polly Chesley (1892–1936), who moved to
India to participate in the anti-colonial movement. Two conversations between Polly Chesley and Gandhi were published in the
Collected Works of Mahatma Gandhi. In Halifax, where the naval
presence was strong, women followed the lead of the Chesleys
to establish a local branch of the Voice of Women, a national peace
organization, in 1960. Fredericton women soon followed suit,
and the mandate of the Bay St. George (Newfoundland) Status
of Women Council married nuclear disarmament with women's
rights. These anti-war groups shared with suffrage activists the
claim that only women could pull nations back from the reckless
sabre rattling of male politicians and set them on an ethical and
peaceful path. More ethnically diverse than suffrage groups, the
Halifax branch was nonetheless predominantly middle class and
university educated.

Campaigns for access to birth control, equal pay for equal work,
minimum standards of living, non-violence, and racial equality
energized 1960s women's rights agendas, which were largely championed by grassroots projects, including women's health services,
rape crisis centres, shelters for domestic violence survivors, peace
marches, and consciousness-raising groups. More formally, these
aims were included in the recommendations of the 1970 Report of
the Royal Commission on the Status of Women, to which women
from the four Atlantic provinces made more than a dozen submissions. Agitation for improved legal rights, including in matrimonial property and minimum wage laws, had remained constant
since the suffrage era and was bolstered by new provincially

funded arm's-length government advisory councils on the status of women (New Brunswick, 1975–2011; Nova Scotia, 1977–; Prince Edward Island, 1975–; and Newfoundland, 1980–). Their quantitative research undisputedly demonstrated the ongoing economic, social, and political inequality of women. Newfoundland's many local advisory councils ensured that feminism penetrated even into small communities, and New Brunswick's provincial council gave much stability to the movement, with the first president serving for a decade. Progressing on what remained largely a parallel track, Indigenous, Black, Acadian, and poor women battled fundamental restrictions against them, including barriers to education and employment, unclear titles to historic land grants, and – for Indigenous women – loss of Indian status if they married out. Only in the second wave were minority women's inequities recognized by the mainstream movement, and still not fully.

As with the first wave, second-wave causes overlapped and conflicted. Muriel Duckworth (1908–2009), founding member of the Halifax Voice of Women and national president from 1967 to 1971, noted that the peace, ecology, and women's movements were "alive and effective because more and more of us see these things as interrelated." Many local groups were nationally and internationally affiliated. As with any large grassroots movement, there were cleavages, including between pro-life and pro-choice feminists, rural and urban women, younger and older women, middle-class and working-class women, racialized and white women, and liberal and radical feminists. Nevertheless, fragmented though it was, the movement covered more bases and involved far more women than the suffrage movement had. In 1990, Nova Scotia alone had 127 women's groups, which had expanded to 178 by 2004. In Prince Edward Island, conservatives temporarily gained the upper hand, not only securing a seat on the Provincial Advisory Council on the Status of Women but barring abortion when it was decriminalized federally in 1969 and even winning an appeal against pro-choice activist Henry Morgentaler in 1996.

INDIGENOUS, BLACK, AND ACADIAN WOMEN:
SYSTEMIC DISCRIMINATION

Early-twentieth-century suffrage agitation excluded Indigenous women who lived on reserves. Suffragists had focused on gaining rights that were equal to those held by male voters and therefore blindly accepted the disenfranchisement of Indigenous men. In addition, the Indian Act (which was not recognized when Newfoundland joined Canada in 1949, so the Act did not apply there) regarded male and female status Indians as wards of the state. This act allowed Ottawa to control their education, cultural and religious practices, land use, and band elections, while denying them the right to vote federally until 1960. Even band council elections excluded women until 1951. The Indian Act continued the connection between Indigenous peoples and the British Crown, as established in the seventeenth century and later represented by the federal government. These structural and cultural ties eclipsed relationships between Indigenous peoples and provincial governments. Because suffrage was a provincial rather than a federal movement, Indigenous women were probably less interested in it than if it had been a federal issue. At the same time, the lack of voting rights provincially or federally was of less concern to them than other human rights violations in the Indian Act that had a more regular and personal impact, including evictions from land, children's forced attendance at residential schools, inadequate health care and educational services, and women's loss of status through marrying out.

During the second wave, Maritime Indigenous women collectively fought these injustices, including through provincial affiliates of the Native Women's Association of Canada, founded in 1974. The Nova Scotia branch, established in 1972 by Helen Martin (1922–93), Annie Johnson, and Martha Julien (1911–98), preceded the national organization. Though Indigenous women in Labrador and Newfoundland did not come under the Indian Act until a 2009 agreement between the Federation of Newfoundland

Indians and Ottawa, they shared other concerns. In 1978, Innu and Mi'kmaw women held a large conference in Nain and thereafter formed several community groups to address the lack of support services, the decline of traditional knowledge and culture, and the prevalence of alcohol and violence. Indigenous women rarely advocated individually, yet two Atlantic Canadians are particularly well known for effecting national change during the second wave: Isabelle Knockwood (1931–2020) and Sandra Lovelace Nicholas.

Exposing residential school abuses became the primary goal of Mi'kmaw activist Isabelle Knockwood after she returned home to Indian Brook Reserve, Nova Scotia, from Boston where she was involved in the American Indian Movement. As she wrote in *Out of the Depths* in 1992, staff at Nova Scotia's Shubenacadie Indian Residential School, which she attended from 1936 to 1947, enforced a "code of silence ... with a combination of physical intimidation and psychological manipulation which produced terror and confusion." Knockwood's work raising awareness of the school's brutal assimilationist agenda was acknowledged with an honorary degree in 2013 and the designation of the school as a national historic site in 2020.

Wolastoqi women activists from the Tobique reserve – including Sandra Lovelace Nicholas – fought against the sexual discrimination of the Indian Act through which Indigenous women lost on-reserve housing and other benefits if they married out. (Mohawk activist Mary Two-Axe Earley started this campaign in 1967.) After Lovelace Nicholas and six other Tobique women protested, occupying the band office for several weeks in 1977, Glenna Perley (1939–95) convinced her to take the complaint further and appeal to the United Nations Human Rights Committee, which ruled two years later that the Indian Act violated international law. It took Parliament until 1985 to finally amend the discriminatory statute. Even so, Ottawa offered few additional resources to accommodate those who regained their status. Many women who returned to their reserves encountered hostility, ostracism, and criticism for using "white laws" to gain their return. In 2005, Lovelace Nicholas became the first Indigenous woman from Atlantic Canada to be appointed to the Senate, where she focuses on, among other things, the crisis of murdered and missing Indigenous women.

Provincial suffrage legislation included Black Atlantic Canadian women, but they continued to face overwhelming racism and human rights violations, especially in Nova Scotia where the Black population was largest. The Ladies Auxiliary of the African United Baptist Association maintained its community reform work into the mid-twentieth century, after hosting the First Congress of Coloured Women in 1920. Two years later, another Black women's auxiliary formed to support children's needs through the Nova Scotia Home for Coloured Children. The Nova Scotia Association for the Advancement of Coloured People was founded in 1945, fortuitously in advance of Viola Desmond's (1914–65) 1946 arrest for sitting in the white section of New Glasgow's Roseland Theatre.

African Nova Scotia journalist Carrie Best (1903–2001) founded the *Clarion* newspaper in 1946 and the *Quiet Corner,* a radio show, in 1954, "to work for the betterment of racial relations." Her coverage of Viola Desmond's arrest and trial helped earn Desmond the moniker "Canada's Rosa Parks," her civil disobedience transpiring a decade ahead of the American Black activist's. Reflecting on how slowly race relations were improving, particularly for Black and Indigenous Canadians, Best commented in 1968,

Canadian society is a white society. Its legislators are white. Its judges are white; its teachers are almost universally white; its police are white; its executives are white; its newsmen are white; its real estate agents are white; its landlords, its school board administrators, its mayors and aldermen, its bankers, its armed forces, and its Prime

Minister are white. They support and perpetuate the institutions and customs that make Canada what it is. Thus they are racists.

It took a long time for mainstream society to recognize the human rights accomplishments of Desmond and Best. The federal government featured their images on postage stamps in 2011 and 2012, and put Desmond's picture on the ten-dollar bill. Google paid tribute to both, with its "Google Doodle" images and stories.

Carrie Mae Prevoe (1903–2001) was raised in New Glasgow, Nova Scotia, a small town with a significant minority African Nova Scotian population that was connected to local railway, mining, and domestic service employment. She married railway porter Albert Best in 1925 and had one child and several foster

Black women's rights proponents emerged during the second wave, including a Nova Scotia branch of the Congress of Black Women, which hosted its national convention in Halifax in 1976, and the Black United Front, a mixed gender group with many female members. Black activists pushed for the establishment of Nova Scotia's Human Rights Commission in 1967. The opacity of some anti-Black racism made it hard to fight. For example, Atlantic Canadian Black women were technically allowed admission to the two most common professions for white women –

children. Self-educated in African American history and culture, Best advocated against racial discrimination from a young age, including lobbying the manager of the local Roseland Theatre in 1941 to stop requiring Black patrons to sit in the balcony away from white patrons. When the manager refused to comply, Best sat in the white section herself with her son, was arrested and charged, and welcomed the opportunity to end this anti-Black injustice. Sadly, she lost her case in 1942 and was even forced to pay the defendant's costs. In 1946, she and her son, Calvert, founded the Clarion *to report on the challenges and achievements of African Nova Scotians. They soon expanded the paper to include coverage of the whole country, renaming it the* Negro Citizen. *The* Clarion's *incisive documentation of Viola Desmond's arrest, jailing, and trial has been credited with the official end of segregation in Nova Scotia, in 1954. Without Best's journalism and the Nova Scotia Association for the Advancement of Coloured People, Desmond's case might have fallen into obscurity, as so many incidents of anti-Black racism had, including Best's own case against the same theatre.*

nursing and teaching – but were almost completely barred from them until the late 1950s. The Provincial Normal School, founded in 1854, did turn out its first female Black graduate in 1927–28 – Madeline Symonds (1905–96). However, most Black women taught in segregated schools on special licences that did not require studying at the Normal School. One of the first Black nurses from the Nova Scotia Hospital School of Nursing, Clotilda Yakim-chuk (1932–2021), graduated in 1957. Neither school admitted to excluding African Nova Scotians, but the segregated public education system prevented their access to prerequisite courses. This kept Black women's waged labour confined to domestic service, a tactic that Bernice Moreau refers to as "educational violence." Most of the Black women whom she interviewed in 1990–91 had attended school decades earlier, where they were not allowed to study math beyond the primary grades and could not study science at all. School segregation continued until 1954 and segregated bathrooms more than a decade longer, along with open discrimination in hiring processes, commerce, and access to housing. Halifax Municipal Council's 1960s destruction of Africville, a Black community for two centuries, and the Province's failure to resolve the land grants of Black Loyalist settlers until 2017 show the breadth and depth of anti-Black, state-sanctioned human rights violations.

Whereas Indigenous and Black residents each composed under 2 percent of every Maritime province, Acadians were a much larger ethnic minority, especially in New Brunswick where they had reached 40 percent by 1960. Nineteenth-century Acadian men had broken into the legal, medical, and political professions, and benefitted from educational opportunities and broader networks provided by the church, but Acadian women were rarely visible in public life until after the Second World War, except as teachers, nurses, and nuns. Only in 1943, through an arrangement brokered with the Religieuses de Notre-Dame du Sacré-Coeur, did Collège Saint-Joseph became the first francophone institution in New

Brunswick to admit female students to university courses, seventy years after women could attend the anglophone Mount Allison. Acadian women's paid employment was limited to domestic service, factory work, child care, retail positions, teaching, and nursing. Predominantly Catholic, they provided some of this work as nuns in Catholic schools and hospitals for minimal salaries, replicating Quebec's Catholic social services model. The socio-economic exclusion caused by the intersection of Acadian ethnicity, francophone language, rural geography, and female gender was addressed only in 1960, when Louis Robichaud (1925–2005), an assertive Liberal Acadian premier, introduced a "Program of Equal Opportunity" aimed at setting minimum targets of social, economic, and cultural opportunities for non-anglophone New Brunswickers. This turning point for Acadian rights led to a second Acadian Renaissance – this one including such women as internationally recognized author Antonine Maillet (1929–) – that synergized with second-wave feminism.

Acadian women (Acadiennes) such as Université de Moncton professor Corinne Gallant (1922–2018) and founding chair of the New Brunswick Advisory Council on the Status of Women, Madeleine Delaney-LeBlanc, led the Maritime feminist movement, with demands often exceeding those of anglophone feminists. Because so much of their oppression was economic and because women had little influence with unions, Acadian women focused on equal pay for equal work in combination with language rights. In 1968, Dames d'Acadie from Campbellton became the first local minority group on the second wave's stage. Branches expanded into Bathurst, Moncton, and Caraquet, and then formed a provincial organization (Fédération des Dames d'Acadie) that affiliated with a national group, Fédération des femmes canadiennes-françaises. Liberté, Égalité, Sororité, Femmes Acadiennes de Moncton, which grew out of a collective response to the Report of the Royal Commission on the Status of Women, concentrated on workplace gender inequality, attracting two hundred women to "New Directions for New Brunswick," a 1974 conference in Memramcook. Subsequent annual conferences organized by the New Brunswick Advisory Council on the Status of Women drew increasing numbers of French- and English-speaking New Brunswick women.

As historian Nicole Lang explains, Acadian feminists preferred a decentralized movement and specifically francophone groups because their language, which had long been threatened, was so key to their identity and culture. Anglophone feminists favoured a more centralized approach of collective action and had limited interest in minority groups. The two groups reached something of a compromise when the New Brunswick Advisory Council on the Status of Women was founded in 1977. Not only was its first president an Acadian woman (Madeleine Delaney-LeBlanc), but its government-funded council offices were located in the Moncton/Dieppe area where many Acadians lived, rather than the largely anglophone provincial capital of Fredericton.

Catholic clergy and politicians did not succeed in delaying enfranchisement in the Maritimes to the extent that they did in Quebec, where non-Indigenous women got the vote only in 1940. However, clerical opposition to suffrage in the Maritimes seems to have encouraged Acadian women's militancy in the second wave compared to their anglophone counterparts. In fact, Acadian feminists often saw anglophone women as belonging to the socio-economic status quo and therefore contributing to their economic discrimination. Even decades after New Brunswick became officially bilingual in 1969, Acadiennes still had fewer career opportunities than anglophone women.

USING THE VOTE

Had suffrage achieved women's equal participation in politics, there would have been no need for second-wave feminism. When women were enfranchised in Nova Scotia, Prince Edward Island, and Newfoundland, they were simultaneously granted the right to run for office, and New Brunswick added that right in 1934, but resistance to electing them remained high. A handful ran in early elections: Bertha Donaldson and Grace MacLeod Rogers (Nova Scotia, 1920); Helena Squires (Newfoundland, 1930); and Frances Fish (New Brunswick, 1935). Of them, only Squires was elected and only for two years. In the Maritime provinces, as much as two to four decades would elapse before a woman was elected. In Newfoundland, the election of Squires was followed by a forty-five-year gap in which no woman won a seat, a hiatus broken only by Hazel McIsaac in 1975, although no one in the dominion voted between 1934 and 1949 when Britain suspended democracy and imposed a commission government to deal with deep government debt. Federally, women became eligible for appointment to the Senate in 1929, but not until the mid-1950s did a woman from New Brunswick or Prince Edward Island sit in the Red Chamber. For Nova Scotia and Newfoundland, the wait was even longer, until 1972 and 1986, respectively. Prince Edward Island and New Brunswick did not elect a female MP until 1961 and 1964, respectively. Nova Scotia and Newfoundland did not follow suit until 1974 and 1993.

To be sure, there were some bright spots toward the end of the twentieth century. Both Nova Scotia and New Brunswick had effective long-term female party leaders: in Nova Scotia, Alexa McDonough (1944–2022) led the provincial New Democratic Party between 1980 and 1994, and federally between 1995 and 2003, whereas Elizabeth Weir (1948–) led the same party in New Brunswick from 1988 to 2004. In 1993, Prince Edward Island became the first – and still the only – Canadian province to have an all-female slate of premier, leader of the Opposition, Speaker of the House, and lieutenant governor. In 2010, Newfoundland became the first Canadian jurisdiction to have all three main political parties led by women. These advances occurred amid a commonplace reluctance to favour female legislators anywhere. For example,

- Until 1996, women never composed more than 6 percent of elected members in the Newfoundland legislature.
- Between 1967 and 1987, only four women were elected to the New Brunswick legislature.
- Before 1993, fewer than 10 percent of Nova Scotia's provincial politicians were female.
- In Prince Edward Island, a woman did not run provincially until 1951 and none was elected until 1970, putting the province in last place for both developments.

For women of colour and Indigenous women, breaking into provincial politics was far harder, just as it was in other provinces and often territories, though Nunavut and the Northwest Territories have distinctive stories to tell. In 1984, Daurene Lewis was elected as mayor of Annapolis Royal, Nova Scotia, making her the first female Black mayor in North America, but she failed to win provincially in 1988. Not until 1998 did Atlantic Canada elect an African Canadian woman provincially, Yvonne Atwell (1943–). No Indigenous woman or man has been elected to an Atlantic Canadian provincial legislature, and just one Indigenous man from the region has won a federal seat, Jamie Battiste in 2017. Female candidates have, however, made some inroads at the band level. The first elected female chiefs in Prince Edward Island, Nova Scotia, and New Brunswick were Mary Bernard, on Lennox Island in 1960; Mary Ellen Pierro, in Wagmatcook in 1962; and Margaret LaBillois, in Eel River Bar in 1971. In 2004, Lennox Island elected the region's first all-female band council.

The political gender equality advocated by many early suffragists remains elusive in the early twenty-first century. Whereas Prince Edward Island and Newfoundland have both elected female premiers, Nova Scotia and New Brunswick are among the five provinces that have yet to take this step. Still more significantly, over the course of more than a hundred elections, women

The Lennox Island Band Council in 2019. *L to r*, Off-Reserve
Councillor Mary Moore Phillips, Chief Darlene Bernard, and
On-Reserve Councillors Tabatha Bernard and Emily Bernard.
Just off the northeast coast of PEI, Lennox Island is home to
approximately 450 Mi'kmaw residents. Darlene Bernard was
re-elected chief in 2022.

have only once made up over 25 percent of the MLAs in any
Atlantic Canadian province. That miserable record is only too familiar, with women in 2021 making up just 34 percent of elected
lower house representatives nationally and 24 percent globally.
In 2022, only between 22 and 31 percent of the MLAs in the four

Atlantic Canadian legislatures were female, in contrast to Quebec and the Northwest Territories, which had the highest rate in the country – 42 and 47 percent, respectively.

Neither did the implementation of suffrage necessarily help related campaigns, such as school trustee appointments or municipal voting. It might seem logical that once women could run in provincial and federal elections and be appointed to the Senate, any controversy about their suitability as school trustees would fall away. Only in 1945, however, were two women, Helen MacDonald (1914–2005) and Dorothy Lantz (1904–94), finally appointed school trustees in Prince Edward Island. By that time, not only had the island WI spent three decades improving education, but MacDonald and Lantz had also created a School Improvement League in 1943. In the same vein, long after most provincial and federal franchises dropped property qualifications, some municipalities made it especially hard for women to qualify. Until 1966, married women who wished to run in Halifax municipal elections were required to have their own property on which they paid the tax, rather than qualifying through property held in their husband's name. Suffrage had not convinced doubters of women's capacity for leadership or the need to alter the status quo.

CONCLUSION

THE MARITIMES AND NEWFOUNDLAND had long and contentious campaigns for female enfranchisement, starting as early as
the 1830s and lasting until the 1960s, when Indigenous women
living on reserves finally got the vote. Given the early enthusiasm,
particularly in Nova Scotia, New Brunswick, and Newfoundland,
why did it take so long to pass suffrage bills? Part of the answer lies
with the first surge of activism in the 1890s and the near passing
of suffrage in the New Brunswick and Nova Scotia legislatures in
1885 and 1893, respectively. That early and unexpected support
triggered a fierce defence of the status quo. Anti-suffragists
worked all the harder to defeat the threat that had almost over-
whelmed them. Even in Prince Edward Island, where advances
were made despite less formal organization, progress stagnated
in the late 1890s. But determined opposition is only part of the
explanation. Ultimately, suffrage was the goal of only a relatively
small group of white, Protestant, mostly middle-class Maritimers
and Newfoundlanders. As years passed, many were exhausted, put
their energies elsewhere, or decided that cautious progress was
the best option. Those problems were exacerbated by inability or
disinterest – so far as the existing records show – in reaching out
to marginalized groups or indeed even to the new generation in
their own communities, with the exception of St. John's.

In Nova Scotia, activists in the Halifax branch of the Local
Council of Women (LCW) believed that caution was essential in
achieving even modest gains. Standing at the heart of provincial
agitation, they understandably feared a backlash after the colos-
sal failure of their hopes in the 1890s. At the same time, Mary

Chesley, who resided outside Halifax, was a forceful and internationally known peace activist and suffragist, the equal of the
better-known Prairie suffragists, including Violet MacNaughton
and Gertrude Richardson, who worked with her to found the Canadian chapter of the Women's International League for Peace and
Freedom. Such energy was not captured by earlier suffrage accounts, most notoriously in Catherine Cleverdon's preoccupation
with regional conservatism. Burnt once, most suffrage leaders –
excluding Chesley – turned to playing a longer game, educating
the public and improving the conditions under which women and
children lived. Activism on other fronts helped ensure that Nova
Scotia settler women fared quite well in the wider movement for
human rights. They achieved admission to universities on par
with or earlier than women in Ontario, and the married women's
property laws that applied to them always included dower law,
unlike in the West, where dower waited until the 1910s. For Nova
Scotians, perhaps more than Canadian suffragists elsewhere,
the First World War, as well as the Halifax Explosion, was key to
pushing support forward. Mary Chesley, however, set the record
straight, unconvinced of the war's necessity and refusing any
framing of the vote as a reward for war work. She insisted that
Nova Scotia women had sought the franchise "not as a gift not as a
favour, but as a debt that is somewhat overdue."

As in Nova Scotia, New Brunswick's suffrage campaign began
in the mid-nineteenth century and generally concluded in about
1920. Between 1885 and 1919, the House of Assembly debated
eight bills and four resolutions on suffrage, a period of greater
legislative activity over a longer span of time than in any other
Atlantic Canadian province. Both suffragists and their opponents mustered strength throughout these years, with less of a
two-phase suffrage movement than in Nova Scotia. The trough
between the bills of the 1890s and 1910s was shorter, and the
Saint John Women's Enfranchisement Association's exploration of
Fabian socialism between 1899 and 1903 helped secure a new

provincial factory act in 1905 and led to a broader appreciation of the work of unions. The presence of the association signalled a radicalism that is more difficult to detect in Nova Scotia. Atlantic Canada's only long-term suffrage group, the association anchored many suffragists as they lobbied politicians and circulated petitions and hosted public events, including visits from the American suffragist Julia Ward Howe and the British suffragette Sylvia Pankhurst. A core group of about ten women led the association for more than three decades, regularly creating synergies with pro-suffrage politicians. The Woman's Christian Temperance Union (WCTU) also played a highly influential role, particularly with its reach into rural communities and with petitions. In contrast, the Saint John LCW took on the cause only in 1910.

No racialized New Brunswick women were invited into the circle of suffrage leadership. In the first several decades after New Brunswick's 1785 creation, its government officials formulated separate policies for white and racialized settlers, which continued with educational segregation and grossly limited opportunities for African New Brunswickers and Indigenous peoples into the 1950s and 1960s. The fact that the Black population of New Brunswick stayed at roughly 1,200 from 1784 to 1961 speaks volumes about how the province treated racialized people. Ultimately, the suffrage movement confronted a deep well of misogyny, racism, and fear. New Brunswick's treasured investment in the conservatism that many associated with Loyalism and property crippled many efforts. The Acadian influence put a further brake on progress toward provincial suffrage. As in Quebec, the Catholic Church virulently opposed female enfranchisement. The outspokenness of Marichette suggests dissent, however, and New Brunswick's Catholic women, like some in Quebec, found outlets for feminism in the expanding work of religious orders. In any case, the province's suffragists ultimately had little reason to trust politicians of any stripe. For all the striking loyalty of some MLAs, the legislature revealed itself as a forum that women, and indeed all disadvantaged groups, had little reason to trust. Achieving full democracy was an uphill fight all the way.

The absence of a suffrage association in Prince Edward Island led historians to assume that it was apathetic concerning women's political rights, further interpreted as being due to its isolation. Needless to say, this explanation failed to recognize the bigger picture. Regardless, the stereotype persisted: until very recently, the online version of the *Canadian Encyclopedia* devoted only one sentence to PEI suffrage, considerably less than for other Atlantic Canadian provinces, and the storyboard for PEI suffrage in Calgary's Heritage Park is a grudging tribute.

Records show that suffrage was part of a long evolution of PEI women's legal and political rights. The characterization of PEI women as uninterested in politics is belied by late-nineteenth-century laws enacted to secure their rights, persistent lobbying to have them appointed as school trustees, a broader reform movement, and the work of the Liberal Women's Club, Women's Institutes, and the WCTU on enfranchisement, as well as the success of suffrage within seven years of the first Canadian province to achieve it. Any depiction of PEI in the early twentieth century as isolated and unaffected by outside influences is nonsense. Many women attended university elsewhere, many national reform and religious organizations had PEI branches, and island women were actively engaged in national and international events such as the First World War. Tantalizing evidence of individual PEI women's ties to the international suffrage movement has also surfaced. In 1900, Charlottetown resident Helen Anderson, whose mother was president of the Charlottetown LCW, attended the annual meeting of the International Council of Women in Paris. And, perhaps most significantly, returning relatives who had left during the years of high outmigration between 1870 and 1930 kept islanders in touch with causes in the United States and the rest of Canada, including in formalized "Old Home Weeks," which were first celebrated in Summerside and Charlottetown in 1904 and

1905. Increasing numbers of tourists also brought the world to the island. Islanders were well connected to regional, national, and international issues, including suffrage, even if they did not agitate as visibly as women did in other provinces.

Newfoundland had a brisk and active suffrage movement that emerged a decade later than in any of the Maritime provinces – but was edgier. Supported by an outspoken women's temperance newspaper that endorsed enfranchisement, Newfoundland achieved two respectable votes on suffrage bills during the early 1890s despite particularly mean-spirited and personal attacks on advocates. Suffrage activism did not drop off at the beginning of the century to the extent that it did in the Maritimes, and then extended longer after the war. Even the herculean efforts of the Women's Patriotic Association and the broader sacrifices made by women, including enduring a 60 percent casualty rate among their male kin, did not convince opponents that they deserved the vote. Newfoundland suffragists remained determined, however, founding a franchise league in 1920. Suffrage was won only in 1925, with a compromise that set the age requirement at five years higher than it was for male Newfoundlanders. And still, a story persisted that Newfoundland women were largely disinterested in enfranchisement and that victory owed nothing to local efforts, as one Newfoundland official claimed in 1949: "My guess is that the extension of the franchise to women in 1925 was simply a repercussion of what was happening in the United Kingdom, Canada, and the United States." Britain's implementation of commission government in Newfoundland between 1934 and 1949 and the resulting fifteen-year disenfranchisement of all men and women may have encouraged forgetfulness of the island's suffrage heroines. In any case, misogyny, the spirit that drove Richard Squires and many others, was the obvious villain.

The campaign for women's rights continued long after most women in Atlantic Canada achieved suffrage between 1918 and 1925. Patriarchy did not end. Neither did any particular kind of feminism ever become uniform. The more pervasive, forceful, and disparate second wave did not have as clear a goal or endpoint as the suffrage campaign had possessed, though 1980s and 1990s neoliberalism certainly dampened it by reducing funding to feminist and other social justice organizations and prioritizing a free-market mentality over equality. Meanwhile, women's representation at all levels of politics lagged behind that of men, and not all elected women were feminists. Atlantic Canada's highly popular Elsie Wayne (1932–2016), mayor of Saint John from 1983 to 1993 and MP from 1993 to 2004, perplexed many in the same way that the iconic Margaret Thatcher did: both were politically and fiscally conservative anti-feminists who refused to acknowledge that the personal was political or that their own political influence was produced by decades of hard work on the part of female activists. Dissatisfied with the second wave's failure to appreciate multiple layers of oppression or gender fluidity, young feminists generated a third wave in the 1990s. A fourth wave, which began in the 2010s, continues to emphasize and tackles issues such as rape culture, often through online activism.

In Atlantic Canada and elsewhere, the threads of what suffragists fought for in the late nineteenth century were pulled through all these waves and remain evident today, including in women's campaigns for greater participation in public life; the end of intimate partner violence; improvements to matrimonial property laws (especially for female farmers); safe and fair employment practices; food security; and access to education, health care, child care, and the professions. At the same time, the shortcomings of early suffragists remain obstacles to an inclusive and cohesive feminist movement, including too little concern for Indigenous and racialized women, most obvious in the missing and murdered Indigenous women and girls crisis, the Black Lives Matter movement, and the failure to adequately address poverty and homelessness. Atlantic Canadian grassroots organizations such as the Nova Scotia Native Women's Association, Women's

Equality PEI, the Single Parent Association of Newfoundland, and New Brunswick's Avenue B Harm Reduction Sex Trade Action Committee are just a few examples of the hundreds of groups currently campaigning for women and gender rights. Other groups, such as the LCW and the Voice of Women, continued since the first and second waves, respectively. Frustration over women's low rates of political representation is addressed in related provincial organizations: Newfoundland and Labrador Equal Voice, Nova Scotia Equal Voice, Women for 50% (New Brunswick), and the PEI Coalition for Women in Government.

More research is needed to understand late-nineteenth- and early-twentieth-century political power and agency outside the white, heteronormative, middle-class experience, for BIPOC (Black, Indigenous, people of colour) women and LGBTQIA2S+ (lesbian, gay, bisexual, trans, queer, intersex, asexual, two-spirited, "plus") people. Likewise, understanding intergenerational activism, including that of daughters of Atlantic Canadian suffragists, could further address the conservative stereotype that haunts the Atlantic provinces, especially given the tantalizing instances of mother-daughter activism. Examples here include Nova Scotia's Mary and Polly Chesley, New Brunswick's Ella and Grace Hatheway, and PEI's Catherine and Helen Anderson. Further research is needed on the motivation for obtaining early women's property rights, especially the degree to which women themselves advocated for them, compared to how much male relatives wished to safeguard the property holdings of wealthy families. Reading against the grain of WCTU and Women's Institutes histories suggests they both served as proxies of women's enfranchisement associations in small communities. More analysis of women's informal political activities in smaller communities could test whether these avenues reduced the need for separate reform and pressure groups.

The enfranchisement campaign ties directly to women's rights issues today. Without suffrage, both as a symbol of citizenship and an actual tool, women could not have made the progress toward equality that they have. Progress remains incomplete, however, as doubters still claim that women lack the capacity for political leadership. The long view of women's rights, as presented in *We Shall Persist*, suggests the incremental nature of progress and the likelihood that we will continue to take two steps forward, one step back.

ACKNOWLEDGMENTS

MANY THANKS TO VERONICA STRONG-BOAG for concep-
tualizing this series and guiding me through every step. I benefitted from the other authors in the series (Denyse Baillargeon,
Tarah Brookfield, Lara Campbell, Sarah Carter, and Joan Sangster),
who inspired and paved the way for me. I am deeply grateful to
Gail Campbell for so generously sharing her vast knowledge of
Atlantic Canadian history – especially on gender and politics –
through the many drafts of this book. The two anonymous peer
reviewers offered dozens of thoughtful comments, suggestions,
and clarifications that strengthened the text and reassured me.
I owe much to the following colleagues and friends at the University of Lethbridge and the University of New Brunswick for
their feedback and encouragement: Lisa Best, Lisa Howard,
Joanna Everitt, Jan Newberry, Janay Nugent, Charlene Shannon-
McCallum, Brian Titley, and Carol Williams. A University of
Lethbridge Research Fund award allowed me to travel to thirteen
different archives in five provinces to complete the research. (In
"Sources and Further Reading," I've named the archivists who
went out of their way in sharing their expertise and collections.) A
University of Lethbridge Chinook Student Research Grant al-
lowed me to hire Carey Viejou to complete detailed newspaper research. Funding from the Vice President's Office at University of
New Brunswick Saint John facilitated hiring two topnotch editors,
Rachel Robinson and Kate Merriman. It was a pleasure to work
with UBC Press, including senior acquisitions editor Darcy Cullen,
copy editor Deborah Kerr, and cover designer Jessica Sullivan.

I thank Andrew Horne for his love and fortitude while living through the long research and writing process with me, as well as my sisters Bethany and Jill for their care and support.

We Shall Persist is dedicated to my parents, Adrienne Ruth Webb MacDonald and Stanley Williams MacDonald, who have encouraged me in pretty much everything I have done.

SOURCES AND
FURTHER READING

INTRODUCTION

The most valuable recently published overviews of women's suffrage in Canada are Joan Sangster, *One Hundred Years of Struggle: The History of Women and the Vote in Canada* (Vancouver: UBC Press, 2018); a two-volume collection of primary documents: Maureen Moynagh and Nancy Forestell, eds., *Documenting First Wave Feminisms*, vol. 1, *Transnational Collaborations and Crosscurrents* (Toronto: University of Toronto Press, 2012); and Nancy M. Forestell and Maureen Moynagh, eds., *Documenting First Wave Feminisms*, vol. 2, *Canada – National and Transnational Contexts* (Toronto: University of Toronto Press, 2014).

The only summary of suffrage in Atlantic Canada before *We Shall Persist* is a chapter in Catherine L. Cleverdon, *The Woman Suffrage Movement in Canada* (Toronto: University of Toronto Press, 1950), 156–213, which accepts the stereotype of regional conservatism, an issue raised in E.R. Forbes, "Introduction," in *Challenging the Regional Stereotype: Essays on the 20th Century Maritimes* (Fredericton: Acadiensis Press, 1989), 7–12. Forbes also critiqued Carol Lee Bacchi, *Liberation Deferred? The Ideas of the English-Canadian Suffragists, 1877–1918* (Toronto: University of Toronto Press, 1989), in Ernest Forbes, "The Ideas of Carol Bacchi and the Suffragists of Halifax: A Review Essay on *Liberation Deferred? The Ideas of the English Canadian Suffragists, 1877–1918*," *Atlantis* 10, 2 (1985): 119–26. Frank MacKinnon, a contemporary of Cleverdon, also embraced the stereotype of Atlantic Canadian disinterest in his *The Government of Prince Edward Island*, Canadian Government Series (Toronto: University Toronto Press, 1951). More recently, the work of some historians and political scientists has perpetuated the stereotype, including Sylvia Bashevkin, *Toeing the Lines: Women and Party Politics in English Canada* (Toronto: University of Toronto Press, 1993); and a recently removed entry in the *Canadian Encyclopedia*: "Suffrage in the Atlantic Provinces and Québec."

In contrast, political scientists Brenda O'Neill and Lynda Erickson engaged 1990s public opinion and voting data to argue that Atlantic Canadian attitudes to female equality differed little from the national average: Brenda O'Neill and Lynda Erickson, "Evaluating Traditionalism in the Atlantic Provinces: Voting, Public Opinion and the Electoral Project," *Atlantis* 27, 2 (Spring 2003): 113–22. Margaret Conrad makes a related argument, claiming that there has been far too little research and attention paid to the Atlantic region: Margaret Conrad,

"'Nothing, of Course, Ever Happens Down There': Atlantic Canada in the National Consciousness," *Canadian Issues/Thèmes canadiens* (Fall 2014): 33–37. This is certainly the case with the historiography (body of published research) of suffrage in the Atlantic region, with a few notable exceptions, including studies published several years ago for Newfoundland and New Brunswick: Margot Duley, *Where Once Our Mothers Stood We Stand: Women's Suffrage in Newfoundland, 1890–1925* (Charlottetown: Gynergy Books, 1993) and Elspeth Tulloch, *We, the Undersigned: A Historical Overview of New Brunswick Women's Political and Legal Status, 1784–1984* (Moncton: New Brunswick Advisory Council on the Status of Women, 1985). Although no comparable investigations exist for PEI or Nova Scotia, important shorter treatments help fill in the picture, including nearly twenty biographies in the *Dictionary of Canadian Biography* and the *Encyclopedia of Newfoundland and Labrador;* articles in the *Canadian Encyclopedia;* and Nova Scotia Legislature, "History of Voting in Nova Scotia," https://nslegislature.ca/about/history/history -voting-nova-scotia.

My response to the shortfall of written histories was to exercise the basic tools of the historian. This task took me to more than a dozen archives across Atlantic Canada, as well as to decades of feminist scholarship, which sharpened my sensitivity to gender differences and intersectional identities. Primary evidence from contemporary newspapers, statutes, government records, minutes of suffrage and social reform groups, memoirs, and biographies appears in each chapter. *We Shall Persist* has also profited from "detective work" made possible by recently digitized sources, such as those found at Ancestry, https://ancestry.ca. Genealogical records are not new, but digitization reduces searches to hours rather than months and extends investigations beyond metropolitan centres and to earlier decades. I have also drawn on unpublished doctoral and master's theses and benefitted from the insights of established (and generous!) scholars, most notably University of New Brunswick professor emerita Gail Campbell and the editor of this series, Veronica Strong-Boag.

Sadly, suffrage leaders generally left fewer records than their opponents, and the less prominent participants – those whose support was limited to attending meetings or signing petitions but who never held executive positions – have left almost no trace. Even data on prominent pro- or anti-suffrage politicians remain scarce. Glaring omissions exist in the record of what motivated major male political supporters, such as Angus McKenzie of Charlottetown or Albert Hemeon of Liverpool. We can only speculate about how the women in their lives may have fostered their sympathy for suffrage, or, more cynically, whether they thought endorsement would garner them female votes.

Historians are handicapped by the ready reliance, particularly in smaller communities, on face-to-face communication and family networks rather than on formal correspondence. Especially in PEI, the suffrage campaign left frustratingly few records. Their absence has sometimes been attributed to local indifference, but that dismissal does not fit with islanders' ongoing enthusiasm for all things political. As someone who was born in PEI, I find it hard to believe that the same people who used pitchforks to protest nineteenth-century absentee landlords, fought a lengthy campaign over abortion services, and regularly reported the highest voter turnout rates in the country stood on the suffrage sidelines! The paucity of information owes more to record keeping than interest. Non-British or non-English-speaking minorities are especially poorly represented. The exceptions of New Brunswick Acadian Émilie LeBlanc (1863–1935), who endorsed suffrage under the pen name Marichette in the 1890s, and the African Nova Scotian Louisa Johnson (?–1911), a Halifax businesswoman, philanthropist, and women's rights advocate, suggest that enthusiasm surfaced beyond the mainstream. See Pierre Gérin, "Une écrivaine acadienne à la fin du XIXe siècle: Marichette," *Atlantis* 10, 1 (1984): 38–45; and Judith Fingard, "Johnson, Louisa Ann," *Dictionary of Canadian Biography*, vol. 14, University of Toronto/Université Laval, 2003–. Although the role of Indigenous women in suffrage efforts remains invisible, their subsequent demands for justice under the Indian Act, which is discussed in this book's final chapter, offer repeated evidence of their capacity for activism. Women who were marginalized by the mainstream developed their own agendas, often focused on survival, and their attitudes toward enfranchisement have not been well preserved.

Other sources for this chapter not already mentioned are Gaynor Rowe, "The Woman Suffrage Movement in Newfoundland" (paper, JL 559/R6/1973, Centre for Newfoundland Studies, Memorial University of Newfoundland, 1973; Terry Bishop, "The Newfoundland Struggle for the Women's Franchise" (submitted to James Hiller, HIST 3120, 10 December 1981), JF848.B58., Centre for Newfoundland Studies, Memorial University of Newfoundland, 1981), and Heritage Park Calgary, "Famous 5 Centre of Canadian Women," https://www.heritagepark.ca/plan-your-visit/attractions-and-exhibits/famous-5-centre-of-canadian-women.

Pages   **"Nowhere has the traditional"**: Catherine L. Cleverdon, *The Woman*
2–3   *Suffrage Movement in Canada,* 2nd ed. (Toronto: University of Toronto
             Press, 1974), 156 (emphasis added).

Page 3   **"Slow to develop"**: in Bashevkin, *Toeing the Lines,* 6.

ONE: SUFFRAGE CONTEXTS AND CHALLENGES IN THE MARITIMES AND NEWFOUNDLAND

I have depended on the best social, political, and economic histories of the Atlantic region: E.R. Forbes and D.A. Muise, eds., *The Atlantic Provinces in Confederation* (Toronto: University of Toronto Press, 1993); Phillip Buckner and John G. Reid, eds., *The Atlantic Region to Confederation: A History* (Toronto: University of Toronto Press, 1995); and Margaret Conrad and James K. Hiller, *Atlantic Canada: A History* (Don

Mills: Oxford University Press, 2010). I also benefitted from excellent monographs
on Nova Scotia, Newfoundland, and PEI: Margaret Conrad, *At the Ocean's Edge: A
History of Nova Scotia to Confederation* (Toronto: University of Toronto Press, 2020);
Sean T. Cadigan, *Newfoundland and Labrador: A History* (Toronto: University of
Toronto Press, 2009); Edward MacDonald, *If You're Strong Hearted: Prince Edward
Island in the Twentieth Century* (Charlottetown: Prince Edward Island Museum and
Heritage Foundation, 2000); and Andrew Hill Clark, *Three Centuries and the Island:
A Historical Geography of Settlement and Agriculture in Prince Edward Island, Canada*
(Toronto: University of Toronto Press, 1959). As there is no recent monograph on
New Brunswick, T.W. Acheson, *Saint John: The Making of a Colonial Urban Community*
(Toronto: University of Toronto Press, 1985), was indispensable. These regional
and provincial histories provided the basis for many of the ideas in this chapter,
supplemented by sources below on specific topics. For dozens more secondary
sources on each Atlantic Canadian province, see the sections for Chapters 2, 3, 4,
and 5 below.

For suffrage, see Catherine L. Cleverdon, *The Woman Suffrage Movement in Canada*
(Toronto: University of Toronto Press, 1950); Margot Duley, *Where Once Our Mothers
Stood We Stand: Women's Suffrage in Newfoundland, 1890–1925* (Charlottetown:
Gynergy Books, 1993); Elspeth Tulloch, *We, the Undersigned: A Historical Overview
of New Brunswick Women's Political and Legal Status, 1784–1984* (Moncton: New
Brunswick Advisory Council on the Status of Women, 1985); Gaynor Rowe, "The
Woman Suffrage Movement in Newfoundland" (paper, Centre for Newfoundland
Studies, Memorial University of Newfoundland, 1973), JL 559/R6/1973; Pierre
Gérin, "Une écrivaine acadienne à la fin du XIXe siècle: Marichette," *Atlantis* 10, 1
(1984): 38–45; and Lois K. Yorke, "Edwards, Anna Harriette," *Dictionary of Canadian
Biography*, vol. 14, University of Toronto/Université Laval, 2003–, http://www.
biographi.ca/en/bio/edwards_anna_harriette_14E.html.

On the relevance of religion to Atlantic Canada, women, and suffrage, see D.G. Bell,
"Allowed Irregularities: Women Preachers in the Early 19th-Century Maritimes,"
Acadiensis 30, 2 (2001): 3–39; Elizabeth Muir and Marilyn Färdig Whiteley, eds.,
Changing Roles of Women within the Christian Church in Canada (Toronto: University
of Toronto Press, 1995), especially the "Introduction," 3–16, the chapter by
Elizabeth Muir, "Beyond the Bounds of Acceptable Behaviour: Methodist Women
Preachers in the Early Nineteenth Century," 161–82, and the chapter by Miriam
H. Ross, "Sharing a Vision: Maritime Baptist Women Educate for Mission, 1871–
1920," 77–98; George Edward Levy, *The Baptists of the Maritime Provinces, 1753–
1946* (Saint John: Barnes Hopkins, 1946); Nancy Christie and Michael Gauvreau,
Christian Churches and Their Peoples, 1840–1965: A Social History of Religion in Canada
(Toronto: University of Toronto Press, 2010); and E.C. Merrick, *These Impossible
Women: 100 Years, the Story of the United Baptist Woman's Missionary Union of the
Maritime Provinces* (Fredericton: Brunswick Press, 1970).

For the material on Indigenous peoples, I supplemented previously mentioned monographs with Judith Fingard, "The New England Company and the New Brunswick Indians, 1782–1826: A Comment on the Colonial Perversion of British Benevolence," *Acadiensis* 1, 2 (Spring 1972): 29–42; and "Indian Population," in "Report of the Special Committee of the House of Commons, 1857," https:// www150.statcan.gc.ca/n1/pub/98-187-x/4151278-eng.htm#part4.

For African Maritime history, I depended on the above monographs (especially Margaret Conrad's *At the Ocean's Edge*), as well as Harvey Amani Whitfield, "African and New World African Immigration to Mainland Nova Scotia, 1749–1816," *Journal of the Royal Nova Scotia Historical Society* 7 (2004): 102–11; Harvey Amani Whitfield, "Black Refugee Communities in Early Nineteenth Century Nova Scotia," *Journal of the Royal Nova Scotia Historical Society* 6 (2003): 92–109; Sylvia Hamilton, "Naming Names, Naming Ourselves: A Survey of Early Black Women in Nova Scotia," in *We're Rooted Here and They Can't Pull Us Up: Essays in African Canadian Women's History,* ed. Peggy Bristow (Toronto: University of Toronto Press, 1994), 13–40; W.A. Spray, *The Blacks in New Brunswick* (1972; repr., Fredericton: St. Thomas University, 2021); David Este and Wanda Thomas Bernard, "Spirituality among African Nova Scotians," *Critical Social Work* 7 (2019); Bernice Moreau, "Black Nova Scotian Women's Experience of Educational Violence in the Early 1900s: A Case of Colour Contusion," *Dalhousie Review* 77, 2 (1997): 179–206; Suzanne Morton, "Separate Spheres in a Separate World: African-Nova Scotian Women in Late-19th-Century Halifax County," in *Separate Spheres: Women's Worlds in the 19th-Century Maritimes,* ed. Janet Guildford and Suzanne Morton (Fredericton: Acadiensis, 1994), 185–210; Ken Donovan, "Female Slaves as Sexual Victims in Île Royale," *Acadiensis* 43, 1 (2014): 147–56; David A. Sutherland, "Race Relations in Halifax, Nova Scotia, during the Mid-Victorian Quest for Reform," *Journal of the Canadian Historical Association* 7, 1 (1996): 39–53; "Looking Back, Moving Forward: Documenting the Heritage of African Nova Scotians," *Nova Scotia Archives,* https://archives.novascotia.ca/african -heritage/settlement/; "Edith Hester Macdonald-Brown," *Her Art Story: Homage to Female Artists,* http://www.herartstory.com/edith-hester-macdonald-brown/; Judith Fingard, "Johnson, Louisa Ann," *Dictionary of Canadian Biography,* vol. 14, University of Toronto/Université Laval, 2003–; and "1906 Expanding History," https://150ans1500euvres.uqam.ca/en/artwork/1906-untitled-by-edith-hester -macdonald-brown/#description.

For the argument on women's worthiness as voters, see Shirley Tillotson, "Relations of Extraction: Taxation and Women's Citizenship in the Maritimes, 1914–1955," *Acadiensis* 39, 1 (Winter-Spring 2010): 27–57. On women as voters and politicians, see Jane Arscott, Manon Tremblay, and Linda Trimble, eds., *Stalled: The Representation of Women in Canadian Governments* (Vancouver: UBC Press, 2013); Sylvia Bashevkin, *Toeing the Lines: Women and Party Politics in English Canada* (Toronto: University of Toronto Press, 1993); Amanda Bittner, "Why Can't We Have

Parent-Friendly Parliaments?" *Policy Options,* 4 March 2019, https://policy
options.irpp.org/magazines/march-2019/why-cant-we-have-parent-friendly
-parliaments/; Louise Carbert, *Rural Women's Leadership in Atlantic Canada: First-
Hand Perspectives on Local Public Life and Participation in Electoral Politics* (Toronto:
University of Toronto Press, 2005); Brenda O'Neill and Lynda Erickson, "Evaluating
Traditionalism in the Atlantic Provinces: Voting, Public Opinion and the Electoral
Project," *Atlantis* 27, 2 (Spring 2003): 113–22; Margaret Conrad, "Remembering
Firsts," in *Making Up the State: Women in 20th Century Atlantic Canada,* ed. Janet
Guildford and Suzanne Morton (Fredericton: Acadiensis Press, 2010), 57–77;
Joanna Everitt, "Gender and Sexual Diversity in Provincial Election Campaigns,"
Canadian Political Science Review 9, 1 (2015): 177–92; Richard E. Matland and Donley
T. Studlar, "Gender and the Electoral Opportunity Structure in the Canadian
Provinces," *Political Research Quarterly* 51, 1 (March 1998): 117–40; "Women in
Canadian Provincial and Territorial Legislatures," *Wikipedia,* https://en.wikipedia.
org/wiki/Women_in_Canadian_provincial_and_territorial_legislatures; and
"Daurene Lewis (1943–2013)," *Dancing Backwards: Her Story Archive,* https://www.
dancingbackwards.ca/biographies-of-canadian-women-politicians/item/
daurene-lewis.

Other sources for this chapter not already mentioned are Heritage Park Calgary,
"Famous 5 Centre of Canadian Women," https://www.heritagepark.ca/plan-your
-visit/attractions-and-exhibits/famous-5-centre-of-canadian-women; "Local
Legislators Hear Delegation of Women in Favour of Suffrage Bill," *Halifax Chronicle,*
12 April 1917; Frank MacKinnon, *The Government of Prince Edward Island: Canadian
Government Series* (Toronto: University of Toronto Press, 1951); and Kenneth Norrie
and Douglas Owram, *A History of the Canadian Economy,* 2nd ed. (Toronto: Harcourt
Brace, 1996).

Page 6   **"With due gratitude":** M.R. Chesley to the editor, *Halifax Herald,* 23
           March 1895.

Page 9   **"Circle of ideas":** Joan Sangster, *One Hundred Years of Struggle: The History
           of Women and the Vote in Canada* (Vancouver: UBC Press, 2018), 8.

Page 15   **"Devoted to the interests":** Susanna McLeod, "Carrie Best," *Canadian
           Encyclopedia,* https://www.thecanadianencyclopedia.ca/en/article/
           carrie-best.

Page 15   **"Black women in North America":** Moreau, "Black Nova Scotian
           Women's Experience," 180–81.

TWO: NOVA SCOTIA

Although I disagree with her argument, Catherine Cleverdon's footnotes and
research notes were useful for leading me to other relevant sources: Catherine
L. Cleverdon, *The Woman Suffrage Movement in Canada* (Toronto: University of

SOURCES AND FURTHER READING   215

Toronto Press, 1950); and Catherine Lyle Cleverdon fonds, R2292-0-7-E, box 1, Library and Archives Canada. Until *We Shall Persist,* no published research other than Cleverdon's described the broad Nova Scotia suffrage movement, but there are many important studies of particular Nova Scotia suffragists and their related organizations. See Sharon M.H. MacDonald, "A Passionate Voice for Equality, Justice, and Peace: Nova Scotia's Mary Russell Chesley," in *Making Up the State: Women in 20th Century Atlantic Canada,* ed. Janet Guildford and Suzanne Morton (Fredericton: Acadiensis Press, 2010), 45–55; Judith Fingard, "The Ritchie Sisters and Social Improvement in Early 20th Century Halifax," *Journal of the Royal Nova Scotia Historical Society* 13 (2010): 1–22; Judith Fingard, "Ritchie, Eliza," *Dictionary of Canadian Biography,* vol. 16, University of Toronto/Université Laval, 2003–, http://www.biographi.ca/en/bio/ritchie_eliza_16E.html; Lois K. Yorke, "Edwards, Anna Harriette," *Dictionary of Canadian Biography,* vol. 14, University of Toronto/ Université Laval, 2003–, http://www.biographi.ca/en/bio/edwards_anna_harriette_14E.html; Janet Guildford, "Edith Jessie Archibald: Ardent Feminist and Conservative Reformer," *Journal of the Royal Nova Scotia Historical Society* 11 (2008): 110–33; "Archibald, Edith Jessie National Historic Person," Parks Canada, https://www.pc.gc.ca/apps/dfhd/page_nhs_eng.aspx?id=1822; Ernest R. Forbes, "Battles in Another War: Edith Archibald and the Halifax Feminist Movement," in *Challenging the Regional Stereotype: Essays on the 20th Century Maritimes,* ed E.R. Forbes (Fredericton: Acadiensis Press, 1989), 67–89; and Heidi MacDonald, "Archibald, Edith," *Dictionary of Canadian Biography* (forthcoming). I found additional biographical information on the suffragists at a database of Canadian censuses offered through Ancestry.ca, "Canadian Census Collection," *Ancestry.ca,* https://www.ancestry.ca/search/categories/canadiancensus/.

On the socio-economic, religious, ethnic, racial, and political contexts of late-nineteenth- and twentieth-century Nova Scotia, I used Phillip Buckner and John G. Reid, eds., *The Atlantic Region to Confederation: A History* (Toronto: University of Toronto Press, 1995); E.R. Forbes and D.A. Muise, eds., *The Atlantic Provinces in Confederation* (Toronto: University of Toronto Press, 1993); Margaret Conrad, *At the Ocean's Edge: A History of Nova Scotia to Confederation* (Toronto: University of Toronto Press, 2020); Patricia A. Thornton, "The Problem of Out-Migration from Atlantic Canada, 1871–1921: A New Look," *Acadiensis* 15, 1 (Autumn 1985): 3–34; Betsy Beattie, *Obligation and Opportunity: Single Maritime Women in Boston, 1870–1930* (Montreal and Kingston: McGill-Queen's University Press, 2000); and Judith Fingard, Janet Vey Guildford, and David Sutherland, *Halifax: The First 250 Years* (Halifax: Formac, 1999).

For evolving franchise requirements and examples of women's early voting, see *Legislative Assembly Election Writs,* 1793, RG 5, Series E, vol. 2, Nova Scotia Archives (many thanks to archivist John MacLeod); *Debates and Proceedings of the Nova Scotia House of Assembly,* 20 November 1806, 8–9; Brian Cuthbertson, *Johnny Bluenose at the Polls: Epic Nova Scotian Election Battles, 1758–1848* (Halifax: Formac, 1994);

Joseph Howe, "A 'Petticoat Government,'" Editorial, *Nova Scotian*, 29 July 1834; and John Garner, *The Franchise and Politics in British North America, 1755–1867* (Toronto: University of Toronto Press, 1969). For women's legal status, see Philip Girard and Rebecca Veinott, "Married Women's Property Law in Nova Scotia, 1850–1910," in *Separate Spheres: Women's Worlds in the 19th-Century Maritimes*, ed. Janet Guildford and Suzanne Morton (Fredericton: Acadiensis Press, 1994), 67–91; and George L. Haskins, "The Development of Common Law Dower," *Harvard Law Review* 62, 1 (November 1948): 42–55.

On Baptist and Wesleyan women's organizations, see *Window on the Past: The Story of the Halifax Wesleyan Female Missionary Society*, 3–5, MC 1, no. 706, Nova Scotia Archives; E.C. Merrick, *These Impossible Women: 100 Years, the Story of the United Baptist Woman's Missionary Union of the Maritime Provinces* (Fredericton: Brunswick Press, 1970); and George Edward Levy, *The Baptists of the Maritime Provinces, 1753–1946* (Saint John: Barnes Hopkins, 1946).

On the two main organizations that supported suffrage, the Halifax Local Council of Women and the Nova Scotia Woman's Christian Temperance Union (and their affiliate branches and departments), see Joanne Veer, "Feminist Forebears: The Woman's Christian Temperance Union in Canada's Maritime Provinces, 1875–1900" (PhD diss., University of New Brunswick, 1995); Tanya Gogan, "The WCTU's Contribution to the Woman's Suffrage Movement in Nova Scotia," *Dalhousie Undergraduate History Society Academic Journal* 3 (1992): 55–64; and "Woman's Christian Temperance Union, Hantsport, Nova Scotia Petition for the Enfranchisement of Women (1878)," in *Documenting First Wave Feminisms*, vol. 2, *Canada – National and Transnational Contexts*, ed. Nancy M. Forestell and Maureen Moynagh (Toronto: University of Toronto Press, 2014), 119; Reports of the Department of Franchise, Woman's Christian Temperance Union, 1910–1918, WCTU Records, MG 20, vol. 356, Nova Scotia Archives; "Public Support of WCTU Hiram MacKay, Letter to Editor," *Halifax Chronicle*, 29 September 1917; N.E.S. Griffiths, *The Splendid Vision: Centennial History of the National Council of Women of Canada, 1893–1993* (Ottawa: Carleton University Press, 1993), 58, 112; Halifax Local Council of Women, Minute Book and Scrapbook, 13 December 1894–1920, MG 20, vol. 535, no. 1, Nova Scotia Archives; Guildford, "Edith Jessie Archibald," 110–33; also see Janet Guildford's *The Magnificent Services of Women: The Halifax Local Council of Women, 1894–2002* (Halifax: Halifax Local Council of Women, 2002); and Janet Guildford, "The Local Council of Women of Halifax: The First Two Decades, 1894–1914," *Historic Nova Scotia*, https://historicnovascotia.ca/items/show/69. On Halifax women's contributions to the First World War, see Forbes, "Battles in Another War," 67–89.

On the media coverage of the advances and setbacks in the suffrage movement, see "Local Council of Women and Woman Suffrage," *Halifax Chronicle*, 1 March 1917; "The Social Service Congress Asks for Votes for Women," *Halifax Herald*, 27 January 1917; "Wolfville Favors Woman's Suffrage," *Halifax Chronicle*, 16 March 1917;

"Suffrage Bill Introduced in the Legislature," *Halifax Chronicle*, 15 March 1917; "Disappointment in the Gallery of the Assembly," *Halifax Chronicle*, 21 March 1917; "Local Legislators Hear Delegation of Women in Favour of Suffrage Bill," *Halifax Chronicle*, 12 April 1917; "Votes for Women Bill Got the Three Months Hoist in Legislature Yesterday Afternoon," *Halifax Chronicle*, 24 April 1917; "Principle of Womanhood Suffrage Affirmed but the Present Bill Rejected in the Real Interest of the Public," *Halifax Chronicle*, 28 April 1917; "Dr. Eliza Ritchie Replies to W.E. MacLellan on the Womanhood Suffrage Question," *Halifax Chronicle*, 2 May 1917; W.E. MacLellan, "Principle of Womanhood Suffrage Affirmed," *Halifax Chronicle*, 28 April 1917; and "Well Known Halifax Woman [Ella Murray] Dies," *Halifax Chronicle Herald*, 1 August 1949.

I depended heavily on transcripts of the suffrage debates in the House of Assembly, suffrage petitions to the House, and bills related to women's rights and suffrage: *Debates and Proceedings of the Nova Scotia House of Assembly*, 1806–1919; *Legislative Assembly Election Writs*, 1793, Nova Scotia Archives; Nova Scotia House of Assembly Petitions, RG 5, Series P, vol. 22, no. 6a, Nova Scotia Archives, https://novascotia.ca/archives/suffrage/archives.asp?ID=10; *An Act for the Protection of Married Women in Certain Cases*, 1866, c. 33; *An Act to Confer upon Female Ratepayers the Right to Vote at Civic and Municipal Elections*, Nova Scotia Statutes, 1887, c. 27; *An Act Respecting the Property of Married Women*, Nova Scotia Statutes, 1887, c. 19; *An Act to Amend and Consolidate the Acts in Respect to the Electoral Franchise*, 26 April 1918, c. 2.

On African Nova Scotian women leaders, see Bridglal Pachai and Henry Bishop, *Historic Black Nova Scotia: Images of Our Past* (Halifax: Nimbus, 2006), 120; "Our History," *African United Baptist Association of Nova Scotia*, https://www.aubans.ca/web/about-us/history/; Judith Fingard, "Johnson, Louisa Ann," *Dictionary of Canadian Biography*, vol. 14, University of Toronto/Université Laval, 2003–, http://www.biographi.ca/en/bio/johnson_louisa_ann_14E.html; and "Maude Sparks" (Halifax), 1911 and 1921 Census of Canada, *Ancestry.ca*, "Canadian Census Collection." On long-standing issues of African Nova Scotians' land grants, see David A. Sutherland, "Race Relations in Halifax, Nova Scotia, during the Mid-Victorian Quest for Reform," *Journal of the Canadian Historical Association* 7, 1 (1996): 35–54; and Jean Laroche, "Proposed N.S. Law Aims to Make It Easier for Black Families to Get Land Titles," *CBC News*, 23 March 2021, https://www.cbc.ca/news/canada/nova-scotia/land-titles-black-communities-bill-ns-legislature-1.5960589.

On women's admission to higher education, see Margaret Conrad, Elizabeth Rice, and Patricia Townsend, eds., *Women at Acadia University: The First 50 Years, 1884–1934* (Kentville: Acadia University, 1984); Jennifer Harris, "'Ushered into the Kitchen': Lalia Halfkenny, Instructor of English and Elocution at a 19th-Century African American Women's College," *Acadiensis* 41, 2 (2012): 45–65; Tori Weldon, "Lalia Halfkenny: An Important History Almost Lost to Time," *CBC News*, 25

February 2021, https://www.cbc.ca/news/canada/new-brunswick/lalia-halfkenny
-first-black-woman-higher-learning-1.5926008; P.B. Waite, *The Lives of Dalhousie
University,* vol. 1, *1818–1925* (Montreal and Kingston: McGill-Queen's University
Press, 1994); Judith Fingard, "College, Career, and Community: Dalhousie Coeds,
1881–1921," in *Youth, University and Canadian Society: Essays in the Social History
of Higher Education,* ed. Paul Axelrod and John G. Reid (Montreal and Kingston:
McGill-Queen's University Press, 1989), 26–50; L.M. Montgomery, "A Girl's Place
at Dalhousie College, 1896," *Atlantis* 5, 1 (1979): 146–53; James D. Cameron, *For the
People: A History of St. Francis Xavier University* (Montreal and Kingston: McGill-
Queen's University Press, 2014); Margaret MacDonell, *Mount Saint Bernard College,
Antigonish, 1897–1947* (Montreal: Congregation of Notre Dame, 1998); and Theresa
Corcoran, *Mount Saint Vincent University: A Vision Unfolding, 1873–1988* (Lanham,
MD: University Press of America, 1999).

On Nova Scotia's first female physician and lawyer, see "Med Corner," *Dalhousie
Gazette,* 3 February 1953, http://dalgazette.com/opinions/from-the-archives-4/;
Lois Kernaghan, "Angwin, Maria Louisa," *Dictionary of Canadian Biography,* vol. 12,
University of Toronto/Université Laval, 2003–, http://www.biographi.ca/en/bio/
angwin_maria_louisa_12E.html; and Barry Cahill, "Frances Lilian Fish: An
Enduring Mystery: Why Nova Scotia's First Woman Lawyer Abandoned the Legal
Profession," *Nova Scotia Barristers' Society,* http://nsbs.org/frances-lilian-fish (page
removed by 11 February 2022).

Other diverse sources for this chapter include "Mary Russell Chesley," in James
Morgan, *The Canadian Men and Women of the Time* (Toronto: William Briggs, 1898);
"Ella May Murray," 1921 Census of Canada, *Ancestry.ca,*https://www.ancestry.ca/
discoveryui-content/view/8111632:8991?tid=&pid=&queryId=d00e2419db8aba
8ad04300406a5bf344&_phsrc=aHe10&_phstart=successSource; Ella Murray to
Catherine Cleverdon, 19 April 1943, Cleverdon fonds; Shirley Tillotson, *Give and
Take: The Citizen-Taxpayer and the Rise of Canadian Democracy* (Vancouver: UBC
Press, 2017), 57; Antoinette Burton, *Burdens of History: British Feminists, Indian
Women, and Imperial Culture, 1865–1915* (Chapel Hill: University of North Carolina
Press, 1994); "History," *Women's International League for Peace and Freedom,* https://
www.wilpf.org/who-we-are/; and Heidi MacDonald, "Maritime Women, the Great
Depression, and the Dominion-Provincial Youth Training Program, 1937–39," in
Guildford and Morton, *Making Up the State,* 131–49.

I would also like to thank archivists Patti Bannister and John MacLeod of the
Nova Scotia Archives, librarian Anne Valderstine of the Nova Scotia Legislative
Library, and freelance historian Sharon MacDonald.

Page 20   **"All women are not":** Mary Fletcher, "Local Legislators Hear Delegation
of Women in Favour of Suffrage Bill," *Halifax Chronicle,* 12 April 1917.

Page 22   **"Scathing attack" ... "With due gratitude":** M.R. Chesley to the editor,
Halifax Herald, 23 March 1895.

Page 23   **"Good if women"**: *Legislative Assembly Election Writs*, 1793, Nova Scotia Archives.

Page 23   **"Several women"**: *Debates and Proceedings of the Nova Scotia House of Assembly*, 20 November 1806, 8–9, quoted in Cuthbertson, *Johnny Bluenose at the Polls*, 9.

Page 29   **"Let loose in a little town"**: *Window on the Past*, 3–5, Nova Scotia Archives.

Page 30   **"We, the undersigned"**: "Woman's Christian Temperance Union, Hantsport, Nova Scotia Petition," in Forestell and Moynagh, *Documenting First Wave Feminisms*, 119.

Page 31   **"Consider [themselves] as members"**: Margaret Conrad, "Introduction," in Conrad, Rice, and Townsend, *Women at Acadia University*, 4.

Page 32   **"That female students shall"**: Waite, *The Lives of Dalhousie University*, 132.

Page 35   **"An Act for the Protection"**: *An Act for the Protection of Married Women in Certain Cases, 1866*, c 33.

Pages   **"It was pure justice"**: *Debates and Proceedings of the Nova Scotia House of*
35–36   *Assembly*, 28 April 1887, 376.

Page 36   **"Insulted by the crowd" ... "greater concessions"**: Ibid., 4 May 1887, 430.

Page 37   **"Pioneer worker"**: MacDonald, "A Passionate Voice," 51.

Page 38   **"Subsumed their grief in service"**: Ibid., 46.

Page 38   **"Controversialist" ... "settlement of national difficulties"**: Morgan, *The Canadian Men and Women*, 183.

Page 38   **"The best interest of the ladies" ... "in the affection"**: Debates and Proceedings *of the Nova Scotia House of Assembly*, 7 May 1891, 114.

Page 39   **"Too many sweeping provisions" ... "A woman could not receive"**: *Debates and Proceedings of the Nova Scotia House of Assembly* , 10 April 1893, 206–7.

Page 41   **"He could not conceive" ... "Rock-a-by baby"**: *Journal and Proceedings Nova Scotia*, 1 March 1895, 83.

Page 42   **"A true helpmate" ... "As a result of the wonderful inventions"**: Halifax Local Council of Women, Minute Book, 13 December 1894, Nova Scotia Archives (emphasis in original).

Page 43   **"Human bondage and servitude"**: Yorke, "Edwards, Anna Harriette."

Page 44   **"Erratic and contentious" ... "feeble-minded"**: Guildford, "Edith Jessie Archibald," 116–18; and Halifax Local Council of Women, Minute Book, 19 January 1911, Nova Scotia Archives.

Page 45 **"We have not taken a very active part"**: Halifax Local Council of Women, Minute Book, 19 February 1903, Nova Scotia Archives.

Page 46 **"Last year I mentioned"**: Reports of the Department of Franchise, 1913, 51, Nova Scotia Archives.

Page 46 **"I cannot think"**: Ibid., 1914, 48.

Page 46 **"One of the great forces"**: Hiram MacKay to the editor, *Halifax Chronicle,* 29 Sept 1917.

Page 47 **"Feeble-mindedness"**: Halifax Local Council of Women, Minute Book, 2 April 1906, Nova Scotia Archives.

Page 47 **"Matter of social justice" ... "exhaustive report"**: Halifax Local Council of Women, Scrapbook, 1911, MG 20, vol. 535, no. 1, Nova Scotia Archives.

Page 47 **"Participating in public life"**: *Halifax Evening Mail,* 24 January 1911, 34, in Halifax Local Council of Women, Scrapbook, 1911, Nova Scotia Archives.

Page 48 **"Until further public opinion"**: Halifax Local Council of Women, Minute Book, 16 February 1911, Nova Scotia Archives.

Page 48 **"Before the time was ripe" ... "one should not wait"**: Ella Murray, quoted in Catherine Cleverdon, *The Woman Suffrage Movement in Canada,* 2nd ed. (Toronto: University of Toronto Press, 1974), 167.

Page 52 **"To Amend the Nova Scotia Franchise Act"**: "Suffrage Bill Introduced in the Legislature," *Halifax Chronicle,* 15 March 1917.

Page 52 **"All women are not heroines" ... "most careful consideration"**: "Local Legislators Hear Delegation of Women in Favour of Suffrage Bill," *Halifax Chronicle,* 12 April 1917.

Page 53 **"Gave it the hoist" ... "would serve no useful purpose"**: "Votes for Women Bill Got the Three Months Hoist in Legislature Yesterday Afternoon," *Halifax Chronicle,* 24 April 1917.

Page 53 **"Well-considered and properly-framed" ... "no intelligent and patriotic member"**: "Principle of Womanhood Suffrage Affirmed but the Present Bill Rejected in the Real Interest of the Public," *Halifax Chronicle,* 28 April 1917.

Page 53 **"Asking in good faith" ... "whose mental powers"**: "Dr. Eliza Ritchie Replies to W.E. MacLellan on the Womanhood Suffrage Question," *Halifax Chronicle,* 2 May 1917.

Page 54 **"The franchise to the better women"**: W.E. MacLellan, "Principle of Womanhood Suffrage Affirmed," *Halifax Chronicle,* 28 April 1917.

THREE: NEW BRUNSWICK

The main sources for this chapter were Mary Eileen Clarke, "The Saint John Women's Enfranchisement Association, 1894–1919" (master's thesis, University of New Brunswick, 1979); Elspeth Tulloch, *We, the Undersigned: A Historical Overview of New Brunswick Women's Political and Legal Status, 1784–1984* (Moncton: New Brunswick Advisory Council on the Status of Women, 1985); and Gail Campbell, "Defining and Redefining Democracy: The History of Electoral Reform in New Brunswick," in *Democratic Reform in New Brunswick,* ed. William Cross (Toronto: Canadian Scholars Press, 2007), 273–99. I also depended on biographies of the leading suffragists: Janice Cook, "Skinner, Emma Sophia (Fiske)," *Dictionary of Canadian Biography,* vol. 14, University of Toronto/Université Laval, 2003–, http://www.biographi.ca/en/bio/skinner_emma_sophia_14E.html; Susan E. Markham, "Peters, Mabel Phoebe," *Dictionary of Canadian Biography,* vol. 14, University of Toronto/Université Laval, 2003–, http://www.biographi.ca/en/bio/peters_mabel_phoebe_14E.html; and Susan McAdam, "In Search of Ella Hatheway, Social Reformer in Early 20th Century Saint John, New Brunswick," *Frank and Ella Hatheway Labour Exhibit Centre,* http://www.wfhathewaylabourexhibitcentre.ca/labour-history/in-search-of-ella-hatheway/. For additional biographical material, I used correspondence from the Catherine Cleverdon fonds, including Miriam Hatheway Wood to Catherine Cleverdon, 22 October 1944, Catherine Lyle Cleverdon fonds, R2292-0-7-E, box 1, Library and Archives Canada; and Canadian census, birth, and death records obtained through *Ancestry.ca.*

For the broader socio-economic, political, and religious historical background to suffrage, I consulted Phillip Buckner and John G. Reid, eds., *The Atlantic Region to Confederation: A History* (Toronto: University of Toronto Press, 1995); E.R. Forbes and D.A. Muise, eds., *The Atlantic Provinces in Confederation,* 2nd ed. (Toronto: University of Toronto Press, 2001); T.W. Acheson, *Saint John: The Making of a Colonial Urban Community* (Toronto: University of Toronto Press, 1985); W.A. Spray, *The Blacks in New Brunswick* (1972; repr., Fredericton: St. Thomas University, 2021); Judith Fingard, "The New England Company and the New Brunswick Indians, 1786–1826: A Comment on the Colonial Perversion of British Benevolence," *Acadiensis* 1, 2 (Spring 1972): 29–42; D. Murray Young, "Gibson, Alexander," *Dictionary of Canadian Biography,* vol. 14, University of Toronto/Université Laval, 2003–; http://www.biographi.ca/en/bio/gibson_alexander_14F.html; T.W. Acheson, "The Great Merchant and Economic Development in St. John 1820–1850," *Acadiensis* 8, 2 (1979): 3–27; Patricia A. Thornton, "The Problem of Out-Migration from Atlantic Canada, 1871–1921: A New Look," *Acadiensis* 15, 1 (Autumn 1985): 3–34; and David Frank, "Provincial Solidarities: The Early Years of the New Brunswick Federation of Labour, 1913–1929," *Journal of the Canadian Historical Association/Revue de la Société historique du Canada* 19, 1 (2008): 143–69.

222 SOURCES AND FURTHER READING

I did extensive archival work. The minutes of the Saint John Women's Enfranchisement Association were invaluable: Saint John Woman Suffrage Association, Saint
John Women's Enfranchisement Association, Minutes, 30 July 1894–1920, fonds
1D201, New Brunswick Museum Archives. I reconstructed the suffrage debates
mostly through the *Synoptic Report of the Proceedings of the House of Assembly of the
Province of New Brunswick* for the years 1885, 1886, 1889, 1894, 1895, 1896, 1909,
1913, 1917, and 1919 *(Synoptic Report)*; articles from the *Daily Telegraph* (Saint John)
for 1895 and the *Telegraph and Sun* (Saint John) from 1916 and 1917; newspaper
sources cited in Catherine Cleverdon, *The Woman Suffrage Movement in Canada*, 2nd
ed. (Toronto: University of Toronto Press, 1974); and Tulloch, *We, the Undersigned.*

To capture the evolution of women's legal rights, I used various statutes: *An Act
for Regulating Elections of Representatives in the General Assembly and for Limiting
the Duration of Assemblies in this Province,* S.N.B. 1791, c. 17, s. 3; *An Act for More
Effectually Securing the Title of Purchasers of Real Estates, against Claims for Dower,*
S.N.B. 1787, c. 9; *An Act for More Effectually Securing the Title of Purchasers of Real
Estates, against Claims of Dower,* S.N.B. 1792, c. 2; *An Act to Secure to Married Women
Real and Personal Property Held in Their Own Right,* S.N.B. 1851, c. 24; *An Act to Extend
the Franchise to Widows and Unmarried Women in Municipal Elections,* S.N.B. 1886,
c. 83; *An Act to Consolidate and Amend the Law Relating to Elections in the General
Assembly,* S.N.B. 1889, c. 3; *An Act Respecting the Property of Married Women,* S.N.B.
1895, c. 24; *An Act for the Protection of Persons Employed in Factories,* S.N.B. 1905, c. 7;
*An Act to Extend the Electoral Franchise to Women and to Amend the New Brunswick
Electors Act,* S.N.B. 1919, c. 113; and *An Act to Amend the New Brunswick Factories Act,*
S.N.B. 1916, c. 40. For background on married women's property law, see Peter
Baskerville, *A Silent Revolution? Gender and Wealth in English Canada, 1860–1930*
(Montreal and Kingston: McGill-Queen's University Press, 2008).

On pre-Confederation women petitioners and voters, see Gail G. Campbell, "Dis-
franchised but Not Quiescent: Women Petitioners in New Brunswick in the Mid-
19th Century," *Acadiensis* 18, 2 (Spring 1989): 22–54; and Kim Klein, "A 'Petticoat
Polity'? Women Voters in New Brunswick before Confederation," *Acadiensis* 36, 1
(1996): 71–75. For the evolving colonial, provincial, and municipal franchise, I referred to John Garner, *The Franchise and Politics in British North America, 1755–1867*
(Toronto: University of Toronto Press, 1969); Acheson, *Saint John;* Gail Campbell,
"'Smashers' and 'Rummies': Voters and the Rise of Parties in Charlotte County,
New Brunswick, 1846–1857," *Historical Papers* (1986): 86–116; and *A History of the
Vote in Canada,* 3rd ed. (Ottawa: Chief Electoral Officer, 2021), 35, https://www.
elections.ca/content.aspx?section=res&dir=his&document=index&lang=e.

For material on the three most prominent women's organizations, the Saint John
Women's Enfranchisement Association, the Saint John Local Council of Women,
and the WCTU (and its many local branches), I depended on Clarke, "The Saint John
Women's Enfranchisement Association"; Saint John Women's Enfranchisement

Association, Minutes, 1894–1920, New Brunswick Museum Archives; R. Philip Campbell, *Challenging Years: Eighty-Five Years of the Council of Women in Saint John, 1894–1979* (Saint John, 1979); N.E.S. Griffiths, *The Splendid Vision: Centennial History of the National Council of Women of Canada, 1893–1993,* (Ottawa: Carleton University Press, 1993); Joanne Veer, "Feminist Forebears: The Woman's Christian Temperance Union in Canada's Maritime Provinces, 1875–1900" (PhD diss., University of New Brunswick, 1995); and New Brunswick Woman's Christian Temperance Union collection, MC63, Provincial Archives of New Brunswick. On the fascinating fictional Marichette, see Pierre Gérin, "Une écrivaine acadienne à la fin du XIXe siècle: Marichette," *Atlantis* 10, 1 (1984): 38–45; and Pierre Gérin, *Marichette: Lettres acadiennes, 1895–1898* (Sherbrooke: Éditions Naaman, 1982).

On women and higher education, see John G. Reid, "The Education of Women at Mount Allison, 1854–1914," *Acadiensis* 12, 2 (Spring 1983): 3–33; David Mawhinney, "Grace Annie Lockhart – A Mount Allison and Canadian Heroine," *Mount Allison University,* https://mta.ca/about/news/grace-annie-lockhart-mount-allison-and-canadian-heroine-mon-05172021-1708; and "Mary K. Tibbits," *University of New Brunswick Archives,* https://unbhistory.lib.unb.ca/Mary_K._Tibbits. On the appointment of school superintendents, see James Collins Miller, *Rural Schools in Canada: Their Organization, Administration and Supervision,* Contributions to Education, No. 61, (New York: Teachers College, Columbia University, 1913).

For politicians on both sides of the debate, see J.A. Gemmill, ed., *The Canadian Parliamentary Companion, 1897* (Ottawa: J. Durie and Son, 1897), *Canadiana,* https://www.canadiana.ca/view/oocihm.32962/3?r=0&s=1; D.M. Young, "Blair, Andrew George," *Dictionary of Canadian Biography,* vol. 13, University of Toronto/Université Laval, 2003–, http://www.biographi.ca/en/bio/blair_andrew_george_13E.html; R.G. Thorne, "Aspects of the Political Career of J.V. Ellis, 1867–1891" (master's thesis, University of New Brunswick, 1981), 32n50; Wendell E. Fulton, "Emmerson, Henry Robert," *Dictionary of Canadian Biography,* vol. 14, University of Toronto/Université Laval, 2003–, http://www.biographi.ca/en/bio/emmerson_henry_robert_14E.html; Provincial Archives of New Brunswick, "Emmerson, Robert Henry (1826–1857)," *Dictionary of Miramichi Biography,* https://archives.gnb.ca/Search/Hamilton/DMB/SearchResults.aspx?culture=en-CA&action=0&page=297; Peter J. Mitham, "Hatheway, Warren Franklin," *Dictionary of Canadian Biography,* vol. 15, University of Toronto/Université Laval, 2003–, http://www.biographi.ca/en/bio/hatheway_warren_franklin_15E.html; David Frank, "Missing Persons and Other Stories in Saint John Labour History" (paper presented at Frank and Ella Hatheway Labour Exhibit Centre, Saint John, 2 September 2013); Miriam Hatheway Wood to Catherine Cleverdon, 22 October 1944, Cleverdon fonds, Library and Archives Canada; Robert Craig Brown, "Pugsley, William," *Dictionary of Canadian Biography,* vol. 15, University of Toronto/Université Laval, 2003–, http://www.biographi.ca/en/bio/pugsley_william_15E.html; C.M. Wallace, "Tilley, Sir Samuel Leonard,"

Dictionary of Canadian Biography, vol. 12, University of Toronto/Université Laval, 2003–, http://www.biographi.ca/en/bio/tilley_samuel_leonard_12E.html.

Other diverse sources for this chapter include Gretchen Wilson, *With All Her Might: The Life of Gertrude Harding, Militant Suffragette* (Fredericton: Goose Lane Editions, 1996); Janice Cook, "New Brunswick Workers in the Early 20th Century," *Silhouettes: The Associates of the Provincial Archives of New Brunswick* 34 (Spring 2012): 2–4, https://archives.gnb.ca/Associates/Newsletters/2012-34-Spring-e.pdf; and Philip Girard and Rebecca Veinott, "Married Women's Property Law in Nova Scotia, 1850–1910," in *Separate Spheres: Women's Worlds in the 19th-Century Maritimes,* ed. Janet Guildford and Suzanne Morton (Fredericton: Acadiensis Press, 1994), 67–91.

I would also like to sincerely thank four archivists: Janice Cook (Provincial Archives of New Brunswick); Felicity Oseochook (New Brunswick Museum Archives); and Patti Auld Johnson and Sass Bergen (University of New Brunswick Archives).

Page 60   **"We want to get to the polls"** [author trans.]: Gérin, *Marichette,* 52.

Page 66   **"Tradesmen, professionals, and senior clerks":** *A History of the Vote in Canada,* 35.

Page 66   **"In the hands of those":** *Synoptic Report 1855,* 59, quoted in Campbell, "Defining and Redefining Democracy," 279.

Page 67   **"Separate property" … "full consent and concurrence":** *An Act to Secure to Married Women Real and Personal Property Held in Their Own Right,* S.N.B. 1851, c. 24.

Page 70   **"Cornerstone of women's equality":** Veer, "Feminist Forebears," 197.

Page 71   **"Men and women should stand":** Ibid., 200n13.

Page 71   **"In mental and in moral power":** Annual Report, WCTU Canada, 1891, 65, quoted in ibid., 202n17.

Page 72   **"Don't you think" … "loafers":** *Synoptic Report 1885,* 3 April 1885, 110.

Page 72   **"Tendency everywhere" … "certain other powers":** *Synoptic Report 1886,* 1 March 1886, 22–23.

Page 74   **"Indian" … "Women actually require":** *Synoptic Report 1889,* 25 March 1889, 65, 73.

Page 74   **"Intolerable reprobate":** Fulton, "Emmerson, Henry Robert," *Dictionary of Canadian Biography.*

Page 75   **"Gentle, home loving women":** *Synoptic Report 1889,* 3 April 1889, 157.

Page 75   **"State of transition":** Ibid., 91.

Page 76   **"In mental and in moral power"**: Annual Report, WCTU Canada, 1891, 65, quoted in Veer, "Feminist Forebears," 202n17.

Page 76   **"At first we asked for the ballot"**: *Charlottetown Daily Patriot,* 22 September 1891, quoted in Veer, "Feminist Forebears," 204.

Page 77   **"Unpopular among the male"**: "Report of the Sackville W.C.T.U. for the Year Ending March 21st 1894," New Brunswick Woman's Christian Temperance Union collection, Provincial Archives of New Brunswick.

Page 79   **"The women citizens of Canada"**: Constitution, art. 2, Saint John Women's Enfranchisement Association, Minutes, April 1894, New Brunswick Museum Archives.

Page 81   **"Rabid enthusiasm for suffrage"**: Campbell, *Challenging Years,* 22.

Page 82   **"You know, men are good for talking"** [author trans.]: Gérin, *Marichette,* 55.

Page 83   **"Has no authority"**: *Synoptic Report 1895,* 25 February 1895, 104–5.

Page 84   **"The full expression of opinions" … "a subsequent bill"**: *Synoptic Report 1894,* 17 April 1894, 157.

Page 84   **"Why should an ignorant footman"**: Ibid., 163.

Page 84   **"Would add the brightest gem" … "exercise of the franchise"**: Ibid., 159.

Page 84   **"The glory of Roman manhood"**: Ibid., 162.

Page 85   **"When we give the vote"**: *Synoptic Report 1895,* 25 February 1895, 102.

Page 85   **"Was an extension"**: Ibid., 103.

Page 86   **"Clear expression of public opinion" … "exclusion justified despotism"**: Ibid, 95–96.

Page 87   **"That in the opinion" and "Was not in the best interests"**: *Synoptic Report 1899,* 13 April 1899, 63.

Page 87   **"As there may be honourable members"**: Ibid., 64.

Page 87   **"Before a change so radical" … "Behind all legislation is physical force"**: Ibid., 60, 65.

Page 89   **"The members"**: Saint John Women's Enfranchisement Association, Minutes, February 1901, 153–54, New Brunswick Museum Archives

Page 89   **"Exceptional circumstances"**: *An Act for the Protection of Persons Employed in Factories,* S.N.B. 1905, c. 7.

Page 90   **"The great sisterhood of women"**: Rose E. Helmes, "Women's Clubs and the Suffrage," *Evening Times*, 19 February 1908, 5, quoted in Clarke, "The Saint John Women's Enfranchisement Association," 81.

Page 90   **"The public work of the country"**: *Daily Telegraph*, 14 May 1908, quoted in Cleverdon, *The Woman Suffrage Movement in Canada*, 186.

Page 91   **"Those masculine-feminine beings" ... "Would anyone say"**: *Synoptic Report 1909*, 27 April 1909, 185–89.

Page 91   **"Help! Police!"**: Miriam Hatheway Wood to Catherine Cleverdon, 22 October 1944, Cleverdon fonds, Library and Archives Canada.

Page 92   **"How can we expect"**: *Saint John Globe*, 18 April 1912, quoted in Cleverdon, *The Woman Suffrage Movement in Canada*, 187.

Page 92   **"Let us withhold"**: Saint John Women's Enfranchisement Association, Minutes, 9 December 1911, quoted in Cleverdon, *The Woman Suffrage Movement in Canada*, 189.

Page 93   **"Does not appear"**: *Daily Telegraph and the Sun* (Saint John), 16 January 1912, quoted in Tulloch, *We, the Undersigned*, 26.

Page 93   **"Just as strong patriotism"**: *Synoptic Report 1913*, 21 February 1913, 23–24.

Page 94   **"It was a completely unknown world"**: Gertrude Harding, quoted in Wilson, *With All Her Might*, 92.

Page 96   **"Half or three quarters of a loaf"**: *Telegraph and Sun*, 7 June 1917.

Page 96   **"A nation which holds women"**: *Synoptic Report 1917*, 6 June 1917, 83.

Page 97   **"Justice and equity"**: "Local Delegation of Women to Urge Giving of Suffrage," *Telegraph and Sun*, 4 June 1917, 10.

Page 97   **"Removed prejudice" ... "in due time"**: "Women Given Same Rights as Men under Federal Act," *Telegraph and Sun*, 21 March 1918, 6.

Page 98   **"The great contributing factor"**: Miriam Hatheway Wood to Catherine Cleverdon, 22 October 1944, Cleverdon fonds, Library and Archives Canada.

Page 98   **"If one was given the franchise"**: *Synoptic Report 1919*, 12 March 1919, 43.

Page 98   **"Women May Vote for Men but Not for Themselves"**: *Telegraph and Sun*, 23 March 1919.

Page 98   **"With franchise extended to women"**: *Synoptic Report 1919*, 14 April 1919, 295.

Page 98   **"Male person"** ... **"person whether male or female"**: *An Act to Extend the Electoral Franchise to Women and to Amend the New Brunswick Electors Act*, S.N.B. 1919, c. 113.

Page 99   **"No person"**: *An Act to Consolidate and Amend the Law Relating to Elections in the General Assembly*, S.N.B. 1889, c. 3.

FOUR: PRINCE EDWARD ISLAND

Of the Atlantic Canadian provinces, the least is written on suffrage and other women's rights in PEI, and what is available can be overly nostalgic. I depended more than in the other chapters on reading late-nineteenth- and early-twentieth-century newspapers (both the *Guardian* and *Patriot*), looking for glimpses of women's agency and the impact of the geography, small population, and culture on how politics worked on a less formal scale than in larger provinces. Elsie Inman's interview, a rare example of an oral interview of a suffragist, was important for this chapter: Interview with Senator Elsie Inman, c. 1976, Women, law and legislation folder, Acc2933/4b, Public Archives and Records Office, Prince Edward Island. It is unfortunate that neither the Women's Liberal Club nor Inman, its best-known executive member, have spurred any published academic material on PEI suffrage. The only published biography of an island suffragist is Jill MacMicken Wilson, "Sterling, Alice Jane (Johnson)," *Dictionary of Canadian Biography*, vol. 15, University of Toronto/Université Laval, 2003–, http://www.biographi.ca/en/bio/sterling_alice_jane_15E.html. Sterling is remembered most for her work with the WCTU.

On PEI women's rights, see Wendy Owen and J.M. Bumsted, "Divorce in a Small Province: A History of Divorce on Prince Edward Island from 1833," *Acadiensis* 20, 2 (1991): 86–104; Beverly Mills Stetson, "Times They're Sure A-changing," *Common Ground* 8, 3 (1977): 5; Beverly Mills Stetson, "Island Women and the Vote," in *Changing Times: Essays by Island Women*, ed. Mari Basiletti, Donna Greenwood, and Beverly Mills Stetson (Charlottetown: Women's Legal Project of PEI, 1977), 1–8; Catherine Cleverdon, *The Woman Suffrage Movement in Canada*, 2nd ed. (Toronto: University of Toronto Press, 1974); and Provincial Advisory Committee on the Status of Women in the Province of Prince Edward Island, *Report of the Provincial Advisory Committee on the Status of Women in the Province of Prince Edward Island*, 1973, HQ1459.P7P72, Robertson Library, University of Prince Edward Island. On the short-lived Charlottetown Local Council of Women, see N.E.S. Griffiths, *The Splendid Vision: Centennial History of the National Council of Women of Canada, 1893–1993* (Ottawa: Carleton University Press, 1993); and "Woman Council Meeting," *Morning Guardian*, 1 February 1904, 4. On PEI Women's Institutes, see "Women's Institutes," *Morning Guardian*, 14 March 1917, 3. On PEI women becoming school trustees, see *An Act to Further Amend the Public Schools Act of 1877 and amendments thereto*, S.P.E.I. 1899, c. 7.

Edward MacDonald, *If You're Strong Hearted: Prince Edward Island in the Twentieth Century* (Charlottetown: Prince Edward Island Museum and Heritage Foundation, 2000), is the best source on twentieth-century PEI; and Andrew Hill Clark, *Three Centuries and the Island: A Historical Geography of Settlement and Agriculture in Prince Edward Island, Canada* (Toronto: University of Toronto Press, 1959), is invaluable for the eighteenth and nineteenth centuries. Other important sources are Phillip Buckner, "The Maritimes and Confederation: A Reassessment," *Canadian Historical Review* 71, 1 (1990): 1–45; Mary K. Cullen, "The Transportation Issue, 1873–1973," in *Canada's Smallest Province: A History of Prince Edward Island*, ed. F.W.P. Bolger (Halifax: Nimbus, 1973), 232–63; Donald Creighton, *The Road to Confederation: The Emergence of Canada, 1963–67* (Toronto: Macmillan, 1964); Frank Schwartz, "An Economic History of Prince Edward Island," in *Exploring Island History: A Guide to the Historical Resources of Prince Edward Island*, ed. Harry Baglole (Belfast, PEI: Ragweed Press, 1977); and Alan MacEachern, "No Island Is an Island: A History of Tourism on Prince Edward Island, 1870–1939" (master's thesis, Queen's University, 1991). As with other chapters, I also depended on Phillip Buckner and John G. Reid, eds., *The Atlantic Region to Confederation: A History* (Toronto: University of Toronto Press, 1995); and E.R. Forbes and D.A. Muise, eds., *The Atlantic Provinces in Confederation*, 2nd ed. (Toronto: University of Toronto Press, 2001).

For women's roles in the land tenure system, often referred to as the land question, see Rusty Bittermann and Margaret McCallum, *Lady Landlords of Prince Edward Island: Imperial Dreams and the Defence of Property* (Montreal and Kingston: McGill-Queen's University Press, 2008); and Rusty Bittermann, *Rural Protest on Prince Edward Island: From British Colonization to the Escheat Movement* (Toronto: University of Toronto Press, 2006). On the land question more generally, see Ian Ross Robertson, "Reform, Literacy, and the Lease: The Prince Edward Island Free Education Act of 1852," *Acadiensis* 20, 1 (September 1990): 52–71; Ian Ross Robertson, *The Prince Edward Island Land Commission of 1860* (Fredericton: Acadiensis Press, 1988); and Harry Baglole, "Cooper, William," *Dictionary of Canadian Biography*, vol. 9, University of Toronto/Université Laval, 2003–, http://www.biographi.ca/en/bio/cooper_william_1867_9E.html.

On women and higher education, see Heidi MacDonald and G. Edward MacDonald, "Gertrude's Complaint: The First Generation of Women Students at St. Dunstan's University," *Island Magazine* 61 (Spring-Summer 2007): 24–34; Heidi MacDonald, "Prince Edward Island Women and University Education off and on the Island to 1943," *Acadiensis* 34, 1 (Fall 2005): 97–101; Lawrence Shook, *Catholic Post-Secondary Education in English-Speaking Canada, a History* (Toronto: University of Toronto Press, 1971); and Judith Fingard, "College, Career, and Community: Dalhousie Coeds, 1881–1991," in *Youth, University and Canadian Society: Essays in the Social History of Higher Education*, ed. Paul Axelrod and John G. Reid (Montreal and Kingston: McGill-Queen's University Press, 1989), 26–50. On the exceptional educational achievements and careers of two PEI women, Annie Marion

MacLean and Florence Murray, see Tiffany Colannino and Suzanne Morton, "MacLean, Annie Marion," *Dictionary of Canadian Biography*, vol. 16, University of Toronto/Université Laval, 2003-, http://www.biographi.ca/en/bio/maclean_annie_marion_16E.html; and Ruth Compton Brouwer, *Modern Women Modernizing Men: The Changing Missions of Three Professional Women in Asia and Africa, 1902-69* (Vancouver: UBC Press, 2002). On PEI women serving in the Red Cross during the First World War, see Katherine Dewar, *Those Splendid Girls: The Heroic Service of Prince Edward Island Nurses in the Great War, 1914-1918* (Charlottetown: Island Studies Press, 2014), 187-222; Hartwell Daley, *Volunteers in Action: The Prince Edward Island Division Canadian Red Cross Society, 1907-1979* (Summerside, 1981); and Adele Townshend, "McLean, Rena Maude," *Dictionary of Canadian Biography*, vol. 14, University of Toronto/Université Laval, 2003-, http://www. biographi.ca/en/bio/mclean_rena_maude_14E.html. On PEI female public health nurses, see Douglas Baldwin, "Amy MacMahon and the Struggle for Public Health," *Island Magazine* 34 (Fall-Winter 1993): 20-27. On the Women's Institute, see Mary Juanita Rossiter, "Couldn't Wait for Institute Nights: The Women's Institutes of Prince Edward Island, 1913-1939" (Honours thesis, Acadia University, 1996).

On PEI's history of slavery, see Harvey Amani Whitfield and Barry Cahill, "Slave Life and Slave Law in Colonial Prince Edward Island, 1769-1825," *Acadiensis* 38, 2 (2009): 29-51. On the slim historiography of PEI law, see J.M. Bumsted, "The Legal Historiography of Prince Edward Island," in *Essays in the History of Canadian Law*, vol. 9, *Two Islands: Newfoundland and Prince Edward Island*, ed. Christopher English (Toronto: University of Toronto Press, 2005), 38-45.

To trace women's rights and suffrage legislation, I studied the following PEI statutes: *An Act to Consolidate and Amend the Several Acts Incorporating the City of Charlottetown*, S.P.E.I. 1888, Cap. 12, s. 24; *An Act to Consolidate and Amend the Acts Incorporating the Town of Summerside*, S.P.E.I. 1886, Cap. 12; *An Act to Amend "The Summerside Incorporation Act, 1886*," S.P.E.I. 1892, Cap. 35; *An Act to Consolidate and Amend the Laws Related to the Conveyance of Real Estate by Women during Their Coverture*, S.P.E.I. 1861, c. 18; *An Act to Facilitate the Conveyance of Real Estate by Married Women*, S.P.E.I. 1880, c. 6 ; *An Act to Amend An Act to Amend the Rights of Married Women in Certain Cases*, S.P.E.I. 1881, Cap. 12; *An Act Relating to the Separate Property and the Rights of Property of Married Women to Property*," S.P.E.I. 1896, Cap. 5, s. 2; *An Act Prohibiting the Sale of Intoxicating Liquor*, S.P.E.I. 1900, Cap. 3; *An Act to Amend "The Prohibition Act, 1900*," S.P.E.I. 1905, Cap. 8; *An Act to Further Amend the Public Schools' Act, 1877*, S.P.E.I. 1899, Cap. 7; *The Election Act*, S.P.E.I. 1922, c. 5; *Seduction Act*, S.P.E.I. 1876, Cap. 4. To describe the legislative debates on suffrage, I depended on the *Journals of the House of Assembly (PEI)* for these dates: 2 May 1894; 10 May 1894; 11 April 1895; and 5 May 1899.

On PEI's unusually long prohibition policy, see Greg Marquis, "Prohibition's Last Outpost," *Island Magazine* 57 (Spring-Summer 2005): 2-9; and "Mr. Bell on Prohibition," *Charlottetown Guardian*, 11 August 1899, 2. On the Woman's Christian

Temperance Union, see Claude Mark Davis, "I'll Drink to That: The Rise and Fall
of Prohibition in the Maritime Provinces, 1900–1930" (PhD diss., McMaster
University, 1990); and Joanne Veer, "Feminist Forebears: The Woman's Christian
Temperance Union in Canada's Maritime Provinces, 1875–1900" (PhD diss.,
University of New Brunswick, 1995).

On the evolution of the franchise in PEI, see Marlene Russell Clark, "Island
Politics," in Bolger, *Canada's Smallest Province,* 289–327; Marlene Russell Clark, "The
Franchise in Prince Edward Island and Its Relation to Island Politics and Other
Political Institutions" (master's thesis, Dalhousie University, 1968); Colin Grittner,
"Working at the Crossroads: Statute Labour, Manliness, and the Electoral Franchise
on Victorian Prince Edward Island," *Journal of the Canadian Historical Association* 23,
1 (2012): 101–30; Colin Grittner, "Macdonald and Women's Enfranchisement," in
Macdonald at 200: New Reflections and Legacies, ed. Patrice A. Dutil and Roger Hall
(Toronto: Dundurn, 2014), 27–57; Frank MacKinnon, *The Government of Prince
Edward Island,* Canadian Government Series (Toronto: University of Toronto Press,
1951); John Garner, *The Franchise and Politics in British North America, 1755–1867*
(Toronto: University of Toronto Press, 1969); Lorna Marsden, *Canadian Women
and the Struggle for Equality* (New York: Oxford University Press, 2012); Attorney
General F.A. Large to Catherine Cleverdon, 13 September 1945, Catherine Lyle
Cleverdon fonds, R2292-0-7-E, box 1, Library and Archives Canada; and [J.S.
DesRoches], *The Report of The Royal Commission on Electoral Reform* (Charlottetown,
JL219.A5R68 1962, Robertson Library, University of Prince Edward Island. For the
1888 municipal vote, see RG 20, City of Charlottetown, Minutes, vol. 9, 20 April
1888, Public Archives and Records Office, Prince Edward Island; and Legislative
Council of Prince Edward Island, *Debates and Proceedings,* 15 April 1888, 86. On
PEI elections, see Don Desserud, "Prince Edward Island," in *Big Worlds: Politics
and Elections in the Canadian Provinces and Territories,* ed. Jared Wesley (Toronto:
University of Toronto Press, 2015), 19–35.

On PEI's most famous author, L.M. Montgomery, and artist Robert Harris, and how
each are tied to women's rights, see "About L.M. Montgomery," *L.M. Montgomery
Institute,* https://lmmontgomery.ca/about/lmm/her-life; Heidi MacDonald, "The
Landscape as Argument in *Anne of the Island:* L.M. Montgomery's Implicit Argu-
ment for University Education for Women," *CREArTA* 5 (2005): 158–66; Mary
McDonald-Rissanen, *In the Interval of the Wave: Prince Edward Island Women's
Nineteenth- and Early Twentieth-Century Life Writing* (Montreal and Kingston: McGill-
Queen's University Press, 2014); Mary Rubio, *Lucy Maud Montgomery: The Gift of
Wings* (Toronto: Doubleday Canada, 2008); Moncrieff Williamson, "Harris, Robert,"
Dictionary of Canadian Biography, vol. 14, University of Toronto/Université Laval,
2003–, http://www.biographi.ca/en/bio/harris_robert_14E.html; Moncrieff
Williamson, *Robert Harris, 1849–1919: An Unconventional Biography* (Toronto:
McClelland and Stewart, 1970); and Tasia Bulger, "In the Spotlight: Conserving

A Meeting of the School Trustees by Robert Harris," *National Gallery of Canada,* 4 April 2017, https://www.gallery.ca/magazine/in-the-spotlight/in-the-spotlight -conserving-a-meeting-of-the-school-trustees-by-robert. On Harris's architect brother, see Robert Critchlow Tuck, "Harris, William Critchlow," *Dictionary of Canadian Biography,* vol. 14, University of Toronto/Université Laval, 2003–, http:// www.biographi.ca/en/bio/harris_william_critchlow_14E.html.

On PEI politicians who supported suffrage, see Harry Tinson Holman, "Bell, John Howatt," *Dictionary of Canadian Biography,* vol. 15, University of Toronto/ Université Laval, 2003–, http://www.biographi.ca/en/bio/bell_john_howatt_15E.html; Wayne MacKinnon, *The Life of the Party: A History of the Liberal Party in Prince Edward Island* (Summerside: Liberal Party of PEI, 1973); "A.B. McKenzie," *Find a Grave,* https://www.findagrave.com/memorial/185365844/a.-b.-mckenzie; and Legislative Council of Prince Edward Island, *Debates and Proceedings,* 15 April 1888, 86. On Andrew Macphail, see Ian Ross Robertson, "Macphail, Sir Andrew," *Dictionary of Canadian Biography,* vol. 16, University of Toronto/Université Laval, 2003–, http://www.biographi.ca/en/bio/macphail_andrew_16E.html; and "Dr Andrew MacPhail's Essays in Fallacy," *Charlottetown Guardian,* 25 August 1910, 2. On influential PEI educator and reformer Alexander Anderson, see Marian Bruce, "Anderson, Alexander," *Dictionary of Canadian Biography,* vol. 15, University of Toronto/Université Laval, 2003–, http://www.biographi.ca/en/bio/anderson_ alexander_15E.html; *Journals of the House of Assembly,* 5 May 1899, 48; Census of Canada, 1881, 1891, 1901, PEI, Queen's West-; "Annual Report of the Department of Education of the Province of Prince Edward Island for the Fiscal Year Ending March 31st, 1946," *Journals of the Legislative Assembly,* 1946, 56–57, https://www.peildo.ca/ islandora/object/leg%3A5964#page/56/mode/2up.

Other diverse sources for this chapter included John Crossley, "Picture This: Women Politicians Hold Key Posts in PEI," (working paper, June 1995), HQ1391. P75C76 1995 PEI SPEC-PE, Robertson Library, University of Prince Edward Island; Betsy Beattie, *Obligation and Opportunity: Single Maritime Women in Boston, 1870– 1930* (Montreal and Kingston: McGill-Queen's University Press, 2000); Phillip Buckner, "The 1870s: Political Integration," in *The Atlantic Provinces in Confederation,* ed. E.R. Forbes and D.A. Muise (Toronto: University of Toronto Press, 1993), 48–81; Ashley Csanady, "Breastfeeding MPs Cause a Stir, but with More Women Running Than Ever in Canada, It Should Be the New Norm," *National Post,* 19 September 2015, http://nationalpost.com/news/canada/canadian-politics/breastfeeding- mps-cause-a-stir-in-parliaments-around-the-world-but-with-more-women- running-than-ever-in-canada-it-should-be-the-new-norm/wcm/cd3ab95c -351f-4708-95d9-efaa8c524b1c; D.A. Muise, "The 1860s: Forging the Bonds of Union," in Forbes and Muise, *The Atlantic Provinces in Confederation,* 1993 ed., 13– 47; and Moncrieff Williamson, *Island Painter: The Life of Robert Harris, 1849–1919* (Charlottetown: Ragweed Press, 1983).

I would like to thank the archivists whose assistance improved this chapter so much: Simon Lloyd (Robertson Library, University of Prince Edward Island); John Boylan (Provincial Archives and Records Office, Charlottetown); Jannah Toms (Provincial Archives and Records Office, Charlottetown); and Alina Ruiz (Mount Saint Vincent Library). Special thanks also to the very generous G. Edward MacDonald, Department of History, University of Prince Edward Island.

Page 107   **"A blood sport"**: MacDonald, *If You're Strong Hearted,* 18.

Page 111   **"The age of Women's Rights"** ... **"closer to the era"** ... **"a drunken reprobate"**: Editorial, *Patriot,* 9 April 1903, 4.

Page 112   **"A very liberal women's property act"**: Stetson, "Times They're Sure A-changing," 5.

Page 115   **"Astonished that honorable members"** ... **"Knowing the little I know"**: Legislative Council of Prince Edward Island, *Debates and Proceedings,* 15 April 1888, 86.

Page 115   **"If the amendment is not intended"**: Charlottetown City Council, Minutes, 20 April 1888, RG20, vol. 9, Provincial Archives and Records Office, PEI.

Page 117   **"Good work"**: *Journal of the House of Assembly,* 10 April 1894, 80.

Page 118   **"Nothing herein contained"**: *An Act to Further Amend the Public Schools' Act, 1877,* Cap. 7.

Page 120   **"Praying that the Legislature"**: *Journal of the House of Assembly,* 2 May 1894, 174.

Page 123   **"Find their desires conceded"**: "Women's Suffrage," *Charlottetown Guardian,* 20 January 1904, 4.

Page 123   **"Showing little mercy"** ... **"trained, original, and exceedingly vigorous mind"**: "Essays in Fallacy," *Charlottetown Guardian,* 25 August 1910, 2.

Page 124   **"General Emmeline Pankhurst"**: "Women Suffragettes Celebrate Fifth Anniversary of the War," *Morning Guardian,* 13 October 1913.

Page 124   **"Not a question"**: "Women, Love, and the Vote," *Charlottetown Guardian,* 21 November 1913, 2.

Page 126   **"For support"** ... **"do the right thing"**: "Letter to School Secretaries," *Morning Guardian,* 15 June 1918, 2.

Page 127   **The "Island's Florence Nightingale"**: "Georgina Pope: A Pioneer of Nursing," *Canadian War Museum,* 13 June 2016, https://www.warmuseum. ca/blog/georgina-pope-a-pioneer-for-nursing-and-for-women/.

Page 129   **"A young fellow" ... "safeguard their own interests"**: "Votes for the Women," *Charlottetown Patriot*, 25 April 1918, 5.

Page 129   **"Risked their lives" ... "If the franchise" ... "The matter was accordingly dropped"**: "Proceedings of the Provincial Legislature," *Morning Guardian*, 15 May 1919, 1.

Page 130   **"A deep interest in the moral progress"**: Editorial, *Charlottetown Guardian*, 21 October 1921, 4.

Page 130   **"Voluntarily and as a matter of justice"**: "Premier Meighen's Manifesto," *Charlottetown Guardian*, October 6, 1921.

Page 131   **"Not less than men's" ... "the shrill contempt"**: Gladys McCormack, "The Changed Position of Women," *Charlottetown Guardian*, 11 December 1920, 5, 8.

Page 132   **"My dear lady"**: "Odds and Ends," *Charlottetown Guardian*, 18 May 1920, 11.

Page 133   **"Wherever a women's institute"**: Editorial, *Charlottetown Guardian*, 19 July 1921, 4.

Page 133   **"Our motto"**: "Ninth Annual Convention PEI Women's Institutes," *Charlottetown Guardian*, 5 July 1922, 1.

Page 133   **"Resolved: That it is expedient" ... "It was Pharaoh's daughter"**: "Proceedings of the Provincial Legislature," *Morning Guardian*, 3 May 1922, 1.

Page 135   **"Any person shall" ... "an Indian ordinarily resident"**: *The Election Act*, S.P.E.I. 1922, c. 5.

Page 136   **"This promise"**: Editorial, *Charlottetown Guardian*, 18 May 1922, 4.

Page 136   **"A great and worthy part"**: "Woman Franchise," *Charlottetown Patriot*, 5 May 1922, 5.

Page 136   **"Many of the ladies"**: "Instructing the Ladies," *Charlottetown Guardian*, 11 January 1923, 4.

Page 137   **"Majority of PEI husbands" ... "most women"**: Interview with Senator Elsie Inman, c. 1976, Public Archives and Records Office.

FIVE: NEWFOUNDLAND

The essential book on Newfoundland women's suffrage is Margaret Duley's *Where Once Our Mothers Stood We Stand: Women's Suffrage in Newfoundland, 1890–1925* (Charlottetown: Gynergy Books, 1993), which includes biographies of the leading suffragists. Duley published three subsequent book chapters related to enfranchisement: "The Rise and Triumph of the Women's Suffrage Movement in Newfoundland, 1909–1925," in *Pursuing Equality: Historical Perspectives on Women in Newfoundland and Labrador*, ed. Linda Kealey (St. John's: Institute of Social and Economic Research, 1993), 15–65; "The Unquiet Knitters of Newfoundland: From Mothers to Mothers of the Nation," in *A Sisterhood of Suffering and Service*, ed. Sarah Glassford and Amy Shaw (Vancouver: UBC Press, 2013), 51–74; and "Armine Nutting Gosling: A Full and Useful Life," in *Creating This Place: Women, Family, and Class in St. John's, 1900–1959*, ed. Linda Cullum and Marilyn Porter (Montreal and Kingston: McGill-Queen's University Press, 2014), 114–43. I also recommend *The Untold Story of the Suffragists of Newfoundland*, a Codlessco docudrama directed by Greg Malone and written and produced by Marian Frances White, 1999.

For additional biographies of suffragists and women's rights leaders, see Helen Woodrow, "Julia Salter Earle: Seeking Social Justice," in Cullum and Porter, *Creating This Place*, 71–88; Anne Hart, "Knowling, Fannie (Fanny) (McNeil)," *Dictionary of Canadian Biography*, vol. 15, University of Toronto/Université Laval, 2003–, http://www.biographi.ca/fr/bio/knowling_fannie_15F.html; and Bert Riggs, "Two Women Who Courted Success," transcribed from the *Telegram* by Barbara McGrath, October 2002, http://ngb.chebucto.org/Articles/2-women.shtml. From the five-volume *Encyclopedia of Newfoundland and Labrador*, see "Ayre (née Miller), Agnes Marion (1890–1940)," vol. 1; "Earle, Julia Salter" (1878–1945)," vol. 1; "Gosling, Armine Nutting," (c. 1863–1942), vol. 2; "McNeil, Frances Knowling," (1869–1928), vol. 3; "Old Colony Club" [Ladies Reading Room], vol. 4; "Women's Patriotic Association, WPA," vol. 5; and "Squires, Helena E, (1879–1959)," vol. 5 in Joseph Smallwood and Robert D.W. Pitt, eds., *Encyclopedia of Newfoundland and Labrador* (St. John's: Newfoundland Book Publishers, 1981–1994), http://collections.mun.ca/cdm/compoundobject/collection/cns_enl/id/2677/rec/1. The following primary sources include additional biographical information on the suffragists: Julia Salter Earle, "War Memorial Suggestion," *Evening Telegram*, 8 March 1919; "Province's First Woman Lawyer Louise M. Saunders Dies at 72," *Daily News*, 15 June 1969; "Jessie Ohman," *Ancestry.ca*, https://www.ancestry.ca/discoveryui-content/view/1013967912:62226?tid=&pid=&queryId=bea56dd5032df6080e4ed7b68d717e98&_phsrc=aHe9&_phstart=successSource; "To the Women Voters of Newfoundland," *Twillingate Sun*, 4 August 1928, 4; "Won by Sacrifice and Service," *St. John's Daily News*, 12 May 1920; and *Proceedings of the House of Assembly and Legislative Council*, 11 March 1910, 427–28. Broader references to suffrage in Newfoundland appear in Francis M. Mason, "The Newer Eve: The Catholic Women's Suffrage Society in England, 1911–1923," *Catholic Historical Review* 72, 4 (1986): 625; and "A Suffrage Victory," *Jus Suffragii*, 25 April 1925, 22.

Several unpublished papers on suffrage topics, housed in the Centre for Newfoundland Studies, Memorial University of Newfoundland, were useful: Janice O'Brien, "Women's Suffrage in Newfoundland" (submitted to Linda Kealy, HIST

3813, 7 April 1982), JF848 .O23 1982 ; Terry Bishop, "The Newfoundland Struggle for the Women's Franchise" (submitted to James Hiller, HIST 3120, 10 December 1981), JF848.B58; and Lillian Bouzane et al., "The Triumphs and Tribulations of the Early Suffragettes and Others, or Go Home and Bake Bread" (play written for the tenth anniversary of the Newfoundland Status of Women Council, November 1982), HQ1459, N4, T65, c. 16.

On Newfoundland women's rights before the suffrage era, see Trudi Johnson, "Women and Inheritance in Nineteenth-Century Newfoundland," *Journal of the Canadian Historical Association* 13, 1 (2002): 1–22; Trudi Johnson, "Defining Property for Inheritance: The Chattels Real Act of 1834," in *Essays in the History of Canadian Law*, vol. 9, *Two Islands: The Legal Histories of Newfoundland and Prince Edward Island*, ed. Christopher English (Toronto: University of Toronto Press with the Osgoode Society, 2006), 192–216; and Trudi Dale Johnson, "Matrimonial Property Law in Newfoundland to the End of the Nineteenth Century" (PhD diss., Memorial University of Newfoundland, 1998). For mid-nineteenth-century Newfoundland rural women's agency, see Willeen Keough, "'Now You Vagabond [W]hore I Have You': Plebeian Women, Assault Cases, and Gender and Class Relations on the Southern Avalon, 1750–1860," in English, *Two Islands*, 237–71. For two relevant primary sources see also *An Act to Amend the Law Related to Married Women's Property*, S.N. 1883, c. 17; and *An Act to Amend the Act 52 Vic., Cap 22 Entitled "An Act to Amend Title III, chap 10, of the Consolidated Statutes Entitled, Of the Law Society, Barristers, and Solicitors,"* 4 July 1895, Cap. 1.

For primary sources on early-twentieth-century women and higher education, see "Our University Girls," *Distaff*, 1917, 3; and *Dalhousie University, Halifax, NS: Directory of Graduate and Former Students of the University, 1937* (Halifax: Dalhousie University, 1937), MS-1-Ref, Box 27, Folder 19, Dalhousie University Archives. And for the first Newfoundland woman to study and practice medicine, Edith Weeks Hooper, see Howard Maxwell Harvey, *Newfoundland and Labrador Days: Historic Notes, Oddities, Recipes, Daily Diary and Calendar for Any Year* (St. John's: Jespersen, 1997), 55. For women's entrance into the profession of law, see the transcription of the legislative debate: *Proceedings of the House of Assembly and Legislative Council*, 11 March 1910, 427–28; and Duley's biography of Janet Miller in *Where Once Our Mothers Stood.*

On prohibition in Newfoundland, see the many articles written by Jessie Ohman in issues of the *Water Lily*, which are available online through the Centre for Newfoundland Studies at Memorial University, https://collections.mun.ca/digital/collection/uchurch/search; and Melvin Baker, "1921 Report of the Commission on the Prohibition Plebiscite Act," *Newfoundland and Labrador Studies* 27, 2 (Fall 2012): 267–79.

The key primary source collection on the Women's Franchise League is correspondence between Fannie McNeil and Prime Minister Richard Squires, as well as related newspaper clippings (including "History of the Woman's Franchise Bill," *Daily News*, 18 August 1921) in the Squires Collection, MF137, Memorial University of Newfoundland Archives.

On the 1921 municipal vote, see Melvin Baker, "William Gilbert Gosling and the Charter: St. John's Municipal Politics, 1914–1921," *Newfoundland Quarterly* 81, 1 (Summer 1985): 19–25. Unfortunately, there are no surviving voters lists from 1925, but there is one for Saint John West in 1928. See "1928 Voter's Index for the Communities in the St. John's [sic] West," *Newfoundland's Grand Banks*, http://ngb. chebucto.org/V1928/1sjw-28vl-idx.shtml.

On Newfoundland women's war work, see Duley, "The Unquiet Knitters," 51–74; Terry Bishop Stirling, "Such Sights One Will Never Forget," in Glassford and Shaw, *A Sisterhood of Suffering and Service*, 126–48; Terry Bishop Stirling, "Women's Mobilization for War (Newfoundland)," in *1914–1918 Online: International Encyclopedia of the First World War*, ed. Ute Daniel et al. (Berlin: Freie Universität Berlin, 2015), http://encyclopedia.1914-1918-online.net/article/womens_mobilization_for_ war_newfoundland. The key primary source is the *Distaff*, 1916–18, published by the Women's Patriotic Association and available at the Provincial Archives of Newfoundland and Labrador (The Rooms). For the broader context, see Mike O'Brien, "Producers versus Profiteers: The Politics of Class in Newfoundland during the First World War," *Acadiensis* 40, 1 (Winter-Spring 2011): 45–69; and Jenny Higgins, "Beaumont Hamel: July 1, 1916," in *Newfoundland and Labrador in the First World War, Newfoundland Labrador Heritage*, http://www.heritage.nf.ca/first-world -war/articles/beaumont-hamel-en.php. For women's work from the 1890s to the 1930s, see Nancy M. Forestell, "Women's Paid Labour in St. John's between the Two World Wars" (master's thesis, Memorial University of Newfoundland, 1987); Nancy Forestell and Jessie Chisholm, "Working-Class Women as Wage Earners in St. John's, Newfoundland, 1890–1921," in *Feminist Research: Prospect and Retrospect*, ed. Peta Tancred (Kingston: Canadian Research Institute for the Advancement of Women/ Montreal and Kingston: McGill-Queen's University Press, 1988), 141–54; and Shelley Smith, "A Better Chance in the Boston States: An Ethnographic Account of Migratory Domestic Service among Newfoundland Women, 1920–1940" (bachelor of arts honour's thesis, Memorial University of Newfoundland, 1984).

For early socio-economic and legal history, including shore rights issues that were debated into the twentieth century, I depended on Jerry Bannister, *The Rule of the Admirals: Law, Custom, and Naval Government in Newfoundland, 1699–1832* (Toronto: University of Toronto Press, 2014); and Peter Edward Pope, *Fish into Wine: The Newfoundland Plantation in the Seventeenth Century* (Chapel Hill: University of North Carolina Press, 2004). For nineteenth- and twentieth-century Newfoundland political, economic, religious, and social history, I relied on Sean Cadigan, *Newfoundland and Labrador: A History* (Toronto: University of Toronto Press, 2009); James Hiller, "Newfoundland Confronts Canada, 1867–1949," in *The Atlantic*

Provinces in Confederation, 2nd ed., ed. E.R. Forbes and D.A. Muise (Toronto: University of Toronto Press 200), 349–81; James Hiller, "Confederation Defeated: The Newfoundland Election of 1869," in *Newfoundland in the Nineteenth and Twentieth Centuries: Essays in Interpretation*, ed. J. Hiller and Peter Neary (Toronto: University of Toronto Press, 1980), 67–94; Melvin Baker, "William Gilbert Gosling and the Establishment of Commission Government in St. John's, Newfoundland, 1914," *Urban History Review* 93 (1981): 25–51; Phillip Buckner and John G. Reid, eds., *The Atlantic Region to Confederation: A History*, 2nd ed. (Toronto: University of Toronto Press, 2001); James Hiller, *The Newfoundland Railway, 1881–1949* (St. John's: H. Cuff, 1981); and *Historical Statistics of Newfoundland and Labrador*, vol. 1. (St. John's: Queen's Printer, 1970). On the story of the last known Beothuk woman, see George M. Story, "Shawnadithit," *Canadian Encyclopedia*, https://www.thecanadianencyclopedia.ca/en/article/shawnadithit; and "Aboriginal Peoples: Fact Sheet for Newfoundland and Labrador," *Statistics Canada*, 14 March 2016, https://www150.statcan.gc.ca/n1/pub/89-656-x/89-656-x2016002-eng.htm. On Chinese Newfoundlanders, see Miriam Wright, "The Chinese Immigrant in the City: Reflections on Race, Class and Gender in the Public Spaces of St. John's, Newfoundland, 1895–1949," *Acadiensis* (blog), 9 January 2017, https://acadiensis.wordpress.com/2017/01/09/the-chinese-immigrant-in-the-city-reflections-on-race-class-and-gender-in-the-public-spaces-of-st-johns-newfoundland-1895-1949/.

On pro- and anti-suffrage politicians, see J.K. Hiller, "Thorburn, Sir Robert," *Dictionary of Canadian Biography*, vol. 13, University of Toronto/Université Laval, 2003–, http://www.biographi.ca/en/bio/thorburn_robert_13E.html; "Peters, John Edgar Picavant," *Encyclopedia of Newfoundland and Labrador*, vol. 4, 261, https://collections.mun.ca/digital/collection/cns_enl/id/2159/rec/17; James K. Hiller, "Squires, Sir Richard Anderson," *Dictionary of Canadian Biography*, vol. 16, University of Toronto/Université Laval, 2003–, http://www.biographi.ca/en/bio/squires_richard_anderson_16E.html; James K. Hiller, "William Gilbert Gosling and the Charter: St. John's Municipal Politics, 1914–1921," *Newfoundland Quarterly* 81, 1 (Summer 1985): 19–25; James K. Hiller, "William Gilbert Gosling and the Establishment of Commission Government in St. John's, Newfoundland, 1914," *Urban History Review* 93 (1981): 25–51; and J.K. Hiller, "Whiteway, Sir William Vallance," *Dictionary of Canadian Biography*, vol. 13, University of Toronto/Université Laval, 2003–, http://www.biographi.ca/en/bio/whiteway_william_vallance_13E.html. For suffrage debates in the House of Assembly, see *Proceedings of the House of Assembly*, 3 March 1910, 427, 707; 20 May 1920, 447; 9–10 March 1925, 291–322; 19 May 1920, 617–30; and 4 May 1921, 277–81. From the *Legislative Council Proceedings*, see 1910, 427–28; and 9 May 1921, 82.

Other diverse sources for this chapter were June Purvis, "Suffragette Hunger Strikes, 100 Years On," *Manchester Guardian*, 6 July 2009, https://www.theguardian.com/commentisfree/libertycentral/2009/jul/06/suffragette-hunger-strike-protest; L.J. Rupp, *Worlds of Women: The Making of an International Women's*

Movement (Princeton: Princeton University Press, 1997); Gina Snooks and Sonya Boon, "Salt Fish and Molasses: Unsettling the Palate in the Spaces between Two Continents," *European Journal of Life Writing* 6 (2017): 218–41; Miriam Wright, pers. email correspondence, 4 May 2017; David Mawhinney, Mount Allison archivist, pers. email correspondence, 15 May 2017; Alana Wicks, City of St. John's archivist, pers. email correspondence, 25 May 2017 and 8–9 July 2019.

I would also like to thank these archivists for their valuable and much-appreciated assistance: Jessie Chisholm (Provincial Archives of Newfoundland and Labrador); David Mawhinney (Mount Allison University Archives); Linda White (Archives and Special Collections, Queen Elizabeth II Library, Memorial University); Paulette Noseworthy (Archives and Special Collections, Queen Elizabeth II Library, Memorial University); and Alana Wicks (City of St. John's Archives).

Page 139 **"Permit her to do …":** Jesse Ohman, "The Woman Suffrage," *Water Lily*, 1, 2 (March 92) 40.

Page 148 **"The idea of [the Atlantic Hotel]":** *Water Lily* 1, 2 (February 1892): 26.

Page 148 **"These license laws" … "meddling in politics":** *Water Lily* 1, 3 (March 1892): 43.

Page 148 **"Drink Traffic College":** *Water Lily* 1, 2 (February 1892): 27.

Page 150 **"If there be any enjoyment":** "The Woman's Suffrage," *Water Lily* 1, 3 (March 1892): 40.

Page 151 **"When a young man arrived":** *Proceedings of the House of Assembly and Legislative Council,* 15 March 1892, quoted in Duley, *Where Once Our Mothers Stood,* 24.

Page 152 **"Women of Newfoundland":** "Local Option and Woman Suffrage," *Water Lily* 2, 1 (January 1893): 8.

Page 152 **"Manhood suffrage for the clown":** Ibid.

Page 153 **"The most reasonable measure":** Ibid.

Page 153 **"Stirred up the sterner sex":** "Woman Suffrage," *The Water Lily 2, 2* (Feb 1893): 25.

Page 153 **"Until woman is politically":** "Woman Suffrage," *The Water Lily 2,* 2 (March 1893): 40.

Page 153 **"Not seeking notoriety":** "Temperance Convention," *Evening Telegram,* 20 April 1893, 4. Also quoted in Duley, *Where Once Our Mothers Stood,* 30n46.

Page 153 **"We have no word":** Evening *Telegram,* April 20, 1893, quoted in Duley, *Where Once Our Mothers* Stood, 30n46.

Page 154   **"Peace of the house" … "could not have been written by a woman"**:
Duley, *Where Once Our Mothers Stood,* 33n61.

Page 154   **"Home comforts" … "going to the ice"**: "Last Night in the Assembly,"
Evening Telegram, 5 May 1893.

Page 154   **"Had he been speaking" … "a failure to do"**: Editorial, *Water Lily* 2,
6 (June 1893): 80.

Page 155   **"Just quieten down, baby"**: "John Crosbie Dead at 88," *CBC News,*
10 January 2020, https://www.cbc.ca/news/canada/newfoundland
-labrador/john-crosbie-obituary-1.5413882.

Page 156   **"In the more practical affairs of life"**: *Water Lily* 2, 6 (June 1893): 77.

Page 156   **"Our University Girls"**: "Our University Girls," *Distaff,* 1917, 3.

Page 157   **"On the same terms as men" … "merely a competition of brain"**:
Proceedings of the House of Assembly and Legislative Council, 11 March
1910, 427.

Page 158   **"Adopting methods" … "gentle sex"**: Ibid., 8 March 1910, 707–8.

Page 159   **"Slavery of the home"**: Duley, *Where Once Our Mothers Stood,* 51.

Page 161   **"In peace and harmony"**: "The Ladies' Reading Room," *Distaff,* 1916, 18.

Page 163   **"Red Cross Room" … "as if on oiled wheels"**: "A Visit to the W.P.A.
Headquarters," *Distaff,* 1917, 4.

Page 164   **"Women have shown so much ability" … "have given for two years"**:
"The Ladies' Reading Room," *Distaff,* 1916, 18.

Page 165   **"Shown their ability and influence"**: "Won By Sacrifice and Service,"
Daily News, 12 May 1920.

Page 168   **"Whereas we regard"**: *Legislative Council Proceedings,* 9 May 1921, quoted
in Duley, "Where Once Our Mothers," 82.

Page 169   **"From this it will" … "prolonging the agony"**: *Proceedings of the House
of Assembly,* 4 May 1921, 277, 281.

Page 170   **"History of the Woman's Franchise Bill"**: "History of the Woman's
Franchise Bill," *Daily News,* 18 August 1921, clipping, Squires Collection,
Memorial University of Newfoundland Archives.

Page 170   **"Dear Sir"**: Fannie McNeil to Richard Squires, 11 June 1921, Squires
Collection, Memorial University of Newfoundland Archives.

Page 170   **"On being ushered"**: "History of the Woman's Franchise Bill," *Daily News,*
18 August 1921.

Page 171   **"The story"**: "Inside History of the Woman's Suffrage Bill," *Daily News,*
18 August 1921.

Page 171   **"All British subjects" … "any such person" … "Words importing the
masculine gender"**: *An Act to Amend and Consolidate the Laws in Relation
to the Municipal Affairs of the Town of St John's,* S.N. 1921, 2 August 1921,
Cap. 13, s. 8.

Page 172   **"Local situation" … "the last to deal"**: "Report of Mrs. Trounson's
Meeting, College Hall, 23 March 1922," Squires Collection, Memorial
University of Newfoundland Archives.

Page 174   **"Families who formerly"**: *Proceedings of the House of Assembly, 1925,*
9 March 1925, 294.

Page 174   **"Every male British subject"**: *An Act to Amend Chapter Three of the Consolidated Statutes of Newfoundland (Third Series) Entitled, 'Of the Election of
Members of the House of Assembly,'* S.N. passed 3 April 1925, Cap. 7, s. 1–2.

Page 175   **"This decision calls"**: "A Suffrage Victory," *Jus Suffragii,* April 25, 22.

Page 175   **"Though we differ:"** *Daily News,* 27 April 1925, quoted in Duley, *Where
Once Our Mothers Stood,* 95.

Page 177   **"Frosty relationship with the League"**: Duley, *Where Once Our Mothers
Stood,* 111.

Page 177   **"I'm here for"**: Bert Riggs, "A Right Honourable, Quiet Lady," transcribed
from the *Telegram* by Barbara McGrath, October 2002, http://ngb.
chebucto.org/Articles/quiet-lady.shtml.

SIX: THE LEGACY OF SUFFRAGE IN ATLANTIC CANADA

Research by several historians and political scientists helped form this chapter.

For comparing the suffrage movement in Canada by region, see Sarah Carter, *Ours
by Every Law of Right and Justice: Women and the Vote in the Prairie Provinces* (Vancouver: UBC Press, 2020), and the four other volumes in this series, which are listed at
the front of this book.

On the significance of women's roles in the emerging profession of social work,
see Suzanne Morton, *Wisdom, Justice, and Charity: Canadian Social Welfare through
the Life of Jane B. Wisdom, 1884–1975* (Toronto: University of Toronto Press, 2014).
On the influential 1950s municipal women politicians Muriel McQueen Fergusson
and Abbie Lane, see Gail Campbell, "'Are We Going to Do the Most Important
Thing?' Senator Muriel McQueen Fergusson, Feminist Identities and the Royal
Commission on the Status of Women," in *Making Up the State: Women in 20th
Century Atlantic Canada,* ed. Janet Guildford and Suzanne Morton (Fredericton:

Acadiensis Press, 2010), 179–96; Judith Fingard, "Women's Organizations: The Heart and Soul of Women's Activism," in *Mothers of the Municipality: Women, Work and Social Policy in Post-1945 Halifax*, ed. Judith Fingard and Janet Vey Guildford (Toronto: University of Toronto Press, 2005), 25–48; David MacDonald, "Ubiquitous Is the Word for Abbie," *Maclean's*, 15 February 1953, 24–25, https://archive.macleans. ca/article/1953/02/15/ubiquitous-is-the-word-for-abbie; and Charles Bruce Fergusson, *Alderman Abbie Lane of Halifax* (Windsor, NS: Lancelot Press, 1976). On Polly Chesley, see Sharon M.H. MacDonald, "Neither Memsahibs nor Missionaries: Western Women Who Supported the Indian Independence Movement" (PhD diss., University of New Brunswick, 2010).

For an overview of second-wave feminism in Canada, see Gail Cuthbert Brandt et al., *Canadian Women: A History* (Toronto: Nelson Education, 2011), especially Part 4, 429–603. On the movement in the Atlantic region, see Janet Guildford, "Persistence on the Periphery: Advisory Councils on the Status of Women in Atlantic Canada to 2000," in Guildford and Morton, *Making Up the State*, 229; Sharon Gray Pope and Jane Burnham, "Change Within and Without: The Modern Women's Movement in Newfoundland and Labrador," in *Pursuing Equality: Historical Perspectives on Women in Newfoundland and Labrador*, ed. Linda Kealey (St. John's: Institute of Social and Economic Research, 1993), 191; Naomi Black, "Feminism in Nova Scotia: Women's Groups, 1990–2004," *Atlantis* 31, 1 (2006): 66–78; and "News Release: Corinne Gallant Receives Human Rights Award," *New Brunswick Human Rights Commission*, 15 September 2014, https://www2.gnb.ca/content/dam/gnb/Departments/hrc -cdp/PDF/communique-human-rights-award-presented-to-corinne-gallant.pdf. On the development of women's studies, see Veronica Strong-Boag, "Mapping Women's Studies in Canada: Some Signposts," *Journal of Educational Thought (JET)/ Revue de la Pensée Éducative* 17, 2 (1983): 94–111. On the Halifax Voice of Women, see Frances Early, "'A Grandly Subversive Time': The Halifax Branch of the Voice of Women in the 1960s," in Fingard and Guildford, *Mothers of the Municipality*, 253–80.

A key source on the Shubenacadie Residential School is Isabelle Knockwood, *Out of the Depths: The Experiences of Mi'kmaw Children at the Indian Residential School at Shubenacadie, Nova Scotia*, 4th ed. (Halifax: Fernwood, 2015). Rita Joe provides a parallel perspective in her autobiography, *Song of Rita Joe: Autobiography of a Mi'kmaq Poet* (Charlottetown: Ragweed Press, 1996), 44–58. For the impact of marrying out on Indigenous women and the solution of Bill C-31, see Fern Marie Paul, "Bill C-31: The Experiences of 'Indian' Women Who 'Married Out'" (master's thesis, University of New Brunswick, 2003), 3–4, 17–22, 90–98; Lisa Perley-Dutcher and Stephen Dutcher, "At Home But Not at Peace: The Impact of Bill C-31 on Women and Children of the Tobique First Nation," in Guildford and Morton, *Making Up the State*, 197–215; and Heather Conn, "Sandra Lovelace Nicholas," *Canadian Encyclopedia*, 10 January 2018, https://www.thecanadianencyclopedia.

ca/en/article/sandra-lovelace-nicholas. On the challenges for and progress of
Indigenous women in the twentieth century, see Martha Walls, "The Disposition
of the Ladies: Mi'kmaw Women and the Removal of the King's Road Reserve,
Sydney, Nova Scotia," *Journal of Canadian Studies* 50, 3 (Fall 2016): 538–65; Martha
Walls, *No Need of a Chief for This Band: The Maritime Mi'kmaq and Federal Electoral
Legislation, 1899–1951* (Vancouver: UBC Press, 2010); *Nova Scotia Native Women's
Association,* http://www.nsnwa.ca/; Lianne C. Leddy, "Indigenous Women and
the Franchise," *Canadian Encyclopedia,* 7 April 2016, https://www.thecanadian
encyclopedia.ca/en/article/indigenous-women-and-the-franchise.

On early- and mid-twentieth-century anti-Black racism and Black Maritime
women's activism, see Sylvia Hamilton, "Naming Names, Naming Ourselves: A
Survey of Early Black Women in Nova Scotia," in *We're Rooted Here and They Can't
Pull Us Up: Essays in African Canadian Women's History,* ed. Peggy Bristow (Toronto:
University of Toronto Press, 1994), 13–40; Constance Backhouse, "'I Was Unable to
Identify with Topsy': Carrie M. Best's Struggle against Racial Segregation in Nova
Scotia, 1942," *Atlantis* 22, 2 (March 1998): 16–26; Claudine Bonner, "Black Women
and the Civil Rights Movement in Nova Scotia," *Acadiensis* (blog), 9 August 2018,
https://acadiensis.wordpress.com/2018/08/09/black-women-and-the-civil
-rights-movement-in-nova-scotia/; Russell Bingham, "Viola Desmond," *Canadian
Encyclopedia,* 27 January 2013, https://www.thecanadianencyclopedia.ca/en/
article/viola-desmond; "Viola Desmond's 104th Birthday," *Google Doodles Archive,*
6 July 2018, https://www.google.com/doodles/viola-desmonds-104th-birthday;
"Celebrating Carrie Best," *Google Doodles Archive,* 17 December 2021, https://www.
google.com/doodles/celebrating-carrie-best; Bridglal Pachai and Henry Bishop,
Historic Black Nova Scotia: Images of Our Past (Halifax: Nimbus, 2006); and "Congress
of Black Women of Canada: Information Booklet," May 1989, https://20gewo36a
26v4fawr73g9ah2-wpengine.netdna-ssl.com/wp-content/uploads/cbwc-1989
-informationbooklet.pdf. On anti-Black racism in education, see Bernice Moreau,
"Black Nova Scotian Women's Experience of Educational Violence in the Early
1900s: A Case of Colour Contusion," *Dalhousie Review* 77, 2 (1997): 179–206; George
D. Perry, *The Grand Regulator: The Miseducation of Nova Scotia's Teachers, 1838–1997*
(Montreal and Kingston: McGill-Queen's University Press, 2013); Peter Millman,
"African Nova Scotian Youth Experience on the Island, the Hill, and the Marsh: A
Study of Truro, Nova Scotia in the 1950s and 1960s" (master's thesis, University
of Lethbridge, 2020); and Sherri Borden Colley, "One of Nova Scotia's First Black
Nurses Recalls Struggles and Triumphs," *CBC News,* 1 February 2018, https://www.
cbc.ca/news/canada/nova-scotia/black-nurse-education-discrimination-graduate
-whitney-pier-1.4512933. On Daurene Lewis, see "Daurene Lewis (1943–2013),"
Dancing Backwards: Her Story Archive, 2020, https://www.dancingbackwards.ca/
biographies-of-canadian-women-politicians/item/daurene-lewis. On long-
standing issues around the land titles of Black Nova Scotians, see Jean Laroche,
"Proposed N.S. Law Aims to Make It Easier for Black Families to Get Land Titles,"

CBC News, 23 March 2021, https://www.cbc.ca/news/canada/nova-scotia/land
-titles-black-communities-bill-ns-legislature-1.5960589.

On Acadian women's higher education, see Elspeth Tulloch, *We, the Undersigned:
A Historical Overview of New Brunswick Women's Political and Legal Status, 1784–1984*
(Moncton: New Brunswick Advisory Council on the Status of Women, 1985). On
Acadian women's leadership in second-wave feminism, see Nicole Lang, "Les
Acadiennes et le Marché du Travail: Les Revendications et les Stratégies des
Militantes (1968–1991)," *Acadiensis* 45, 2 (2016): 100–17; and Anne Brown, "Les
Iniquites Socio-economiques et le Partenariat Communautaire chez les Femmes
Francophones et Acadiennes de l'Atlantique," *Atlantis* 30, 3 (2006): 45–53. On New
Brunswick's Acadian premier and the program of "equal opportunity," see Della
M.M. Stanley, *Louis Robichaud: A Decade of Power* (Halifax: Nimbus, 1984); and
Della Stanley, "The 1960s: The Illusions and Realities of Progress," in *The Atlantic
Provinces in Confederation,* 2nd ed., ed. E.R. Forbes and D.A. Muise (Toronto: University of Toronto Press, 2001), 421–59. For an overview of Acadian demography,
see Muriel K. Roy, "Demography and Demolinguistics in Acadia, 1871–1991," in
Acadia of the Maritimes: Thematic Studies from the Beginning to the Present, ed. Jean
Daigle (Moncton: Chaire d'études acadiennes, Université de Moncton, 1995),
135–200.

On the rate of women's election to provincial legislatures, see Amanda Bittner,
"Why Can't We Have Parent-Friendly Parliaments?" *Policy Options,* 4 March 2019,
https://policyoptions.irpp.org/magazines/march-2019/why-cant-we-have-parent
-friendly-parliaments/; and "Women in Canadian Provincial and Territorial
Legislatures," *Wikipedia,* https://en.wikipedia.org/wiki/Women_in_Canadian_
provincial_and_territorial_legislatures. For the very late removal of the requirement that married women must hold property to vote municipally, see Shirley
Tillotson, "Relations of Extraction: Taxation and Women's Citizenship in the
Maritimes, 1914–1955," *Acadiensis* 39, 1 (Winter-Spring 2010): 27–57.

Page 184   **"Well-corseted pleasant-looking":** MacDonald, "Ubiquitous Is the
Word."

Page 184   **"Unprecedented experiment":** Strong-Boag, "Mapping Women's
Studies," 100.

Page 186   **"Alive and effective":** Brandt et al., *Canadian Women,* 522n6.

Page 188   **"Code of silence":** Knockwood, *Out of the Depths,* 12.

Page 189   **"To work for the betterment of racial relations" ... "Canadian society is
a white society":** Backhouse, "'I Was Unable to Identify with Topsy,'" 23.

Page 192   **"Educational violence":** Moreau, "Black Nova Scotian Women's
Experience," 184.

244 SOURCES AND FURTHER READING

CONCLUSION

The sources for this chapter include the companion volume in this series: Sarah Carter, *Ours by Every Law of Right and Justice: Women and the Vote in the Prairie Provinces* (Vancouver: UBC Press, 2020); Catherine Cleverdon, *The Woman Suffrage Movement in Canada*, 2nd ed. (Toronto: University of Toronto Press, 1974); Cleverdon's research correspondence in the Catherine Lyle Cleverdon fonds, R2292-0-7-E, box 1, Library and Archives Canada; W.A. Spray, *The Blacks in New Brunswick* (1972; repr., Fredericton: St. Thomas University, 2021); Edward MacDonald, *If You're Strong Hearted: Prince Edward Island in the Twentieth Century* (Charlottetown: Prince Edward Island Museum and Heritage Foundation, 2000); and Mary K. Cullen, "The Transportation Issue, 1873–1973," in *Canada's Smallest Province: A History of Prince Edward Island*, ed. F.W.P. Bolger (Halifax: Nimbus, 1973), 232–63. On Mary Russell Chesley's involvement in the Women's International League for Peace and Freedom, see "History," *Women's International League for Peace and Freedom*, https://www.wilpf.org/who-we-are/our-herstory/. Material on the activism of suffragists' daughters is from Helen Anderson's report on attending the International Council of Women meetings in Paris during Paris Expo 1900 in "City and Country," *Charlottetown Guardian*, 11 February 1901, 8; and David Frank, "Missing Person: Grace Hamilton Hatheway," *Acadiensis* (blog), 26 April 2021, https://acadiensis.wordpress.com/2021/04/26/missing-person-grace-hamilton -hatheway/.

Page 200 **"Not as a gift"**: "Women Plead Earnestly for the Right to Vote," *Halifax Herald*, 12 April 1917.

Page 203 **"My guess is"**: R.A. MacKay to Catherine Cleverdon, 13 April 1949, Catherine Lyle Cleverdon fonds, Library and Archives Canada.

PHOTO CREDITS

Page 7   "Petition from Residents of Lunenburg County in Favour of Female
          Suffrage," 1917, 1, Nova Scotia House of Assembly Petitions. Nova Scotia
          Archives, RG 5, series P, vol. 22, no. 6a.

Page 21   Edith Jessie Archibald, c. 1910. Nova Scotia Archives, Photographic
          Collection: People: Archibald, Mrs. Charles.

Page 40   "Woman's Suffrage," *Halifax Herald,* 11 April 1893.

Page 55   "Wives and Husbands to Be Entered on Voters' List," *An Act to Amend and
          Consolidate the Acts in Respect to the Electoral Franchise,* 26 April 1918,
          Statutes of Nova Scotia, c. 2, 27. Nova Scotia Archives.

Page 56   "Sons and Daughters to Be Entered on Voters' List," *An Act to Amend and
          Consolidate the Acts in Respect to the Electoral Franchise,* 26 April 1918,
          Statutes of Nova Scotia, c. 2, 27. Nova Scotia Archives.

Page 59   Ella Hatheway, c. 1885, unknown photographer, Frank and Ella Hatheway
          Trust. On display at the Frank and Ella Hatheway Labour Exhibit.

Page 68   Historic Sites and Monuments Board of Canada plaque honouring Grace
          Annie Lockhart. Mount Allison University.

Page 101 Senator Elsie Inman, 1955. Public Archive and Records Office (PEI),
          P0007155, Acc3791/384/1. Copyright holder: Portigal & Ayers
          Photographers Ltd.

Page 113 Sister Bernice Cullen, from a photo montage of the graduating class of
          1941. St. Dunstan's University Archive, Robertson Library, University of
          Prince Edward Island.

Page 120 Robert Harris, *A Meeting of the School Trustees,* 1885, oil on canvas,
          102.2 × 126.5 cm. Purchased 1886, National Gallery of Canada.

Page 128 Nursing Sister Rena McLean in front of No. 2 Canadian Stationary
          Hospital, France, c. 1916. Private collection of Katherine Dewar.

Page 131 Gladys McCormack, 1920, *Folia Montana* (1920), 23. Mount Saint Vincent
          Archives.

Page 139 Julia Salter Earle, 1925. Private collection of Marion Frances Wright.

Page 148 "The Drink Traffic College, N.F.L.D.," *Water Lily* 1, 2 (February 1892): 27. Memorial University Digital Archives Initiative.

Page 149 Cartoon, *Water Lily* 2, 9 (September 1893): 128. Memorial University Digital Archives Initiative.

Page 160 Armine Nutting Gosling, c. 1882–86, unknown photographer. Archives and Special Collections, Memorial University Libraries, MF-409.

Page 164 Cover of *A Pair of Grey Socks*. Centre for Newfoundland Studies Archives, Queen Elizabeth II Library, Memorial University. Memorial University Digital Archives Initiative.

Page 179 PEI's Famous Five in 1993. Public Archives and Records Office, Prince Edward Island, Acc4321/1.

Page 182 Muriel McQueen Fergusson, c. 1960s. University of New Brunswick Archives and Special Collections, UA PC 2, no. 109.

Page 190 Canada Post stamp honouring Carrie Best, 2011. Copyright holder: Canada Post Corp.

Page 197 First all-female Lennox Island Band Council in 2019. Personal collection of Darlene Bernard.

INDEX

Note: "(f)" after a page number indicates an illustration.

Macdonald, John A. (prime minister),
123
Macdonald-Brown, Edith, 15
MacEwan, Harvey, 129
MacKintosh, Emma, 42–43
MacKintosh, James Crosskill, 42
MacLean, Annie Marion, 112–13
Maclean's (newspaper), 184
MacLellan, W.E., 53, 54
MacMahon, Amy, 132
MacNaughton, Violet, 200
Macphail, Andrew, 123–24
Maillet, Antonine, 60, 193
male suffrage, 16, 23, 85, 106, 187
Manitoba franchise, 3, 50, 181
Manning, Sarah, 78
Marichette, 60, 82–83, 201
Maritime WCTU: leadership, 29–30, 44,
70–71; suffrage movement, 76, 78,
117, 120, 125
Maritimes, the: See Atlantic Canada;
individual provinces
marriage: abuse, 137, 185, 204; debt, 34,
35, 67, 79, 110, 111; desertion, 9, 34,
146; divorce, 8, 34, 111; education,
112; husbands, incapacitated, 35, 36;
Indian Act, 178, 180, 188–189; legal
status of wives, 8–9, 22, 27, 34, 109,
110; municipal franchise, 95;
pro-suffrage rationale, 115; public
office, 126, 198; single women, 36, 87,
146, 159. See also dower laws; married women's property law; widows
married women's property law: anti-
suffragist rationale, 87; eighteenth-
century reforms, 102; Newfoundland,
progressiveness of, 145–46; protection from husbands, 34–35, 66–67,
79, 111–12; selling property, 110; suffrage, precursor to, 16, 60–61, 110–11,
122, 145–46; voting legislation, 39,
135; women in public office, 198. See
also property ownership legislation

Marshall, Clara Bell, 31
Martin, Alexander, 115
Martin, Helen, 187
maternity leave, 184
McClung, Nellie, 125
McClure, Firman, 45
McCormack, Gladys, 130, 131(f), 132
McCurdy, Susannah Lynds, 10
McDonough, Alexa, 195
McGill University (QC), 112
McIsaac, Hazel, 195
McKenzie, Angus B., 100, 114–15, 116
McLean, Rena, 127, 128(f), 129
McNeil, Fannie Knowling, 141, 166, 168,
170, 175
McNeil, Hector, 168
medicine, 33, 127, 156. See also nursing
Meighan, Arthur (prime minister), 130
Memorial University College (NL), 156
Memorial University (NL), 184–85
Methodists: education, 68, 176; social
reform, 9, 10; suffrage, 28–29, 110,
118, 162, 167
Mi'kmaq people: band council elec-
tions, 196, 197(f); demographics in
Atlantic Canada, 13–14, 62, 105,
144; history pre-settler, 22, 103, 141;
Mi'kmaw women's activism, 188;
racism, 26, 27, 102, 104
militancy: British suffrage, 92–93, 94–
95, 124, 131, 158, 159; feminism, 194
Miller, Janet (Ayre, Murray), 157–58
Miller, Maria Morris, 27
missionaries, 10, 29, 31, 113
Mitchell, Anna Barnes, 166
Mitchell, James, 86
Mohawk people, 188
Moncton (NB), 81, 194
Monroe, Walter Stanley, 173, 174
Montgomery, Lucy Maud, 107, 108
Montreal (QC), 32, 65
morality of women: men's, superior
to, 82, 92, 126, 136, 152–53; peace

194–98. *See also* Liberal Women's Club; Prince Edward Island WCTU
Prince Edward Island WCTU: Charlottetown, 110, 116; suffrage, 103, 111, 120–22, 125, 128; temperance, 103, 117, 125
Prince of Wales College (PEI), 108, 112, 118, 121
prisoners, 98, 99, 124
pro-suffrage rationale: domestic labour, 159; education, 18, 39, 74–75, 84, 85; First World War, 96, 133, 162, 165–66, 168; higher education, 153, 158; intelligence, 131, 141, 153, 157; moral women vs immoral men, 153, 154; morality, 90, 100, 130, 168, 173; motherhood, 22, 118, 131, 147, 152; petition, 168–69; religion, 134, 151; social reform, 125, 133; taxes, 115, 154, 158, 169, 174; taxes without representation, 84, 86, 91; votes for party responsible, 115, 122, 134, 154, 173; working women, 173–74
pro-suffragists: in New Brunswick, 73–75, 83–88, 90–91; in Newfoundland, 151–52, 153–54, 157–58; in Nova Scotia, 22–23, 37–41, 45, 52; in Prince Edward Island, 110–11, 114–15, 121–22, 128–30, 133–35. *See also* Bell, John Howatt
Program of Equal Opportunity (NB), 63, 193
prohibition: as catalyst for suffrage, 103, 106, 125; franchise, anti-suffrage pushback, 151; Newfoundland, women's activism, 146, 148–49, 155; Prince Edward Island, 106, 107–8, 117, 121, 122; property ownership, 111; referendum franchise, 151–53, 153–55; victory as rationale for no other franchise, 103, 117; wartime, 165. *See also* alcohol; temperance movement
property acts: New Brunswick, 61, 67; Newfoundland, 145, 146; Nova

Scotia, 34, 35, 36; Prince Edward Island, 110
property ownership legislation: Black Canadians' enfranchisement, 55; children of property owners, 56(f); feminist activism, 185–86, 204; labour, 106–7; male franchise, 63–64; municipal franchise, 16–17, 99, 171–72, 198; poll taxes, 16–17, 116; as protection from husbands, 34–35, 67, 111, 205; provincial franchise, 27, 61, 98; provincial suffrage and single women, 37, 91; selling property, 110; single women, franchise, 16, 35–36, 102, 114, 135; single women, municipal franchise, 35–36, 115, 116; widows, 16, 36, 115, 145; women in public office, 174, 198; women's rights, precursor to, 8–9, 79–80, 146. *See also* married women's property law; *individual provinces*, property ownership
Protestants: Catholics, disputes with, 13, 107, 118; higher education, 32; internal disputes, 44–45; social reform, 9–10, 29, 119. *See also* religion; WCTU (Woman's Christian Temperance Union)
Provincial Advisory Council on the Status of Women (PEI), 186
provincial franchise: Atlantic Canadian provinces, 1, 5, 19; Black Canadians, 36, 55, 62, 63, 64, 107, 189; federal franchise, 4, 8, 14, 133, 187; ignored, 129; Indigenous peoples, 1, 14, 55, 99, 174, 176; minorities, 16, 27, 63, 174, 176; municipal franchise, 36, 37, 73, 75, 158; property ownership legislation, 27, 37, 61, 91, 98. *See also individual provinces*, enfranchisement; *individual provinces*, suffrage movement
Prowse, Samuel, 118

public office, women in: anti-suffragist, 156, 176–77; eligibility, 98, 135, 174; ethnic minorities, 2, 196; Famous Five, 179(f); Indigenous peoples, 135, 188–89; marriage, 126, 198; MLAs, 134, 156, 176–77; MPs, 134, 164; municipal roles, 139(f), 175–77, 183, 184; post-suffrage, 194–98, 204, 205; Senate, 101(f), 137, 183, 188–89
Pugsley, William, 72, 87–88, 90

Quebec: Atlantic Canadian history, 26, 27, 63, 65, 70; Catholicism, 113–14, 193, 201; First World War, 127; franchise, 3, 126, 175, 194; Innu people, 144; Montreal, 32, 65; post-suffrage, 134, 197–98; prohibition, 125, 165
Quiet Corner (radio show), 189

racialized women: enfranchisement, 19, 102, 135, 180–81, 182; feminist activism, 185, 204; public roles, 2, 15, 178, 180, 188–89, 189–91; rights, lack of, 17, 34, 144; working women, 183–84. *See also* ethnic minorities; Indigenous women
racism: activism against, 185, 189–92; Black Maritimers, 14–15, 189, 191; ethnic minorities, 13, 16, 27, 29, 176, 201; Indigenous enfranchisement, 1, 13–14, 74; slavery, 3, 14–15, 27, 62, 104
Red Cross, 50, 54, 127, 132, 162
referenda, 95, 96, 140
Reid, Marion, 179(f)
Religieuses de Notre-Dame du Sacré-Coeur (NB), 192–93
religion: education, 117–18; missionaries, 10, 29, 31, 113; Nova Scotia suffrage, 22, 25, 42; Protestant controversy, 44–45; social reform, 9–10, 25; suffrage rationale, pro and anti, 134, 151; temperance, 28–30. *See also individual denominations*

Report of the Royal Commission on the Status of Women (1970), 185, 193
reserves: federal franchise, 1, 55, 99; marriage, 178, 180, 188–89; provincial franchise, 55, 99, 102, 103, 135, 176, 199; suffrage, exclusion, 187
residential/assimilationist schools, 14, 62, 187, 188
Richardson, Gertrude, 200
Ritchie, Eliza: about, 4, 24–25, 57; LCW, 42, 44–45, 47, 48, 49; suffrage advocacy, 52, 53–54, 103
Ritchie, Ella, 24–25, 42
Ritchie, Mary, 24–25, 42
Roberts, William, 96
Robichaud, Louis J., 63, 193
Robinson, John A., 158
Rogers, Benjamin, 115
Rogers, Grace MacLeod, 195
Roseland Theatre (NS), 189, 191
Royal Red Cross, 127
Russell, Benjamin, 52, 53
Ryan, James, 66

Sackville LCW (NB), 81
Saint-Basile (NB), 70
Saint John Evening News (newspaper), 90
Saint John Globe, 92
Saint John LCW (NB): about, 61, 76, 80–82, 147, 201; Saint John Women's Enfranchisement Association, 80–81, 88–89, 90, 92; suffrage, endorsement, 90
Saint John (NB), 63, 64, 70–71, 92–93, 95
Saint John Telegraph (newspaper), 95
Saint John Wartime Prices and Trade, 183
Saint John Women's Enfranchisement Association (NB): about, 76, 77–80, 82, 200–1; disrespect towards, 91–92; gains, 95–96; hiatus and revival, 89–90; LCW, 80–81, 88–89, 90, 92; leadership, 59(f), 61, 77–78, 81, 97;